IMPROVED VILLAGE TECHNOLOGY
FOR WOMEN'S ACTIVITIES
A manual for West Africa

IMPROVED VILLAGE TECHNOLOGY
FOR WOMEN'S ACTIVITIES
A manual for West Africa

Prepared under the auspices of the
International Labour Office and the
Government of Norway joint Africa
Regional Project on Technological Change,
Basic Needs and the Condition of Rural
Women

INTERNATIONAL LABOUR OFFICE   GENEVA

ILO
Improved village technology for women's activities: A manual for West Africa
Geneva, International Labour Office, 1984

/Manual/, /Choice of technology/, /Food processing/, /Food products/, /Rural women/, /West Africa/. 08.06.2
ISBN 92-2-103818-1

ILO Cataloguing in Publication Data

Printed by the International Labour Office, Geneva, Switzerland

IMPROVED VILLAGE TECHNOLOGY
FOR WOMEN'S ACTIVITIES IN WEST AFRICA

(A manual of tools, equipment and methods
for the processing of traditional products)

Contents

Appendices

PREFACE

Notwithstanding some recent efforts, there continues to be a dearth of practical guidelines and manuals relating to the improvements in traditional technologies for the particular benefit to special disadvantaged groups like rural women. It is hoped that this manual prepared by Ms. Yvette Stevens of the ILO Technology and Employment Branch, will fill a gap. The manual is one of the outcomes of the ILO's Africa Regional Project on Technological Change, Basic Needs and the Condition of Rural Women funded by the Government of Norway implemented under ILO's World Employment Programme; the other two being an analytical research volume and a summary of highlights of the project findings. The African Regional Project lasted for nearly three years, consisting of an interdisciplinary team of an engineer (Yvette Stevens), an economist (Vivianne Ventura-Dias) and a sociologist (Eugenia Date-Bah), and was guided by Iftikhar Ahmed of the ILO Technology and Employment Branch.

The ILO/Norway project was started in 1980 as a response to various recommendations at international conferences for interational agencies like the ILO to give greater emphasis to the impact of science and technology on the socio-economic conditions of women. For example, the resolution adopted by the UN Conference on Science and Technology for Development (UNCSTD) 1979 recommended that UN bodies like the ILO, dealing with science and technology, should continually review the impact of their programmes on women. Subsequently, the World Conference of the UN Decade for Women (Copenhagen, 1980) recommended that "the ILO in co-operation with pertinent (UN) bodies should develop studies to assess the working and employment conditions of rural women".

This manual is different from existing ones because of its specificity and sub-regional focus. It is based on field work undertaken in the project countries (Ghana and Sierra Leone) and benefitted additionally from a field visit to Senegal.

Following are its special features: (a) the target audience consists of government institutions, rural extension services, financial institutions, women's small-scale processing enterprises and manufacturing firms; (b) focuses on four important processing activities - cassava, vegetable oil, coconut and fish undertaken by rural women in West Africa; (c) covers the range of technologies available in the sub-region; (d) makes a quantitative comparison of the performance of both traditional and improved technologies and provides information on the advantages and disadvantages of each; (e) describes the basic design features of improved and traditional tools and equipment, materials and parts required for their fabrication; and (f) provides sources of equipment.

The practical value of the manual is enhanced by the inclusion of information on concrete possibilities for the utilisation of agricultural wastes and the by-products of women's processing activities. The manual is expected to contribute to TCDC-type of exchange of information on both the traditional and improved technologies not only in this sub-region but in the rest of Africa where these processing activities are common. Operationally, this manual is serving as an important input to the on-going ILO field-based technical co-operation project in Ghana (financed by the Government of the Netherlands) which is promoting the wider use of technologies in rural households through practical demonstrations, supply of prototypes, provision of a package of material inputs and institutional support (e.g. extension, finance, marketing, and improved raw material supply, etc.) in relation to five significant processing activities undertaken by Ghanaian rural women.

Geneva, March 1984

A.S. Bhalla,
Chief,
Technology and Employment Branch.

PART I: INTRODUCTORY

Chapter 1

INTRODUCTION

BACKGROUND

The crucial role of women in West African communities has been well documented.[1] In spite of certain peculiarities of individual countries, a definite pattern of the sexual division of labour emerges from the literature.

In production, rural women are mainly responsible for activities such as planting and weeding in farms, food preparation and processing, water collection, fish-smoking and processing of a variety of other products.

In most West African countries at the village level these tasks are still performed by the traditional methods which, although cheap, are characterised by high labour and time use, poor hygiene and low productivity. In some cases, these methods are burdensome and are hazardous to the health of the processors.

One way of improving the women's welfare, in terms of an increase in their output or in a reduction in the strain and physical injuries associated with their tasks, is to improve the technologies used by them.

However, certain constraints limit the type and nature of improvements which can be introduced. First, given the level of poverty of the rural population in West Africa, it becomes imperative that costs are kept low; second, due to the scarcity of mechanical and artisanal skills in the rural areas, improved equipment must not require sophisticated maintenance and repair. Third, the foreign exchange constraints dictate that as far as possible, technological solutions must be sought from within the countries using materials and skills that can be locally procured or developed.

The above three considerations suggest that short-term technological solutions to the problems facing rural women in the performance of their activities can only be found in the introduction of simple, non-capital intensive technologies.

WHY ANOTHER MANUAL?

A wealth of literature on improved technologies exists for farming, cooking and water collection. (See for example de Lepelure et.al., 1981;

VITA, 1978, Van Dijk, 1978, etc.) Therefore this category of activities is not covered by this manual which is focused instead on food processing. For West Africa, traditional food processing mainly involves the following activities:

- cassava processing
- vegetable oil production
- cereals processing
- fish processing.[2]

Although components of food processing are included in available documentation on village technologies, (see for example VITA, 1975, Brace Research Institute 1975, Gandhian Institute of Studies in India 1973) the range of technologies covered do not have relevance to West Africa. Area-specific manuals are needed to permit the presentation of relevant information which would be valuable to specific areas - in this case to West Africa. However, it could be useful in other areas as well since, although the group of activities are relevant to this region, no single activity is unique to West Africa.

Articles and leaflets exist which examine certain operations involved in food processing at the village level in West Africa. However, there is no detailed documentation of the traditional methods of production The required specific improvements are not always well-defined and the special advantages of traditional methods are not always borne in mind in the choice from alternatives. In many instances this has led to 'improved' technologies being rejected by the rural women. This manual recognises the existence of information gap in regard to traditional technologies and attempts to fill this gap. In one single document it brings together various tools, equipment and methods in use in food processing in West Africa; it also discusses a number of practical possibilities which could contribute to the design development, manufacture and application of technology at the local level.

PURPOSE

The purpose of the manual is threefold: <u>firstly</u> it aims to disseminate information required for technology transfer among countries of West Africa,[3] or from other countries; <u>secondly</u> it seeks to provide designers and developers in each country with description and performance figures of traditional processing methods[4], highlighting the particular problems encountered as well as the trends in improved technology development;

<u>thirdly</u>, it affords extension officers and rural development agents or educators an opportunity to learn about the existing technology alternatives and their specific advantages and disadvantages, thus enabling them to make a choice of technology to suit specific conditions of use.

DEFINITIONS AND CONCEPTS

<u>Village technology</u> is defined, for the purpose of this manual, as technology (traditional or improved) which can be applied at low cost and which utilises locally acquired materials and skills.

A village technology is described as <u>improved</u> if it provides an improved level of performance in terms of scale of operation, energy use, time use, labour use, efficiency, quality of output, ease of use or safety in use as compared to the traditional technology.

A village technology is defined as <u>upgraded</u> if an improvement in the performance as described above is brought about merely by a modification of the traditional technology, that is, without basically changing the underlying principles of operation.

These definitions are by no means rigid, and the concrete form of improved village technology would vary with time. If rural women's incomes and productivity are increased as a result of using an improved village technology or for any other reason, then they would be able to purchase more expensive equipment; training programmes could lead to an increased level of skills of local craftsmen and research and development could reveal better methods of performing traditional tasks. A manual such as this one therefore would require constant improvements. The technologies presented here are seen merely as a first step in raising the living standards of women in the rural areas of West Africa.

SOURCES OF DATA

The data used in the preparation of this manual were collected as follows:
(a) Survey undertaken in rural areas of Ghana and Sierra Leone.
(b) Review of technologies in use through field visits to Ghana, Sierra Leone and Senegal.[5]
(c) Data from R and D institutions in West Africa collected through interviews, mailed questionnaires and analysis of documentary material.
(d) Available manuals, leaflets and publications (for a complete list, see references).

DESIGN OF THE MANUAL

In the second chapter the main operations involved in women's traditional food-processing activities are highlighted and indicators as well as other factors to assess the performance of different technologies in the various operations are given. Considerations for the selection of improved technologies in women's activities are also included.

Chapters three to seven are concerned with the specific activities studied. Each of these chapters starts with a description of the traditional methods of performing the activities together with some performance figures. They then go on to describe improvements to the traditional technologies as well as other technological alternatives which could be adopted, outlining basic design features, materials and parts required for their fabrication, the manufacturing processes involved, some indicators as well as their specific advantages and disadvantages. Comparison of the performance figures of both traditional and improved technology types are included in each of these chapters.

Chapter eight discusses possible uses of the by-products of food-processing activities, mainly as fuel, fertilisers and animal feed.

Chapter nine examines the R and D efforts in the countries of West Africa in the area of village technology. It also discusses problems of equipment manufacture within the region.

The concluding chapter ten makes specific recommendations for development, manufacture and choice of village technology in West Africa.

A GUIDE TO USERS

In Chapters 3 to 8 descriptions of village technology equipment are provided under the headings: <u>Description and Design Aspects</u>, <u>Materials and Parts</u>, <u>Manufacture</u>, <u>Specific Advantages</u>, <u>Disadvantages</u> and <u>Output.</u> The list of contents provides general guidelines to the location of information concerning equipment for specific operations. For a given operation, a number of technological alternatives are presented in the text under specific headings.

The information contained in these six chapters is adequate to give an appreciation of the characteristics of each equipment. For more detailed information references are provided in the notes and at the end of the manual.

Where appropriate, names of known suppliers are given (their addresses are listed at the end of the Manual). It may be noted that this list is far from being exhaustive and that it does not imply a special endorsement of these suppliers by the ILO. Omissions should in no way be construed as being representative of ILO's disapproval. Where no name of suppliers is indicated, the equipment is either in prototype stage or is manufactured indigenously within the villages.

NOTES TO CHAPTER 1

1   See, for example, Akande 1981; Date-Bah, 1981; Stevens, 1981; Tadesse, 1981; Traore, 1981; and Macormack, 1982.

2   A wide range of technologies for fish processing is presented in Allal, 1983.

3   Technology transfer in the area of traditional processing has been minimal. For instance, the hand-operated cassava grater, which has been in use in Nigeria since the 1940s, is only being recently developed in Sierra Leone.

4   Based on a survey of rural areas in Ghana and Sierra Leone.

5   The drawing on the technological experiences of Senegal (made possible by field visits during the author's participation in a regional seminar on women in Dakar) enhances the practical and geographical significance of the manual.

Chapter 2

ASSESSMENT OF TECHNOLOGIES FOR RURAL WOMEN'S ACTIVITIES
AND CONSIDERATIONS FOR IMPROVEMENT
OF TRADITIONAL METHODS

GENERAL

The processing activities of rural women in West Africa can be divided
into a number of operations (Stevens, 1981). These operations are basically:
- cooking
- water collection and transportation
- drying of products
- smoking
- peeling/cracking/shelling
- milling/grating
- sieving/filtering
- dehusking of grains
- pressing (e.g. oil or cassava dough)

Each operation can be regarded as a technological process. In any
technological process, there are inputs and outputs and the function of the
technique is to transform the inputs into the outputs. The inputs can be
material inputs, energy inputs, time input, labour inputs, or other auxiliary
inputs. The outputs can be divided into main products and by-products. The
technical assessment is concerned with the best utilisation of any particular
input combination.

Consider a particular process or equipment which can be schematically
represented thus:

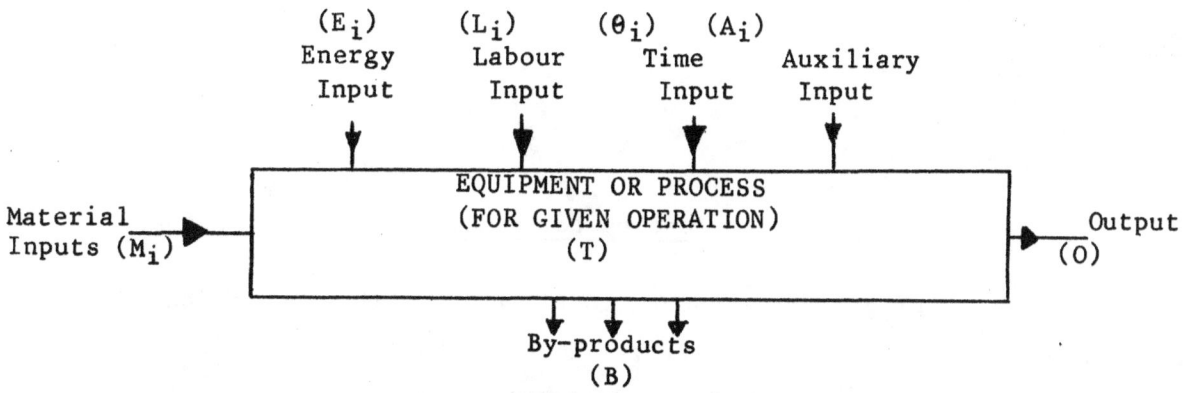

Fig.1 Schematic representation of a technological
process

The output and by-products would depend on the input factors and the equipment or process itself. Mathematically this can be expressed thus:

$$0 = f(M_i, E_i, A_i, T, \theta_i, L_i) \dotfill (1)$$
$$B = f(M_i, E_i, A_i, T, \theta_i, L_i) \dotfill (2)$$

The <u>material inputs</u> here are defined as the raw materials which are to undergo some transformation as a result of the technological process.

The <u>energy input</u> is taken here to mean input of fuel, electricity, solar energy, electricity, etc. It however excludes human energy for reasons of analysis.

The <u>time input</u> is the overall time required for the technological process.

The <u>labour input</u> is the number of man hours spent in the process.[1]

The <u>auxiliary inputs</u> are taken here as inputs which act as catalysts in the technological process. For example, water to facilitate milling of grains.

The <u>outputs</u> are the main products of the process.

The <u>by-products</u> are other products of the process which can be usable or non-usable.

Where a required output is obtained as a result of a number of processes, each process would have its own inputs which will be provided partly as a result of one or more processes, and its outputs which may serve as inputs to other processes. If the processes are in series, then they can be represented thus:

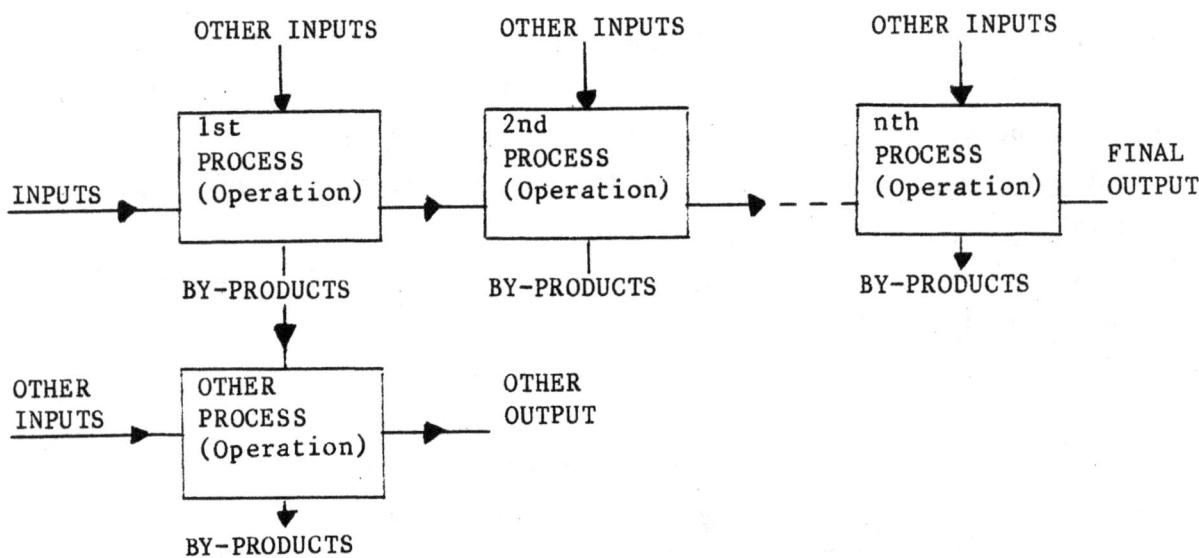

Fig. 2 <u>Chain of processes leading to production of given outputs</u>

Where a chain of processes (operations) leads to the production of a final product it is called an activity. Thus shelling of maize is an <u>operation</u>, but maize processing to produce kenkey is an <u>activity</u>. An activity, by definition, consists of a number of operations.

The functions (1) and (2) are complex ones since the five forms of inputs depend on other external factors. For instance, the material inputs would depend on its source, variety and 'history'. In addition, some of these input variables are interrelated, as for example, the time input might depend on the amount of energy used for the process. The inputs themselves might depend on the nature of the process or the type of equipment.

In order to study the effect of any one of the input variables on the output, the other inputs have to be controlled. For instance, the dependence of the output on the variation of the energy input can be investigated if the material, labour and time and auxilliary inputs are kept constant for a given process.

The output itself, as well as the by-products can be assessed by their quality and quantity. The units in which these are measured would depend on the process.

A given technological innovation is designed to give specific results. It might be required for instance, to (a) decrease or increase labour requirements for a given output; (b) decrease time spent on a given operation; (c) reduce energy requirements for a given output; (d) increase the quality and quantity of the output for a given material input etc. It can also be a combination of these functions. Depending on which of these is of concern, the relationships to be assessed can be determined.

Also a number of methods or equipment for performing the same functions can be assessed and compared. Possible indicators of merits and demerits could be the requirements of the energy, labour, time, auxilliary inputs required to produce a given output given the same material inputs. Other indicators for assessing a technology (both qualitatively and quantitatively) are given below.

METHODOLOGY AND CRITERIA

The variables and factors which are required for assessing village technology can be classified as:
- Figures of merit which tell how effectively the inputs are being converted into the output. These are quantifiable variables which can usually be measured by tests.
- Other miscellaneous factors both quantifiable and non-quantifiable, which although not directly relating the inputs to the outputs are essential in

the assessment of the technology. Some of these variables have socio-economic and health implications.

A. Figures of merit of village technology for various operations

a) Technical efficiency: This has to be defined for each operation. Where a power driven equipment is used the Power Efficiency would be defined as:

$$\eta_p = \frac{\text{output power}}{\text{input power}}$$

This ratio would reflect how usefully the power (energy) is being utilised. In the assessment and comparison of village equipment which requires different inputs of 'power', it is not always meaningful to talk about the power efficiency since an important factor here is which kind of power is used. For instance, if there are two devices for the same operation which utilise solar energy and diesel respectively, each with its own efficiency of power use, the solar powered equipment could be recommended even though its power efficiency might be less than that of the diesel-powered equipment for the obvious reason that the solar energy is free whilst the diesel is not. Power efficiency becomes important only for comparison of equipment using the same source of power, to ensure maximum utilisation of the given source of power.

Where fuel is used the heat efficiency can be defined as:

$$\eta_h = \frac{\text{Useful Heat}}{\text{Heat produced}}$$

For food processing devices which basically extract certain components from the input (e.g., in oil presses).

Extraction efficiency $\eta_e = \dfrac{\text{output obtained}}{\substack{\text{output obtainable} \\ \text{(present in input)}}}$

In dehusking operations, the dehusking efficiency is described as:

$$\eta_{deh} = \frac{\text{weight of cleaned grain}}{\text{weight of given uncleaned grain}} \ \%$$

In operations where the input is merely "transformed" from one state to the next, such that no part of the material input contributes to the by-product, efficiency will not be defined unless fuel or power source is used in which case the power and heat efficiencies would be assessed, e.g., in milling.

(b) Quality of output: The measure of quality would depend on the particular end product:

e.g.   rice milling: percentage of grains broken

        stoves: amount and content of smoke

        crop dryers: final moisture content

                  food value of crops.

In order to assess in terms of the quality of the output one has to determine the acceptable quality in each case. On the basis of these the class of the produce can be established.

e.g., for grain milling

        Class I grain   grain with less than X% of broken grain

        Class II   (X - Y)% of broken grains etc.

If the quality index is lower than the acceptable standard then it can be concluded that the technology is not serving its purpose and is inappropriate.

(c) <u>Energy utilised per unit of output</u>: In devices where there is an energy input but the transformation of energy is not the main function, it might be useful to know how effectively the energy is used in the process. This variable would account for energy use.

(d) <u>Time required to produce unit output</u>: In the village setting this variable is to be considered where time is an important factor in a given operation. The inverse relationship of output produced in unit time is used in the following chapters and is referred to simply as <u>output</u>.

(e) <u>Labour required to produce unit output</u>: (Labour productivity).

(f) <u>Quantity of auxiliary inputs required per unit of output</u>

Table 2.1 shows important indicators for the different operations involved in traditional processing activities.

Table 2.1 <u>Some useful indicators for assessment of the technologies for single operations</u>

1. Cooking	a) Heat efficiency b) 'Class' of cooking method (determined by methods of smoke disposal, ease of use, etc)
2. Water collection	a) Volume of water collected per hour per person (animal) b) Power efficiency (in case of pumps)
3. Water transportation	a) Volume of water transported per hour per person b) Power efficiency (in case of power driven pumps)
4. Drying	a) Final moisture content b) Time required for unit weight of product to reach final moisture content c) Fuel used per unit weight of food dried d) 'Class' depending on stable moisture content

5. Food smoking
    a) Final moisture content
    b) Time required for unit weight of food to reach acceptable moisture content
    c) Fuel used per unit weight of food smoked
    d) 'Class' of smoked food depending on food value of the products

6. Milling/grating
    a) Weight of food milled per unit time per person
    b) 'Class' determined by the fineness of the product
    c) Power efficiency in case of power-driven mills

7. Dehusking
    a) Weight of grain dehusked per unit time per person
    b) 'Class' determined by percentage breakage
    c) Dehusking efficiency

8. Oil pressing
    a) Extraction efficiency
    b) 'Class' determined by FFA content and food value of the oil
    c) Fuel used per unit weight of oil produced

9. Shelling/peeling
    a) Shelling/peeling efficiency
    b) Weight of food shelled/peeled per unit time per person

B. Other Miscellaneous Factors for assessing Village Technology

Other factors which are to be considered in the assessment of technologies for single operations are:

(e) Power source

(f) Overall dimensions and weight

(g) Materials required for manufacture

(h) Ease of manufacture

(i) Ease of repair and maintenance

(j) Complexity of design

Factors (e) to (f) are important considerations which should be taken into account in the design of equipment for village use. All six of them would depend on factors such as locally available power sources, materials and skills. Since they all have cost implications they will affect the capital, operating, repair and maintenance costs of the technology.

(k) Use of by-products

(l) Quantity of by-products

(m) Quality of by-products

(k), (l) and (m) which refer to by-products are also important considerations, especially where the by-products have special uses.

(n) Degree of pollution and production of harmful by-products

(o) Safety for use: This can be expressed in qualitative terms as simply either safe or unsafe. This assessment would be based on accepted principles

of safety for that particular type of equipment (these are usually laid down
in the form of safety standards or safety regulations).

(p) <u>Breakdowns</u>: This is important in assessing village technology as the
quality of a device would depend on its ability to operate trouble-free for
given periods of time. This is not always possible to judge beforehand as an
equipment would require prolonged use in considerable numbers before any
evaluation could be done.

The <u>Equipment Shutdown Ratio</u> could be defined as the number of failures
reported in unit operating time

i.e. Esd = <u>No. of failures</u>

Total operating time

(q) <u>Physical strain</u> involved in performing the operation. This could only be
measured through physiological studies.

(r) <u>Sociocultural factors</u> such as social norms and taboos, accustomed social
organisation of work and local tastes.

IMPROVEMENT OF VILLAGE TECHNOLOGY

In the selection of alternative technology for a given activity, the
whole chain of operations involved has to be considered. The chain of
operations could be assessed in terms of all the various inputs and the final
output. Consider an activity consisting of n operations which can be
performed in series:

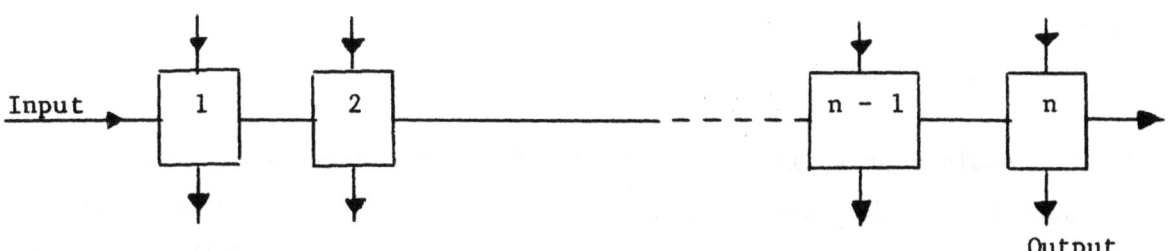

Then one can determine total values of the input variables of such an
activity. The total time required would be given as:

$$\theta \text{ TOTAL} = \sum_{i=1}^{n} \theta_i$$

where θ_i is the time required for the ith operation

Similarly,

$$E \text{ TOTAL} = \sum_{i=1}^{n} E_i$$

$$L \text{ TOTAL} = \sum_{i=1}^{n} L_i$$

$$A_{TOTAL} = \sum_{i=1}^{n} A_i$$

Other output and input relationships would be those of total conversion efficiency (which would depend on the efficiency of each operation in the chain). Other factors such as quality of the output are also affected by all n operations in the chain.

Having considered the total values of the various variables involved, the decision on which factors require to be improved could be based on the following considerations:

(a) For activities performed purely as household chore. Emphasis is to be placed on reduction of labour and time use (assuming labour could be diverted to other uses or for leisure), physical strain, use of all inputs and on rendering the activity more hygienic and safe to perform.

(b) For activities performed purely for income generation. Here the emphasis is on increasing production, and on lowering the cost of production. (These do not exclude other considerations but are considered overidding).

(c) In between these two extremes are activities for which products are used both for home consumption and for sale. These fulfil a final function as household chores and income-generating activities. They can be considered as case (b) since an increase in production or a decrease in production cost would lead to increased incomes for the women.

Women's household chores

For household chores, it can be assumed that the quantity of material to be processed remains the same since the household size does not change with the introduction of an improved technology. The main purpose of the improved technology should be to relieve the 'drudgery' associated with such tasks. Drudgery is usually as a result of long hours of work (due to low labour productivity) and physical strain.

For many household chores, the primary objectives in improving technologies are thus to relieve time spent on given activities (increase labour productivity) and to reduce the strain associated with them. However, in cases where inputs are inefficiently used in the traditional methods of performing household chores, the primary objectives could be expanded to include minimisation of these inputs for the required output. Thus in cooking, primary consideration could be given to minimising fuel use thus leading to <u>income preservation</u> (if firewood is bought) or thus relieving labour (if firewood is fetched).

In the selection of alternative technologies for a specific activity the existing technologies for all the operations have to be studied. It might be that not all of the operations require improvement. Those which do require to be ameliorated and the improvements required are identified.

For the sake of simplicity let us suppose that a given activity is particularly time-consuming (θ total is high). A closer look at the operations might reveal that the kth operation is the most time consuming ($\theta_k \approx \theta$ total).

In the selection of an alternative technology to replace that used in operation k, due consideration has to be given to the other operations in the chain. For instance, if the new technology is such that its capacity cannot be meaningfully utilised within one household, a more appropriate choice has to be made or alternatively it could be chosen to serve more than one household. Thus, whereas a hand-operated maize mill of 10 kg/hour output could be chosen for household ownership, one which grinds 400 kg of grain per hour could be introduced for communal use. For m households, the chain of operations can then be represented as:

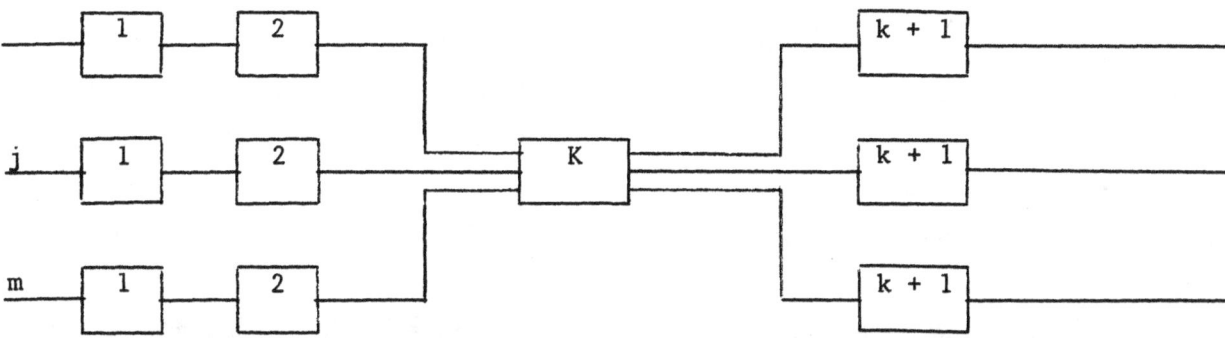

If a charge is levied for communal use of the equipment, a trade-off has to be made between the cost of renting and the time saved in the activity. In any case the women can revert to the traditional technology for performing operation 'k' when money is not available.

It is worthwhile noting that for household chores the economic benefits might not be altogether apparent and this might create problems in the introduction of alternatives. Caution therefore has to be taken to demonstrate the usefulness of the new technology, highlighting its effect on income preservation and on released time for other activities which might contribute to income generation or the improvement of the general welfare of women (for example, time released for rest and relaxation, participation in adult literacy or other educational programmes).

Women's income-generating activities

Under this category is considered any activity performed wholly or partly for the generation of income. In this case the primary objectives would be to increase production and decrease production costs (by increasing productivity).

For income-generating activities, the selection of improved technology becomes much more complicated. Whereas in the case of household chores the quantity of raw materials to be processed remains fixed, in income-generating activities, an increase in raw material to be processed is to be envisaged in order to raise the incomes and hence the quality of life of the women. It would be necessary to determine the proposed scale of the activity in order to determine which technological alternatives could be adopted.

This could be determined from marketing studies (revealing market outlets and size as well as percentage of the market which could be captured by the producer(s)), raw materials availability, initial capital affordable (by individuals through loans), transportation, existing and obtainable skills and individual ambitions. On the basis of these considerations the proposed scale of production can be established.

If several technological alternatives exist for the given scale of production, the next step would be to ascertain that for each of these alternatives the requirements of labour energy, water and other auxiliary inputs for this proposed scale can be met. For alternatives which cater for the proposed scale and for which all the inputs can be ensured, cost and return analyses could be done to determine the most profitable technology to adopt. Such analyses would include the following:

Costs

    (i) Depreciation on building (if required to house equipment usually 5% annually assuming a 20-year life linearly depreciated).

  (ii) Depreciation on equipment (10% annually assuming 10 year life).

 (iii) Labour costs (including paid 8 costed non-paid labour)

  (iv) Fuel costs

   (v) Other energy costs

  (vi) Cost of raw materials

 (vii) Cost of auxiliary inputs

(viii) Cost of repair and maintenance

  (ix) Transportation costs

   (x) Loan repayment costs (where credit is required to purchase equipment).

Returns

  (i) Sale of products

 (ii) Sale of by-products

Items (i) and (ii) in the statement of costs can be affected by factors such as:

- complexity of the designs
- overall dimensions and/or weight
- ease of manufacture/construction
- materials required for the manufacture/construction

Items (iii) to (viii) will be determined by:

- power source type
- total energy use
- total labour use
- total time use
- total auxilliary inputs
- number of breakdowns
- ease of repair and maintenance

The returns for a given set of inputs can be affected by:

- quantity and quality of the output

  (efficiency of conversion of raw material to output)

- quantity and quality of by-products

Here a compromise might have to be struck between these two factors. While the main output should normally receive prior consideration, it might be expedient to strike a balance in order to obtain by-products which could find use in the market.

In income-generating activities where one equipment replacing an operation is of excess capacity for a single producer, communal ownership (as discussed under household chores) can also be recommended. In that case the charge for equipment hire would be included in the statement of costs.

The selected technology for a given activity would consist of a set of equipment which perform the required operations for that particular activity at the required scale of production and at lowest cost.[2] In the final selection, thought should be given to aspects such as safety, convenience and hygiene and socio-cultural factors which are not reflected in cost and return analyses. A trade-off might have to be accepted between net calculated profits and, for instance, conformity with social practices in a particular community. This might be necessitated by the need to ensure acceptance of the technology within the society.

In the following chapters (3 to 8) technology alternatives for various operations are presented wherever available values of some of the variables discussed in this chapter are included. Others are assessed qualitatively under the headings specific advantages and disadvantages.

NOTES TO CHAPTER 2

1 It is assumed here that some part of a technological process might not require human participation or supervision.

2 Or highest profit. If the returns could be increased through improved technology then even with the same production cost the technology would make the women better off.

PART II: TECHNICAL

Chapter 3
CASSAVA PROCESSING

INTRODUCTION

Cassava (manihot esculenta) is a starchy root crop grown widely in West Africa. Its ability to thrive on poor soil and under severe drought conditions make it invaluable in some areas where good soil and water are unavailable. This crop matures and is harvestable in 6-24 months. There are two main varieties of cassava: the 'sweet' and 'bitter' cassava. The 'sweet' variety can be eaten raw or slightly boiled or processed into cassava dough or gari, while the 'bitter' variety is of necessity always processed into cassava dough, gari, or starch.

Cassava contains cyanogenic glucoside a poisonous substance which is usually removed by processing. It is a perishable crop[1] which is susceptible to rapid deterioration. A physiological type of deterioration causes decoloration of the tubers and commences as soon as 24 hours after harvesting. Another type of deterioration, caused by microorganisms (fungi and bacteria) develops 5-7 days after harvesting (FAO and UNEP, 1981).

TRADITIONAL PROCESSING

The steps involved in the traditional methods of processing cassava in West Africa are shown in Fig. 3.1.

Peeling of cassava

Traditionally peeling of cassava is done by knife or cutlass (depending on the size of the tuber) and by hand. A slit is made with the knife or cutlass and the skin can then usually be pulled off by hand. For some variety the peels cannot be easily removed by hand and the whole process is done by knife or cutlass.

Sundrying of cassava. Preparation of dried cassava flour.[2] (Lines A and B in Fig. 3.1).

After peeling the cassava is washed and chopped into small cubes of approximately 2 mm and sundried. Drying is done by spreading the cassava on a variety of surfaces: on bare tarred surfaces, mats, wire nets, cemented drying floors, or on tables. Rarely is cassava dried over a wood fire.

To make dried cassava flour the dried cassava is pounded in the traditional mortar with a pestle.

Fig. 3.1: Stages in cassava processing in West Africa

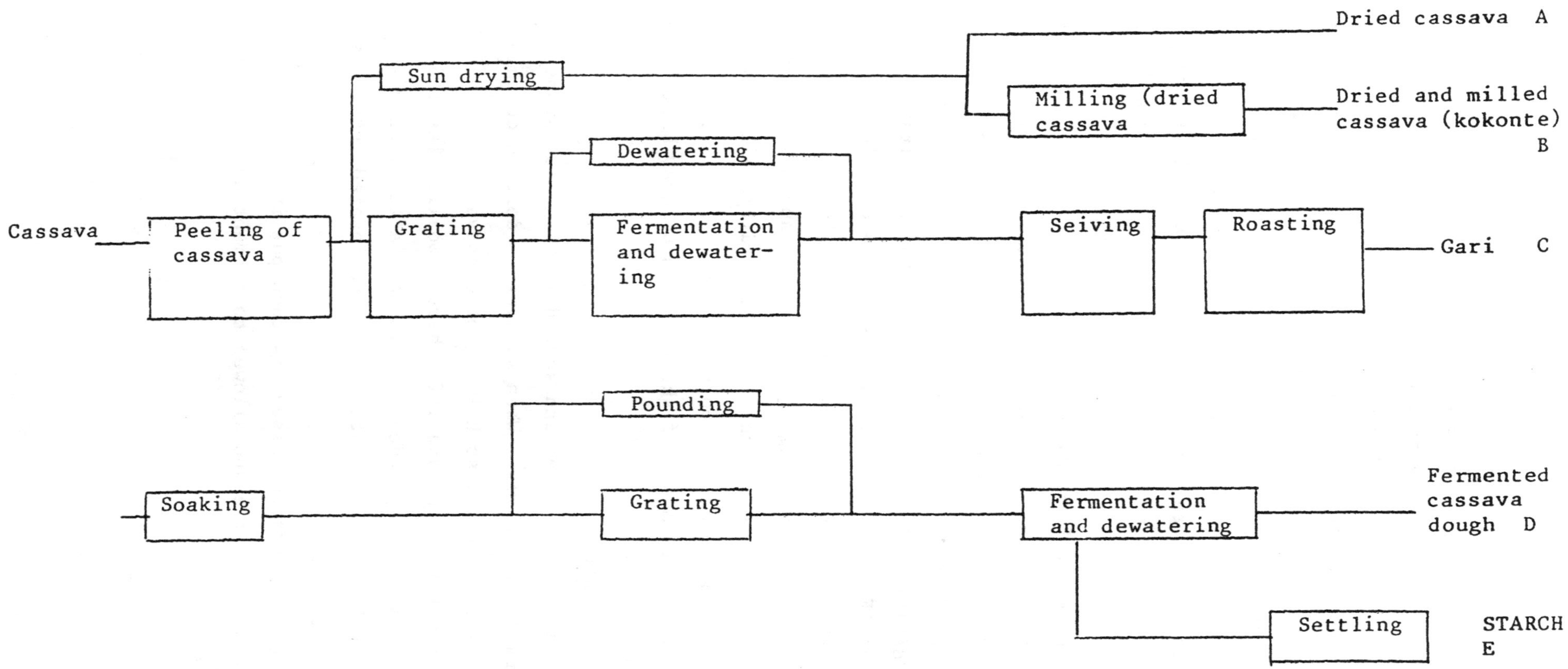

<u>Gari[3] Preparation.</u> Line C Fig. 3.1).

To prepare gari peeled cassava is washed and grated. Traditionally, a perforated metal pan (see Fig. 3.2) is used. The cassava tubers are rubbed against the rough surface of the grater by the processor who assumes a standing position, bending over as shown (Fig. 3.2).

The processes of fermentation and dewatering are done in parallel. Fermentation gives rise to a gari product which is slightly sour due to the production of lactic acid. While this sour taste is preferred in some countries (e.g. Ghana and Nigeria) in others (e.g. Sierra Leone) this is not the case and therefore short periods of dewatering are required.

The grated cassava is put in jute bags, baskets and metal containers and heavy weights (usually stones) are put on top of it (Fig. 3.36) over a period of 1-6 hours (when fermentation is not required) or 1-5 days (when fermentation is required). Another traditional method of dewatering is by means of bush sticks which are placed on both sides of jute bags and tied together by ropes as shown in Fig. 3.3(a). The periods allowed for dewatering/fermentation are the same as for the first method.

Raffia (Fig. 3.4) and metal sieves are used for sieving the dewatered dough, which is broken up into tiny pieces for the purpose.

Roasting or 'garifying' of the dough causes gelatisation and dextrinisation of the starch. This is traditionally done over a three-stone fire in earthenware or iron pots and metal pans (Fig. 3.5). During roasting stirring is done by means of short wooden spoons, broken calabash pieces or metal spoons.

<u>Fermented cassava dough[4].</u> (Line D, Fig. 3.1).

The cassava is peeled and soaked in 44 gallon drums, metal/plastic containers or in streams. When soaking is done in containers about 16 gallons of water is required to soak 10 kg of cassava, and when it is done in streams, cassava is put in sacks and left there. Soaking lasts for 2-7 days after which the cassava is pounded in a mortar (after longer soaking periods when the cassava is soft) or grated with a perforated metal grater (after shorter soaking periods).

The pounded/grated cassava is then put into baskets and sacks, covered with leaves or plastic and allowed to ferment and dewater over a period of about 3 days.

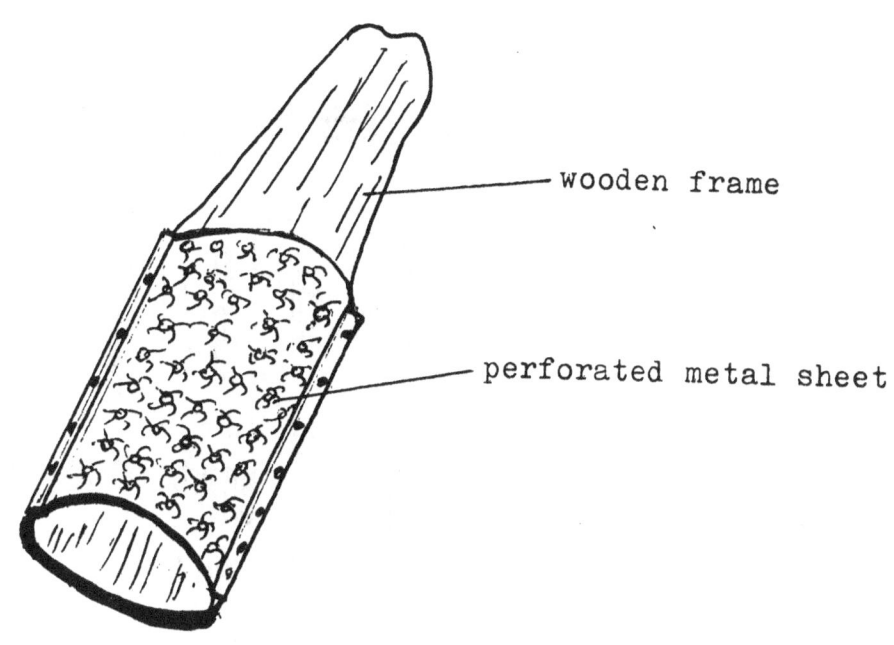

wooden frame

perforated metal sheet

Fig. 3.2 The traditional cassava/coconut grater in use in West Africa

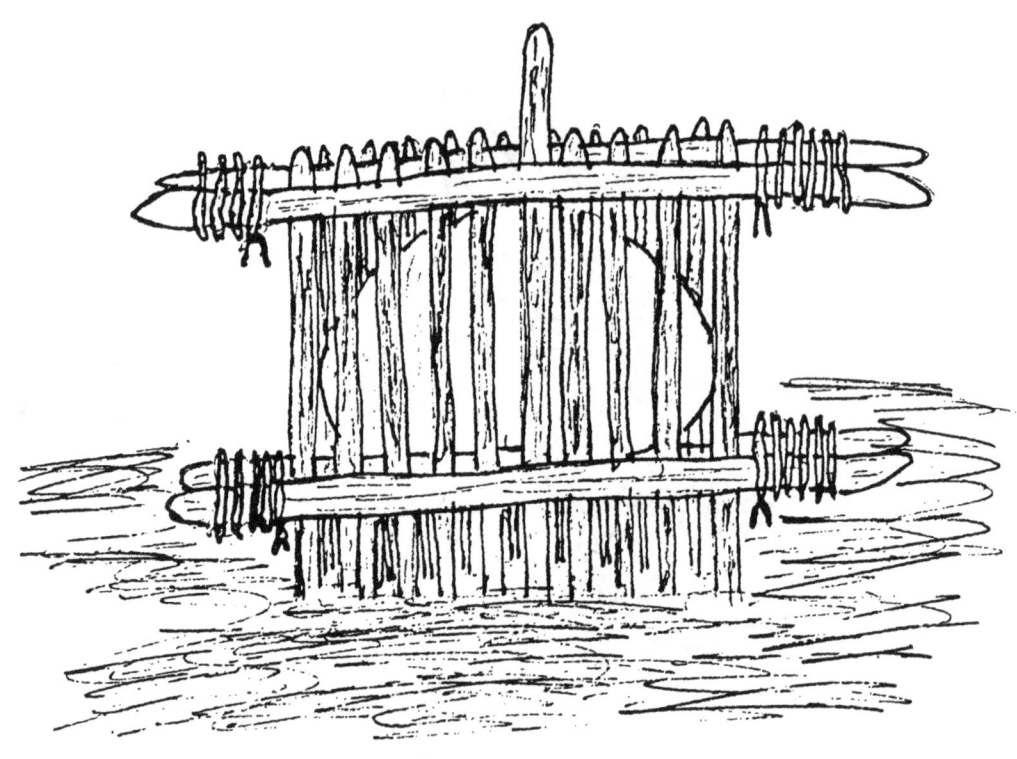

Fig. 3.3 <u>Traditional methods of pressing cassava dough</u>

Fig. 3.4 <u>Traditional raffia sieve for seiving gari</u>

Fig. 3.5 <u>Roasting or 'garifying' of grated and pressed</u>
<u>cassava</u>

Technical Performance

The operations involved in the traditional processing of cassava are
shown in Table 3.1. The values of the technical variables defined for these
operations in Chapter 2 are estimated and presented in Table 3.1.

Table 3.1

Performance Figures of Traditional Methods

of Cassava Processing [5]

No.	Operation	Technical Variable	Units of Measurement	Value
1	Peeling of cassava	Time required by individual to peel 10 kg of cassava	minutes	34 (Output 17.6 kg/hr)
2	Sundrying of cassava	Time required to dry cassava to final (equilibrium) moisture content	hours	4 days (dry season) 8 days (rainy season)
3	Pounding of dried cassava	Time required by individual to pound 10 kg of dried cassava	minutes	18 (Output 33 kg/hr)
4	Grating of cassava	Time required by individual to grate 10 kg of fresh raw cassava	minutes	50-100 (Output 6-12 kg/hr)
5	Dewatering (Pressing)	Time required to dewater 10 kg of grated cassava	hours days	1-6 without fermentation 1-5 with fermentation
6	Sieving	Time required by individual to sieve 10 kg of dewatered dough	hours	1.6 (Output 6 kg/hr)
7	Roasting	Time required for an individual to roast 10 kg of dewatered dough	hours	2-3 (Output 3-5 kg/hr)
		Final moisture content in gari	%	16

| 8 | Soaking (for preparation of fermented cassava dough | Period of soaking | days | 2-7 |
| 9 | Grating of soaked cassava (preparation of fermented cassava dough | Time required[6] to pound 10 kg of soaked cassava | days | See Fig. 3.6 |

Advantage of traditional methods of cassava processing

- the tools and equipment utilised are cheap.

Disadavantages of traditional methods of cassava processing

- cassava grating and pressing are time-consuming and strenuous.
- frequent lacerations of the fingers are inevitable with hand graters.
- processing is unhygienic (especially in sun drying, dewatering, and soaking in streams of cassava).

IMPROVED EQUIPMENT FOR CASSAVA PROCESSING

Traditional methods utilised in cassava processing have been discussed. The setbacks of these methods have to be eliminated through the use of improved equipment. This equipment is therefore required to:
- relieve the strain of cassava grating
- save time in processing
- render the processing more hygienic
- reduce the effects of smoke and heat on the processors.

Cassava peelers

Design of cassava peelers pose special problems since the roots occur in a variety of shapes and sizes. Peelers which have been tried have had a high percentage of wastage, as compared to hand peeling.[7] Since peeling is not complete with peelers, additional labour has to be utilised to finish the process.

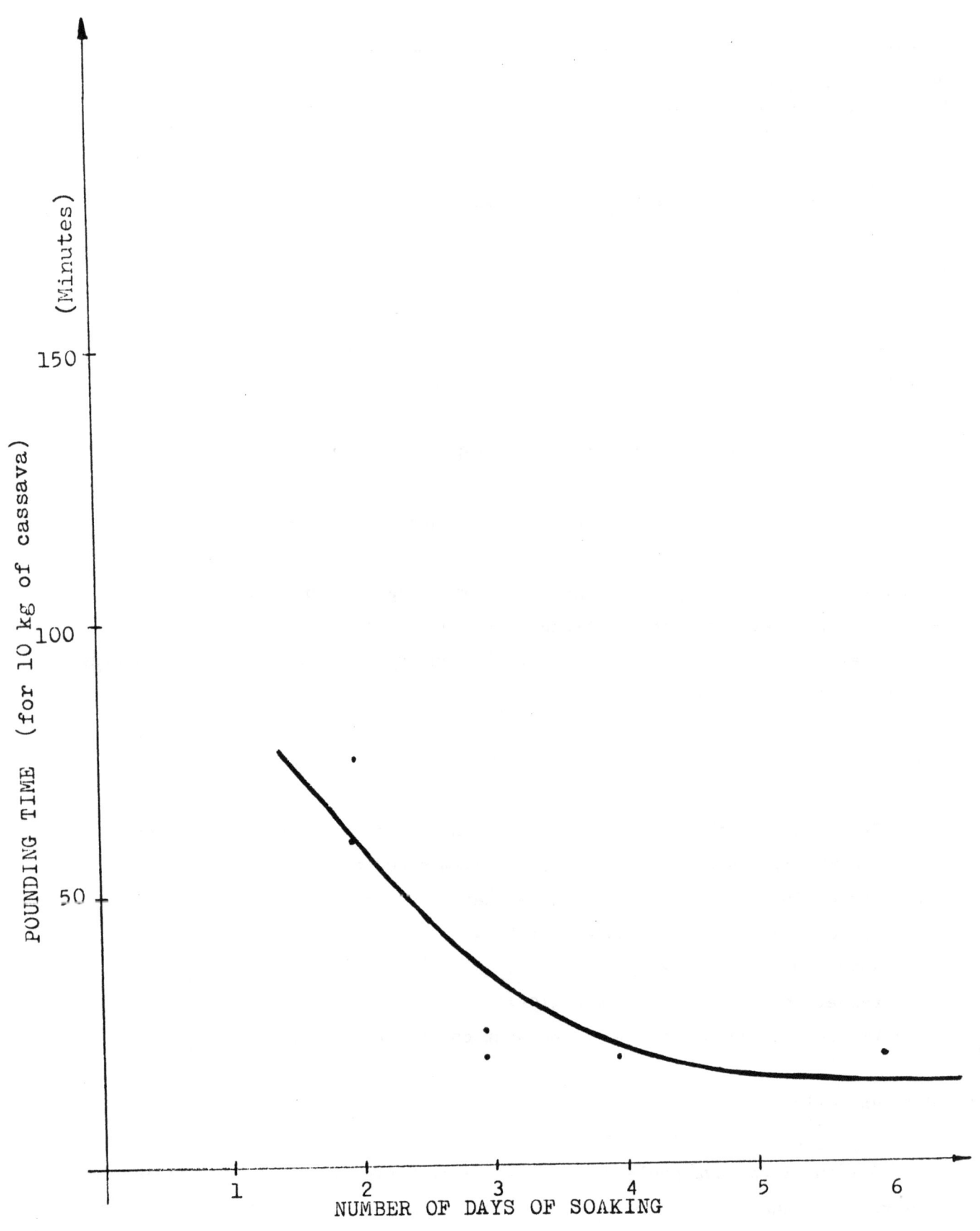

Fig. 3.6   Relationship between time required for pounding soaked
cassava and the length of the soaking period

Cassava graters

A number of mechanised cassava graters exist in the market.
Hand-operated graters have been in use in Nigeria since the 1940s. The type
of graters described here can be either hand/pedal-operated or driven by
motors/engines.

Pedal-operated grater

Description and
design aspects:

One variety of cassava graters is that designed by S.W.
Eaves and used in Zaria, Nigeria. It consists of a
vertical disc with grating slits rotated by means of
pedal power as shown in Fig. 3.7. The cassava is fed in
through the hopper. Detailed engineering drawings of
such a grater are to be found in Eaves, 1976 (ITDG).

Materials and
parts:

Sheet metal, steel pipes; bicycle mechanism.

Manufacture:

Sheet metal bending; cutting and welding.

Specific advantages:

Manufactured from easily available materials and bicycle
scrap.

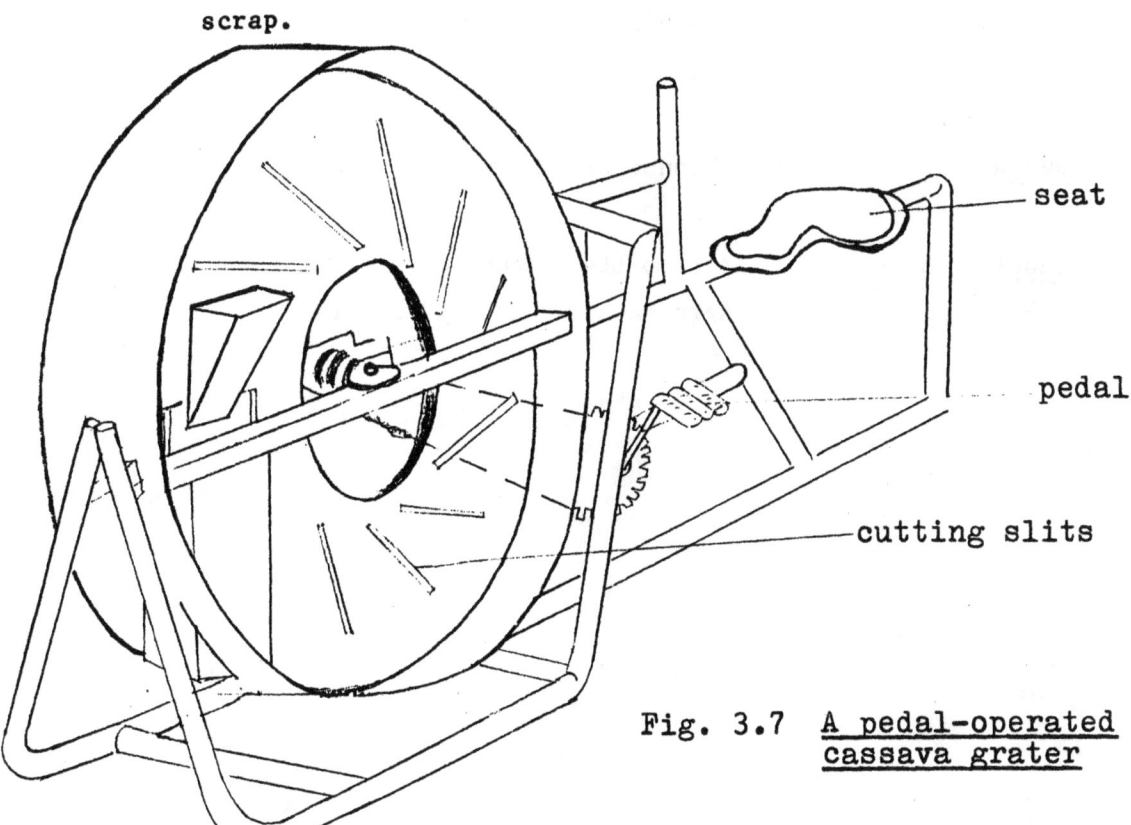

seat

pedal

cutting slits

Fig. 3.7 A pedal-operated
cassava grater

The Wadhwa cassava grater (Ghana)

Description and design aspects:	This is a disc grater which consists of a perforated steel sheet clasped over a wooden block, powered by a 5 h.p. diesel engine. It is made mainly of sheet metal and a hopper is used to connect the vertical shaft of the machine to that of the engine (see Fig. 3.8). The grated cassava flows out through a chute by gravity.
Materials and parts:	Sheet steel, steel pipes, wood, belt and pulley transmission mechanism, motor/engine.
Manufacture:	Sheet metal bending equipment, cutting and welding.

An improvement of this type of grater is one in which the disc is covered with aluminium sheet over which is clasped the perforated galvanised metal sheet. This facilitates cleaning of the press and ensures that the wooden disc does not absorb the cassava liquid during pressing. The hopper is also lined with aluminium for the same reason. Although more hygienic this type of grater would increase the cost of the equipment.

Specific advantages:	Ease of disassembly and access to grating surface for cleaning. Top loading utilises gravity feed thus reducing hazard of lacerations of fingers.
Output:	1 tonne of cassava an hour.
Suppliers:	Agrico Ltd., Ghana. Agro Machines Ltd., Liberia.

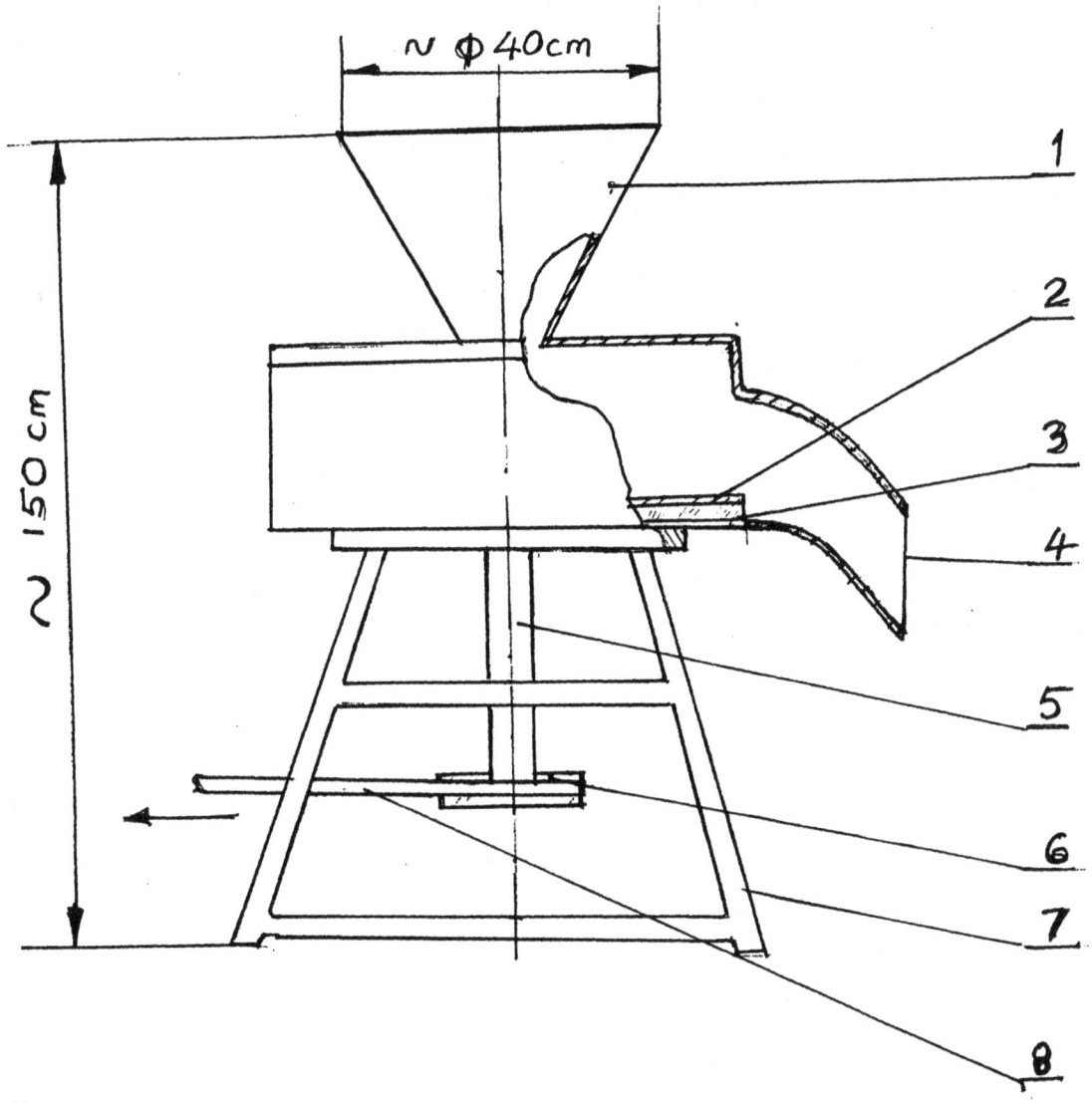

Fig. 3.8 A Horizontal disc cassava grater
(Agrico type)

1. Hopper
2. Perforated sheet metal
3. Wooden disc
4. Outlet for grated cassava
5. Rotating shaft
6. Pulley
7. Stand
8. Belt to engine or motor shaft

(TAEC) cassava grater (Sierra Leone)

Description and design Aspects:	This is also a drum grater in which the drum rotates in a vertical plane (see Fig. 3.9). The cassava is fed laterally into the machine. The rotating drum with its attached perforated grate is powered by a 4 h.p. diesel engine or electric motor and its shaft is directly connected to that of the engine or motor.
Materials and parts:	Wood, angle-iron, sheet metal, belt and pulley, motor/engine.
Manufacture:	Sheet metal bending and cutting equipment; welding; basic carpentry tools.
Special advantages	Wide use of wood which is locally available in many countries in the region.
Disadvantage:	Difficulty to clean the grating surface. Since the tubers are hand held there is wastage as the end bits cannot be grated without the risk of lacerating the fingers.
Output:	500 kg of cassava per hour.

A suggested improvement of this grater would be a wooden plate attached to a handle designed such as to fit into the hopper. This could be used to press the end bits of tuber against the grating surface (Fig. 3.9b).

Supplier: Tikonko Agricultural Extension Centre, Sierra Leone.

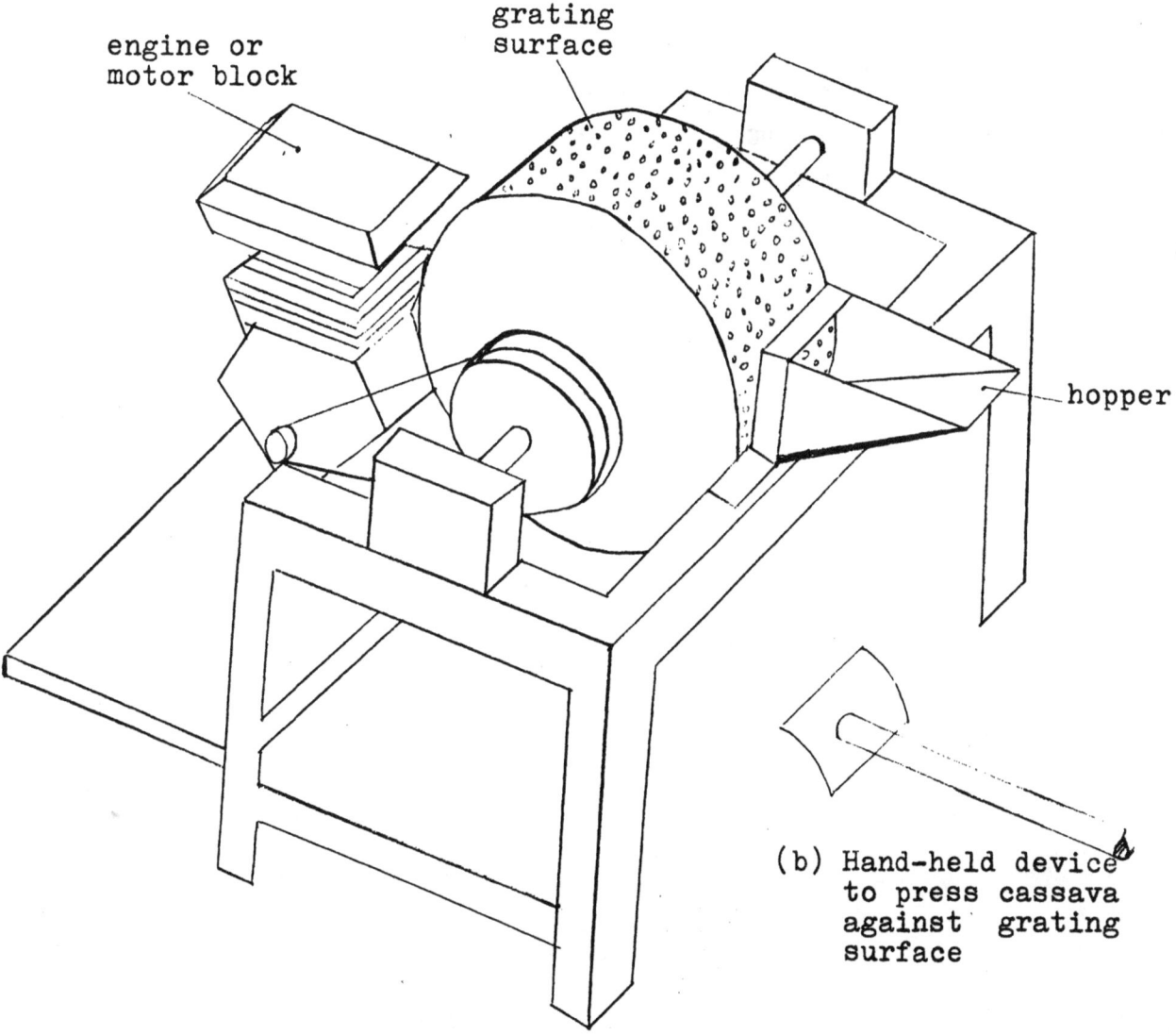

engine or
motor block

grating
surface

hopper

(b) Hand-held device
to press cassava
against grating
surface

Fig. 3.9: A vertical drum cassava grater
(Tikonko Agricultural Extension Centre, Sierra Leone)

Fofie's cassava grater

Description and design aspects:	This type is a rotating drum grater. The drum which is of 30 cm diameter and 30 cm in length is driven by a 2.2 h.p. motor. The cutting elements are sections of used sawmill band blades which are set into the surface of the drum parallel to the drum axis, 5 cm apart. At hand level a sliding block holds the cassava against the grating drum to prevent laceration of the fingers during grating.

Pressing of grated cassava

Upgraded Traditional Press

Description and design aspects:	An upgrading of the traditional sticks-and-rope press was recently developed by the Tikonko Agricultural Extension Centre in Sierra Leone. It consists of two wooden/metal frames as shown in Fig. 3.10. To one of the frames is attached a number of screw threads which go through holes in the other frame. Hand screws are used to hold both frames together such that pressure is exerted on the grated cassava dough placed between them. The cassava dough is put in sacks.
	Even though the time required for pressing the dough is not significantly affected by the use of this method, the time and labour required to set up the equipment for this operation is considerably reduced. Thus in cases where fermentation of the dough is required, (pressing time does not need to be reduced) both time and labour can be saved by using this upgraded traditional press.
	It is specifically recommended for use by single processors.
Materials and parts:	Wood; bolts and hand (wing nuts).
Manufacture:	Basic carpentry equipment. Due to the swelling of wood during pressing, one development of this press is the use of metal strips welded together. (fig. 3.11a)
Special advantages:	Time and labour-saving.
Disadvantage:	Wooden variety 'swells' due to soaking which reduces the effective pressure on the dough.
Supplier:	Tikonko Agricultural Extension Centre, Sierra Leone.

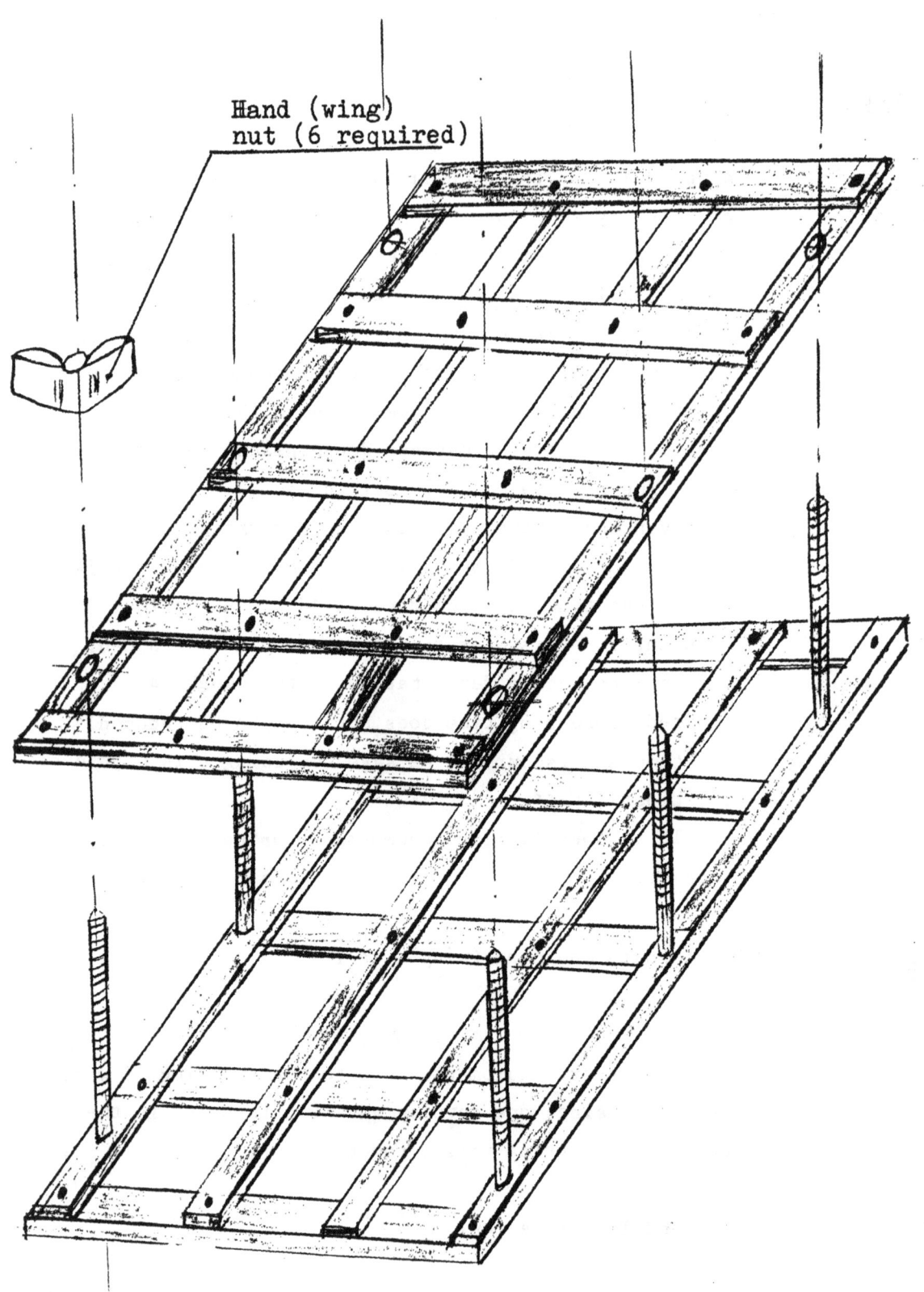

Hand (wing)
nut (6 required)

Fig . 3.10 An upgraded traditional press for cassava dough

The Wedge Press

Description and
aspects of design:
Another development of the traditional method of
pressing is the wedge press which has been used in China
for oil pressing (Boatwright, 1979). One such press is
shown in Fig. 3.11. The wooden wedges are driven in by
hammer from both sides and provide the necessary
pressure for removing the fluid, which can be collected
for making starch. In the diagram trees are used to
provide support. However logs can be installed for this
purpose. If the water is required for starch
preparation, container to collect this water should be
included.

Materials and
parts
Wood (pressure block and beam and wooden wedges). Tree
stump or wooden support.

Manufacture:
Basic wood cutting tools.

Specific advantages:
Low cost. Ability to press a few sacks of dough in one
batch.

Disadvantage:
The wedges need to be hammered into place.

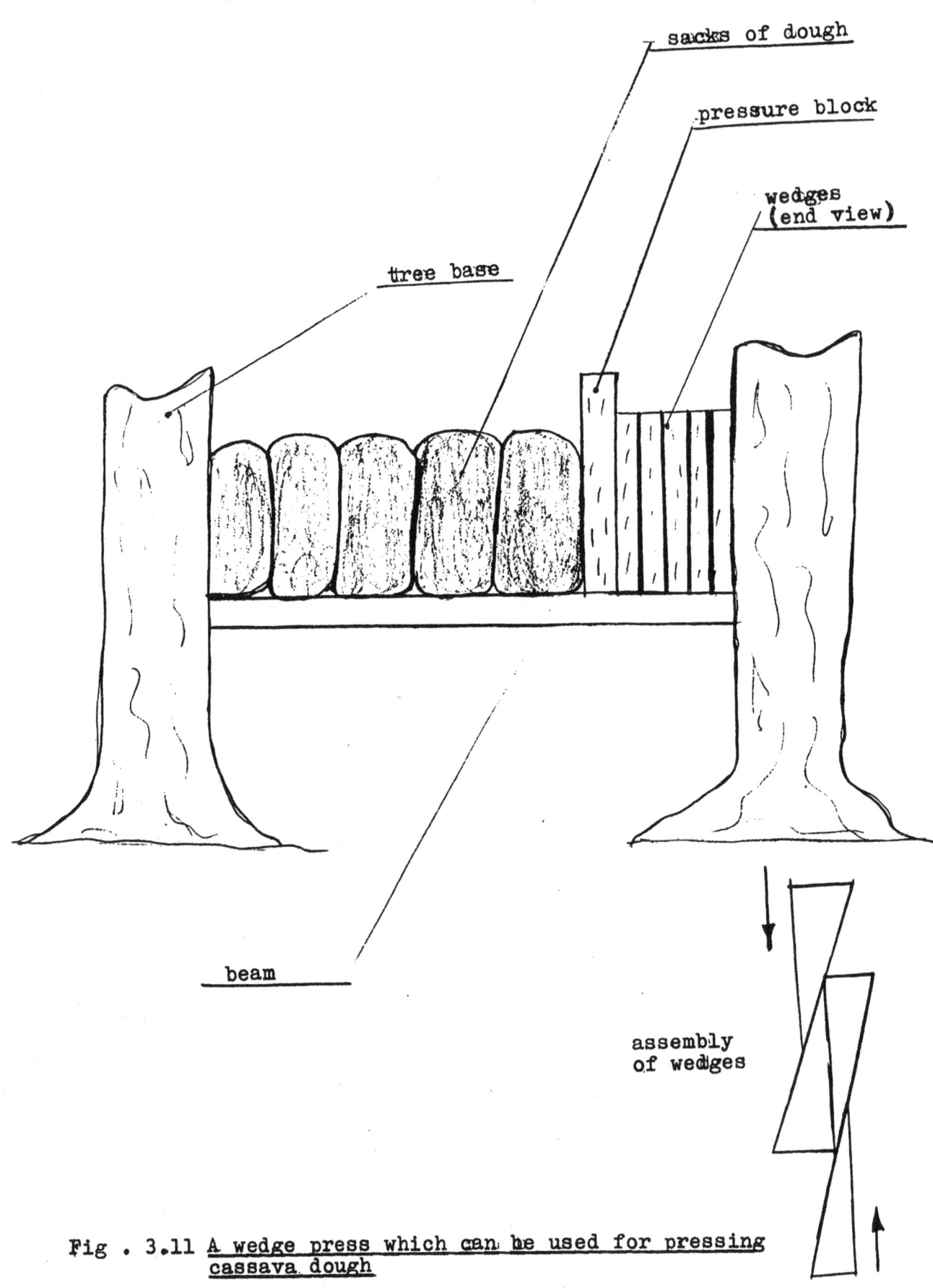

Fig . 3.11 A wedge press which can be used for pressing cassava dough

Fig. 3.11(a) <u>A metal version of the upgraded press
showing hand nuts</u>

Fig; 3.11(b)   <u>The wooden upgraded press</u>

The Screw Press

Description and
design aspects:

The screw press, as the name implies, produces pressure by means of screws. Fig. 3.11 shows one version of a screw press for cassava dough. When the hand bar is rotated pressure is exerted on the dough and the liquid flows out through the holes in the container. The cassava dough is placed in sacks as above.

Materials and parts: Sheet metal plates, steel bars, bolts.

Manufacture:

Welding equipment; lathe for cutting screw thread sheet metal bending and cutting equipment.

Specific advantages: High rate of fluid extraction, thus reducing the time required for pressing.

Disadvantage:

Dough can only be pressed in batches, the size of which is determined by that of the container. For large-scale processors this might be tedious.

Suppliers: (See screw presses for oil extraction).

One type of screw press for cassava dough has been developed and is being field tested by the Department of Agricultural Engineering, Njala University College. This is shown in the foreground of fig. 3.11(b).

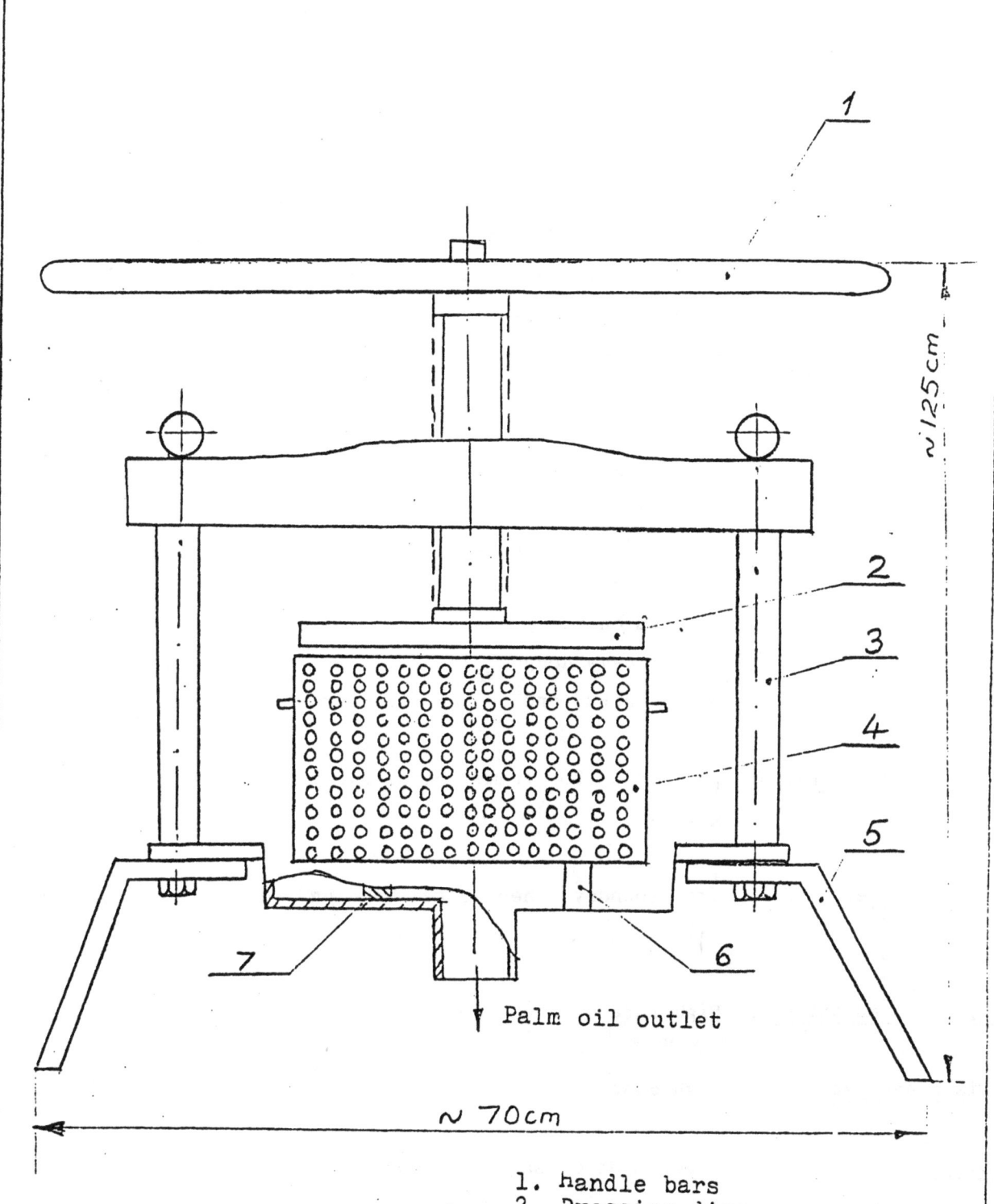

Palm oil outlet

1. handle bars
2. Pressing disc
3. Bar support
4. Cylinder with holes for dekernelled palm fruits
5. Stand
6. Support
7. Tray for palm oil collection

FIG.3.12 A screw press for cassava dough

(not to scale)

The Hydraulic Press

Description and
design aspects:

The hydraulic press increases the applied force without
increasing the work output and is based on Pascal's
principle that fluids transmit pressure equally in all
directions. Fig. 3.13a shows the principle of operation
of such a press. A small pump (power or hand-operated)
is the basic feature of this press. The press has a
cylinder and plunger (press ram) which are similar to
the pump but much bigger, with a substantially greater
plunger area.

A hydraulic press developed by Agrico Ltd. of Ghana
is shown in Fig. 3.13b.

The dough is placed in jute bags and placed in the
container. When the hand lever is operated pressure is
exerted on the pressing disc and this is lowered on to
the cassava dough. The water is collected at the bottom
of the press and can be used for making starch.

Materials and parts: Cast iron (for frame) metal sheets, hand pump, pressure
guage.

Manufacture: Iron foundry, sheet metal bending and cutting equipment,
welding.

Specific advantage: High rate of fluid extraction.

Disadvantage: High cost.

Output: 1 tonne of cassava dough per hour.

Suppliers: Agrico Ltd., Ghana.
Agro Machines Ltd., Liberia.

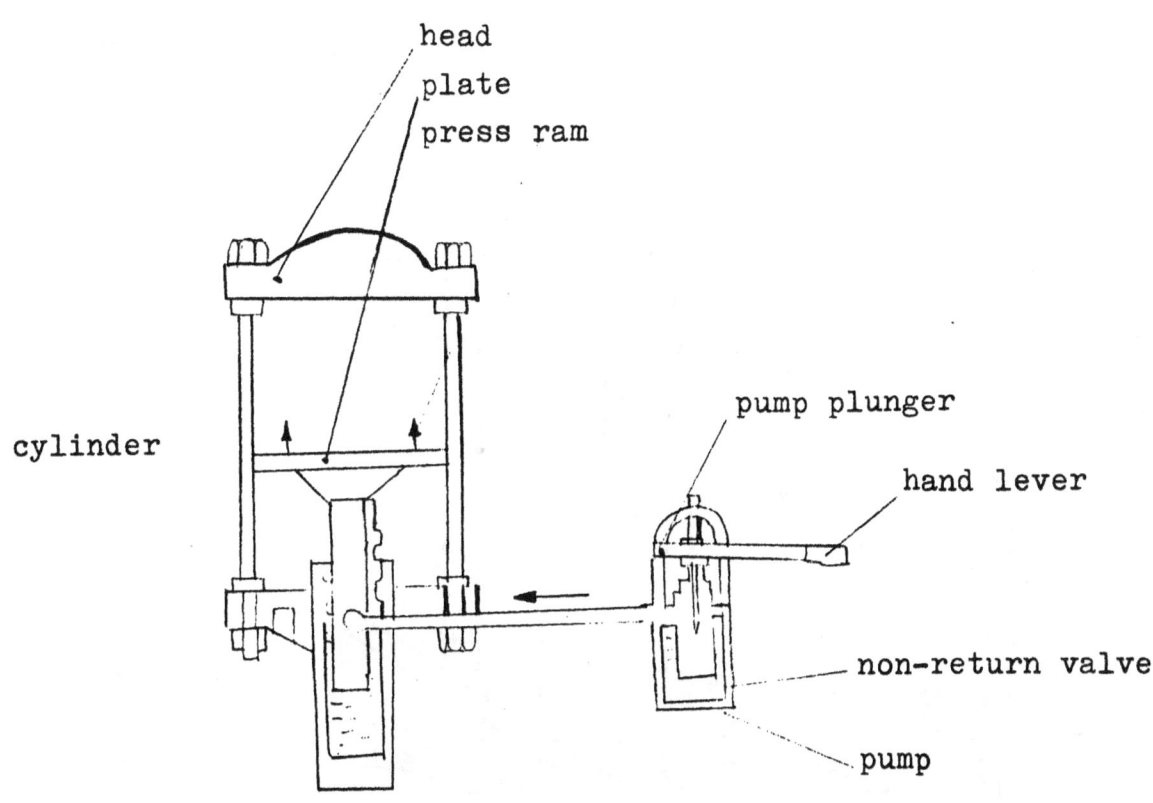

head
plate
press ram

cylinder

pump plunger

hand lever

non-return valve

pump

Fig. 3.13a: The hydraulic press

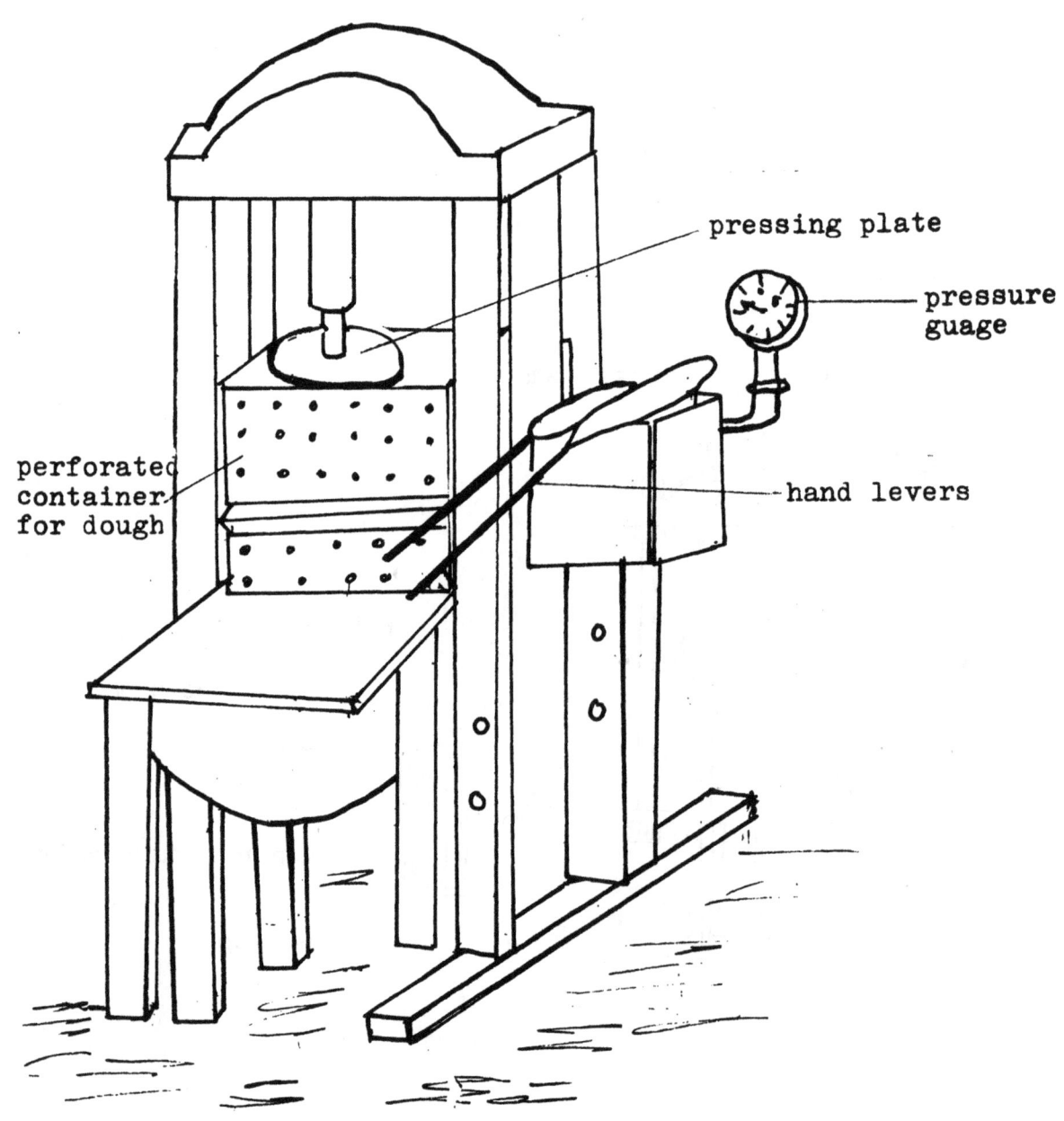

pressing plate

pressure
guage

perforated
container
for dough

hand levers

Fig. 3.13(b) The Wadwa hydraulic press for cassava dough

Sieving of pressed cassava dough

The Rotating Sieve (Fig. 3.14)

Description and
design aspects:

A rotating sieve has been developed by Agrico Ltd. of Ghana. It consists of a drum containing a cylindrical sieve made from wire netting. The dough is introduced through the hopper and when the hand bar is rotated it is sieved. The sieved dough comes out through the outlet as shown in the figure.

Materials and Parts: Wire mesh, 44-gallon drum, sheet metal, steel pipes.

Manufacture: Welding.

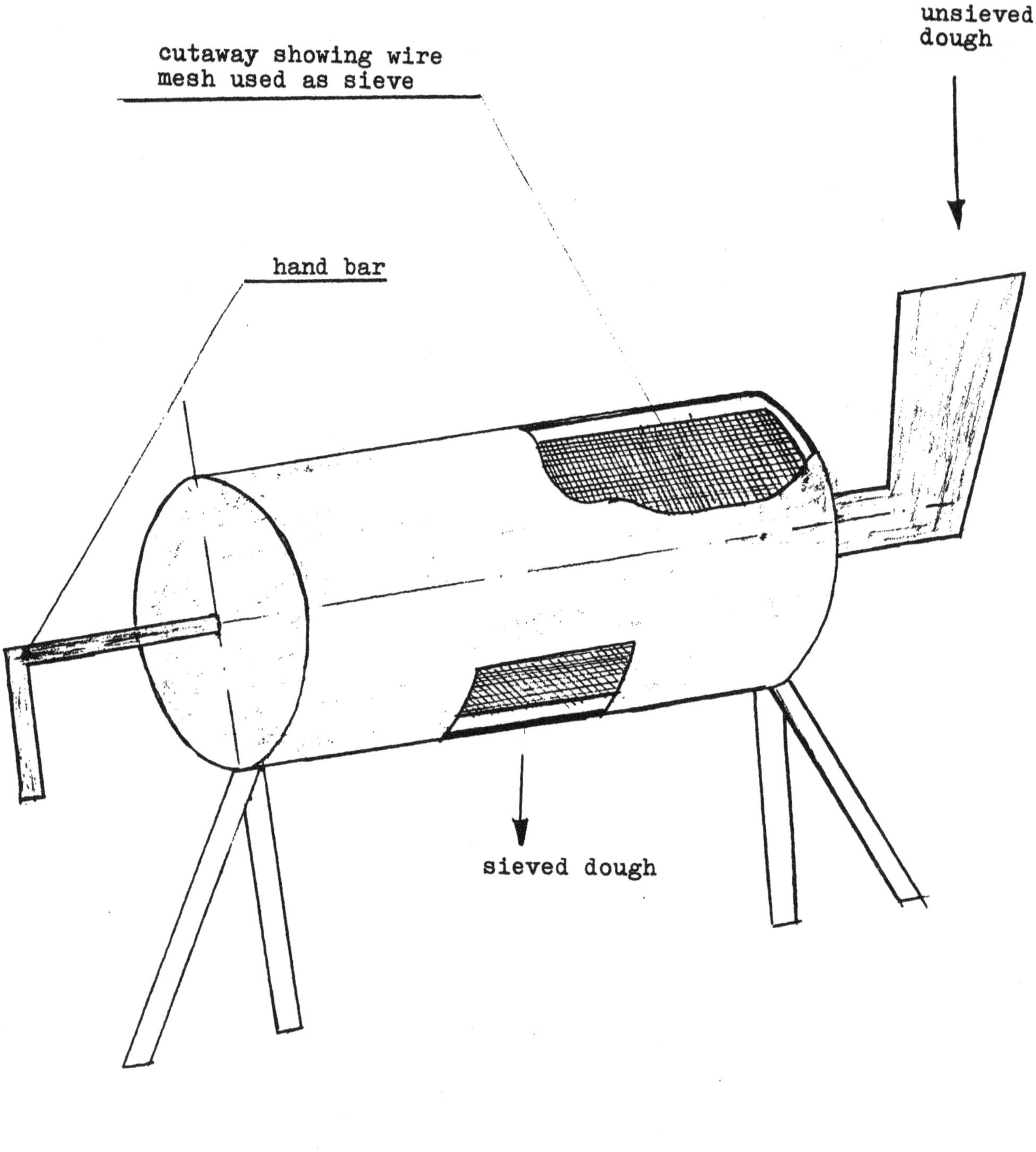

cutaway showing wire
mesh used as sieve

unsieved
dough

hand bar

sieved dough

Fig 3.14   Basic features of hand-operated rotating drum sieve

**Fig. 3.15   Wadhwa power-operated
sieve**

Power operated Sieve

Description and
design aspects:

One variety is developed and manufactured also by Agrico
Ltd. In this version a power operated sieve is used
(see Fig. 3.15). The sieved dough comes out through the
lower outlet while the residue is removed via the upper
outlet.

Materials and parts:

Sheet metal, angle-iron, belt and pulley mechanism,
motor/engine.

Manufacture:

Welding, sheet metal cutting and bending.

Specific advantage:

Low cost.

Suppliers:

Agrico Ltd., Ghana.
Agro Machines Ltd., Liberia.

Gari roasters

Roasting pan and stirrer set

Description and design aspects:	A special gari-making pan and stove set are shown in Fig. 3.16. Due to the ease of manufacture such a set can be produced by local artisans. The Agrico variety incorporates a chimney which reduces the smoke. The height of the chimney has to be such as to produce optimum air flow in order to burn the fuel efficiently and maintain constant temperature.
Materials and parts:	Sheet metal, mud and straw/cement sand and stones, wood.
Manufacture:	Sheet metal bending and welding, simple masonry for building stove walls and basic carpentry tools for handle construction.
Specific advantages:	Long stirrer prevents burning of the fingers during roasting as well as enabling the processors to be at some distance from the heat. Chimney arrangement reduces the effects of smoke on the processors.
Disadvantage:	The brick/cemented walls are affected by the heat and have to be rebuilt often.

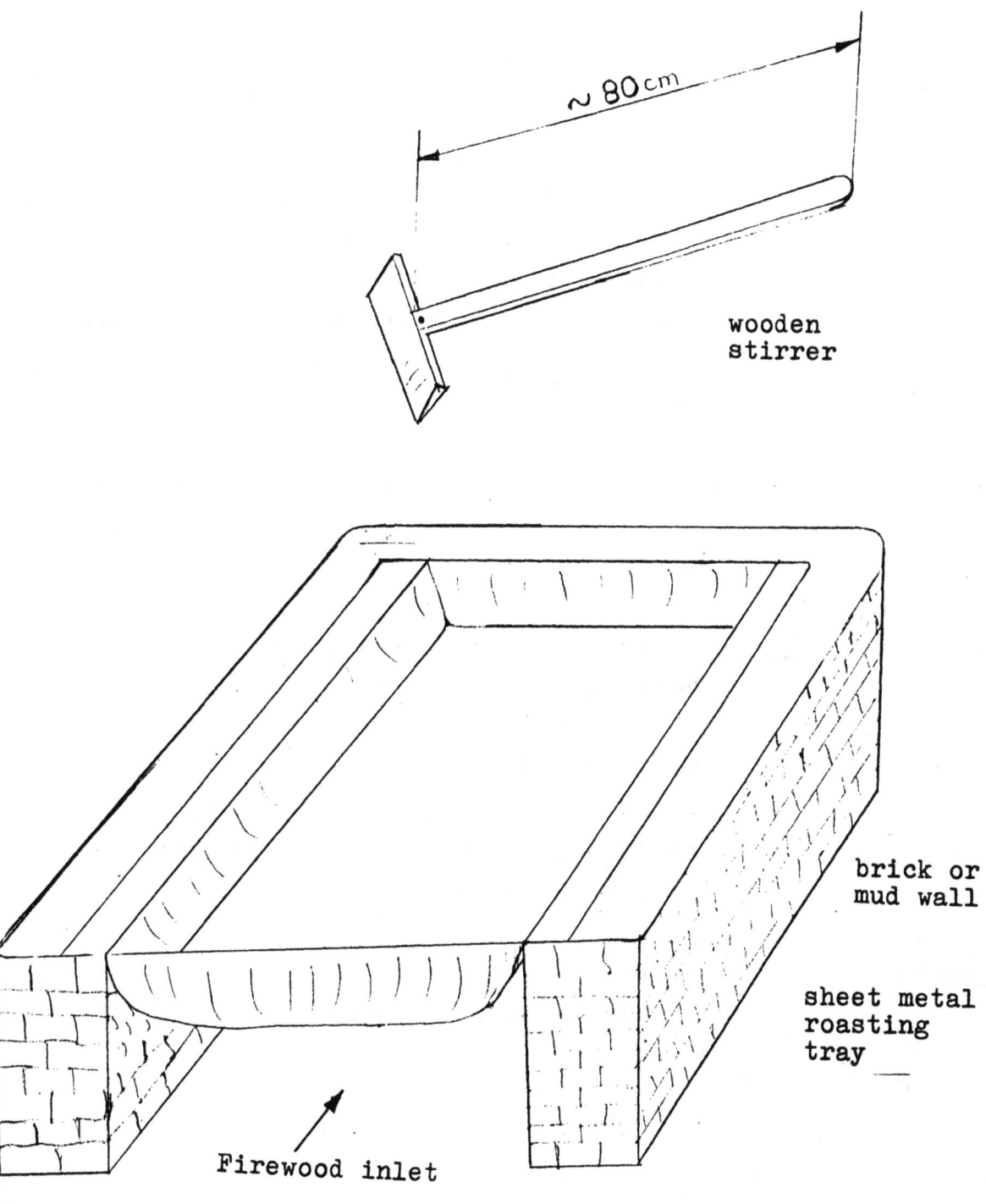

~ 80 cm

wooden
stirrer

brick or
mud wall

sheet metal
roasting
tray

Firewood inlet

Fig. 3.16 <u>Special gari-making pan and stove set</u>
<u>with stirrer</u>

Rotating gari roaster

Description and design aspects:	A type of roaster now in the prototype stage is the rotating roaster, the basic features of which are shown in Fig. 3.17. The sieved gari is fed through a sliding door (not shown) into the drum where it is consinuously stirred by means of stirrers while heat is applied at the bottom. The roasted gari is removed by a second sliding at the base of the drum.
	To minimise fuel use the drum could be made to stand on a brick structure as used for the pan in Fig. 3.16.
Materials and parts:	Metal pipes (rods), 44-gallon drum, metal sheets.
Manufacture:	Welding, sheet metal bending and cutting equipment.
Specific advantages:	Processor is less affected by the heat. More gari can be roasted per processor.
Disadvantage:	Slow turning of the handle would lead to 'caking' of the gari. Also dough requires to be quite dry before roasting. The 'stirrers' need to be carefully designed to ensure continuous stirring.
Supplier:	Agrico Ltd., Ghana. Agro Machines Ltd., Liberia.

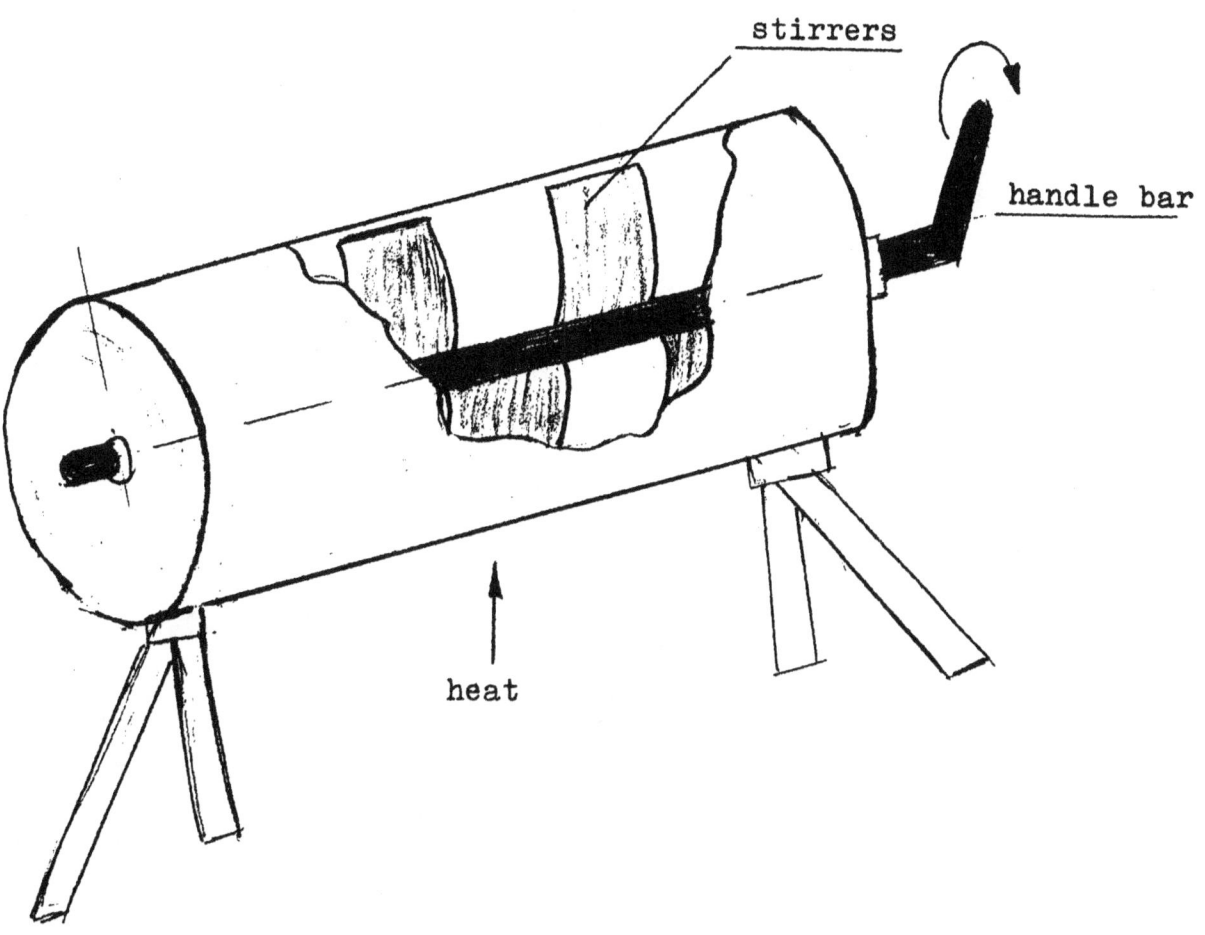

Fig . 3.17. **The basic features of a prototype rotating roaster for gari**

COMPARATIVE PERFORMANCE OF TRADITIONAL AND IMPROVED TECHNOLOGIES

The alternative equipment for processing cassava are compared to the traditional methods in Table 3.2.

It can be seen from this table that the improved technologies either affects the performance figure or reduces certain hazards associated with the traditional technologies.

Table 3.2 Comparison of some figures of merits
of alternative technologies for cassava processing

Operation	Figures of merit	Methods	Values of figures of merits	Comments
(1) Peeling of cassava	Time required to peel 1 kg of cassava	Using knives and hand (sweet variety) Using knives (bitter variety)	(3-4) mins 15 mins	
(2) Sundrying of cassava	Time required to dry given quantity of	(i) in open air (ii) using solar dryer (fig.)	4 days (dry season) 8 days (rainy season) N/A	Figures refer only to Ghana and Sierra Leone
(3) Milling of sun-dried cassava	Time required to mill 10 kg	(i) Mortar and pestle (ii) Power-operated grinding mill	18 mins N/A	These are the plate or hammer mills used for maize (see chapter)
(4) Grating of cassava	Time required to grate 1 kg of cassava	(i) Traditional grater (ii) Hand-operated grater (iii) Mechanised grater (fig. 3.8) Agrico (iv) Mechanised grater (fig. 3.9) TAEC	(10-15 mins) 0.46 mins 0.06 mins 0.12 mins	It is assumed that the "fineness" of the final product is the same in all cases
(5) Pressing of grated cassava	Time required to press 10 kg of grated cassava	(i) Traditional rope and stick (ii) Traditional stones (iii) Wooden frame press (fig. 3.10) (iv) Screw Press (fig. 31.12) (v) Hydraulic Press (fig. 3.13)	 (1-6) hours (30-60) mins 1.2 mins	Reduction of moisture content from 60% to 30% (50% reduction). This is when fermentation is not done simultaneously. Setting up of the operation is made considerably easier.

NOTES TO CHAPTER 3

1 Traditionally, this crop is left unharvested or deliberately buried underground as means of storage.

2 This is known as kokonte in Ghana, attieke in Ivory Coast, 'lafun' in Nigeria.

3 Or gari, farine de manioc, farinya, etc.

4 Called 'foofoo' in Sierra Leone.

5 Source: Survey of villages in Ghana and Sierra Leone.

6 This time varies considerably with length of periods of soaking (see fig. 3.6).

7 (ref. Kaplinsky, 1974).

Chapter 4

VEGETABLE OIL PREPARATION

The major types of vegetable oil produced in West Africa are palm oil, palm kernel oil, coconut oil, groundnut oil and cocoa butter. Only the first three are included in this section.

The fruit of the oil palm (Elaeus guineensis), which grows extensively in West Africa, is very rich in oil obtained both from the exocarp (palm oil) and from the kernel (palm kernel oil). The traditional processes through which the two types of oil are obtained in Ghana and Sierra Leone are outlined in the block diagram of fig. 4.1. The traditional West African oil palm grows wild in the rain forests and an improved (hybrid) variety is cultivated on plantations in both countries. The fruit from the improved variety is characterised by its thicker exocarp and smaller endocarp, as compared to the traditional variety.[1]

Coconut (cocos nucifera) grows widely along the coastal regions in West Africa. Its meat can be processed into coconut oil.

TRADITIONAL METHODS OF PALM OIL PREPARATION

Description

Line A of fig. 4.1 shows the stages in palm oil preparation. The palm fruits which are harvested in bunches are covered with leaves and left to stand in the sun for 1-15 days (average 3 days). This enables the fruit to shrink and loosen from the bunch, after which they are removed with axes (Sierra Leone), cutlasses (Ghana and Sierra Leone), by hitting on a hard surface (Sierra Leone) and by hand (Ghana and Sierra Leone). Removal of the palm fruits from one bunch takes between 10 and 120 minutes, depending on the breed of palm, the size of the bunch, the length of time after harvesting the fruit, and the method of removal. The fruits are then either boiled or fermented.

Boiling is done mainly in 44-gallon drums although metal containers, earthenware pots and the traditional "iron pot"[2] are sometimes used. For the traditional variety, fruits from an average of 24 bunches are boiled, while for the improved variety fruits from an average of 13 bunches are boiled.[3] The fruit is boiled for 5-10 hours usually on a three-stone fire.

Fig.5.12 Palm oil and palm kernel oil preparation and use of by-products

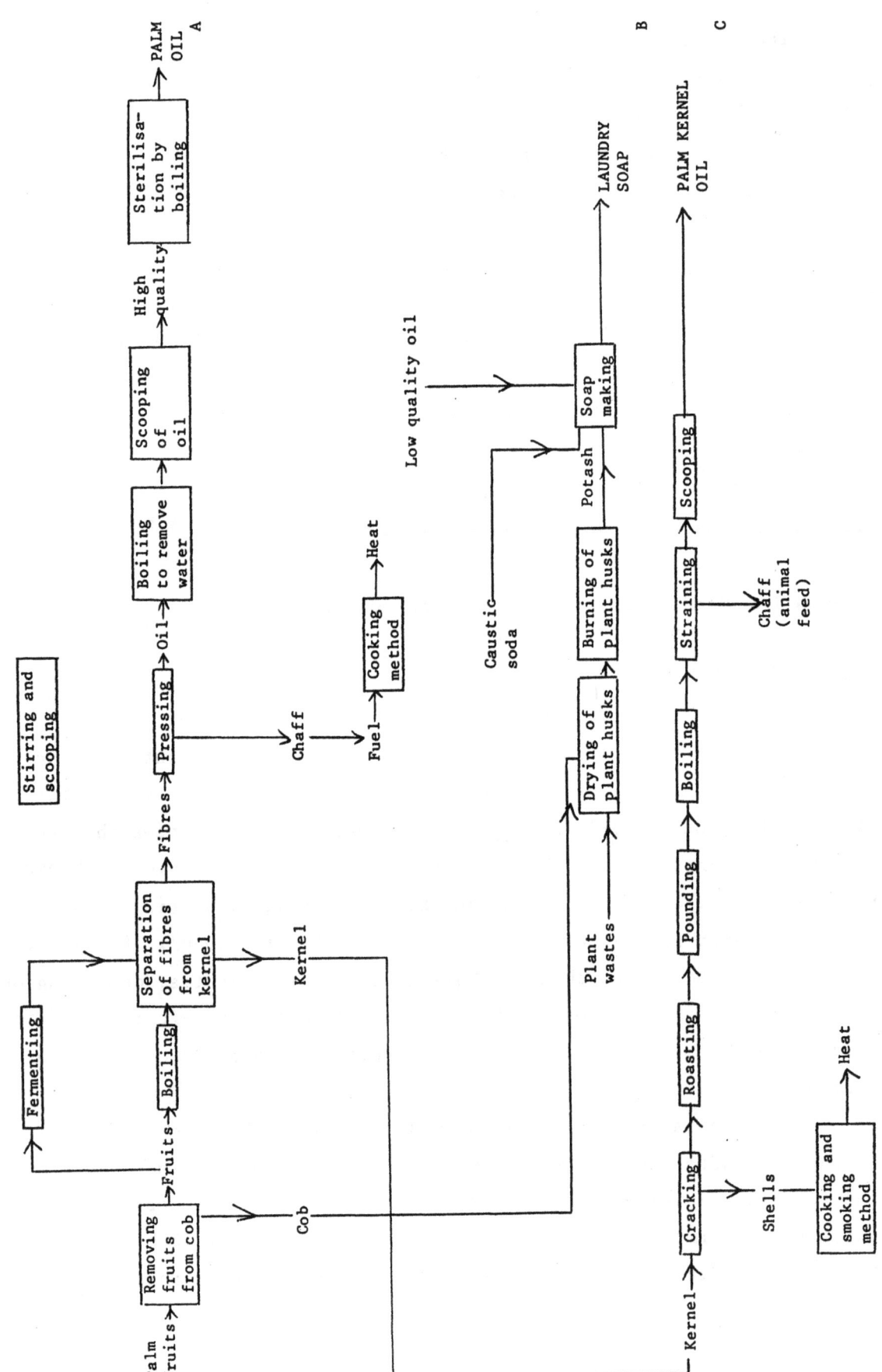

Fermentation of the fruit is sometimes done as an alternative to boiling. This is done by covering the fruits in a hole in the ground and leaving them for 1-10 days.

After boiling or fermentation the next stage of the process involves the separation of the oily fibrous exocarp from the kernel. This is done by either pounding in a mortar or by trampling in a pit. Pounding in a mortar is done for 10-15 minutes. After pounding the kernel is separated from the fibre by hand and the fibre is put in a container with hot water. Average mortar capacity per pounding is approximately 30 kg.

The standard pit used in Ghana is a circular one 0.7 metres in depth and with a diameter of 1 metre which is paved inside with stones (fig. 4.2). The boiled fruits are put in the pit and the processor enters and tramples the fruits while also hitting them with a wooden pestle. The process takes 30-60 minutes, during which water is poured into the pit from time to time. The capacity of the pit is about 90 kg of palm fruits.

In Sierra Leone the "pit" is a rectangular structure which varies in size and is built to a height of 0.8 metres above the ground (fig. 4.3). Men stand in the pit and trample on the boiled or fermented fruit while holding on to wooden supports. At intervals water is poured into the pit in order to increase the yield. The length of time spent on this process depends on the size of the pit, the quantity of palm fruits and the number of processors.[4] The average time was recorded as 50 minutes,[5] for average pits of 300 kg of palm fruits.

Separation of the oil from the fibres, kernels and water mixture is done by scooping with a small calabash and sieving with a basket sieve. The scooping takes less than an hour.

The oil is then boiled in 44-gallon drums and other metal containers. After boiling for about an hour the oil is allowed to cool. The thicker, lower-quality oil sinks to the bottom and the lighter oil which is at the top is scooped out. The lower-quality oil is used for making soap.

Technical performance

The palm oil yield from the traditional methods was estimated by the number of bunches of palm fruits required to produce one gallon of oil. This assumes the standard bunch, which can be taken as an average bunch size. Taking an average figure of 15 kg of fruit per bunch[6] the average yield of the hybrid fruits is estimated at 60 kg of fruit per gallon (4.45 litres) of oil. For the traditional variety of palm fruits, this figure is estimated at 80 kg of palm fruits per gallon of oil.

An estimation from the figures given in Larousse Agricole for the percentage by weight of oil in palm fruit bunches gives the amount of oil available in a palm fruit bunch as 24 per cent for the hybrid variety and 19 per cent for the traditional African variety.[7] Thus, the average extraction efficiency of the traditional methods of production can be estimated to be 30 per cent in Ghana and 29 per cent in Sierra Leone, taking the specific gravity of the oil as 1.0 (that is 1 gallon or 4.45 litres of oil weighs 4.45 kg). One can thus conclude that the extraction efficiency defined as the ratio of the weight of oil extracted to the weight of oil extractable (or present in the pulp) is practically the same for the methods of production used in both countries and is estimated at 30 per cent on average.

Firewood is used for boiling the palm fruits as well as for evaporating the water from the oil and sterilising it. The average firewood used per gallon of oil produced was reported to be 9 kg in Ghana and 7 kg in Sierra Leone. Since basically the same method of cooking (the three-stone method) is used in both countries, the difference of 1 kg per gallon of oil can be explained by the fact that boiling times are longer in Ghana.[8]

Advantages

- the methods are inexpensive, the only costs involved being those of the 44-gallon drums or other containers, the mortar and pestle (which find other uses in the home), and the pits which are constructed from local materials by the village artisans.
- with the enlargement of the pits a greater number of people can participate in the pulp removal and the scooping of the oil.
- a large quantity, (up to 35 bunches) can be processed in one batch in the pits.

Disadvantages

- the efficiency (approximated at 30 per cent) is low since a large percentage of the oil in the coloidal water solution cannot be scooped out.
- the method of trampling fruits is unhygienic.
- it is time consuming, requiring long hours of boiling (on an average 10 hours in Ghana and 6 hours in Sierra Leone).
- labour, fuel and water use is high.

TRADITIONAL METHOD OF PALM-KERNEL OIL PREPARATION

Description

The palm kernels are cracked after being sun dried . The traditional method of cracking is by placing the nuts on a flat, hard surface (usually of stone) and hitting them with a rock. When this method of cracking is utilised 80-95 per cent of the nuts come out whole. A handful of kernels at a time is put on the flat surface and hit with a smaller stone, this cracks them and the nuts are released. In the areas studied in Ghana, after cracking one batch of kernels, the nuts and broken shells are put away to be sorted out only when the cracking of a whole basket is completed. In Sierra Leone sorting is done immediately after cracking open one batch (handful) of nuts. The average time taken to produce 15 kg[9] of cracked nuts was reported to range between 3-5 hours.

The cracked nuts are further sun dried and roasted over a fire. Roasting is mainly done in sheet-metal pans. Other containers used are earthenware containers and the traditional "iron pots". Wooden spoons are mostly used as stirrers but calabash pieces are also used for stirring the nuts during roasting. Roasting is done for 1-4 hours.

After roasting the nuts are ground by mortar and pestle. It takes on average 1.6 hours to pound 12 kg of palm nuts. The pounded nuts are put into water and boiled. After boiling the oil which floats at the top is scooped out with calabashes, metal spoons, wooden spoons and metal "three-penny" pans.[10] It takes on average 1.1 hours in Ghana and 2 hours in Sierra Leone to scoop out one gallon of oil from the boiling mixture.

Fuel is utilised in the traditional production of palm-kernel oil for roasting the nuts and boiling the milled nuts/water mixture.

The total firewood used for palm-kernel oil production is estimated to be 6 kg - 7 kg per gallon of oil produced.

Technical performance

The quantity, by weight of nuts, required to produce a gallon[11] of palm-kernel oil was reported on average to be 27 kg in Ghana and 18 kg in Sierra Leone. Assuming a 60 per cent, by weight, oil content of the palm nuts (Agrico, 1977) these figures represent efficiencies of 27 per cent and 41 per cent respectively.

While roasting is necessary to release the oil in the nuts, it was observed that optimum values of roasting temperatures and roasting times exist. One explanation for this could be that at high temperatures and during prolonged drying periods some of the oil content of the nut is vapourised during roasting, a fact which is confirmed by the thick characteristic-smelling fumes which escape from the roasted nuts.

Advantages

- it is inexpensive as all the equipment utilised in the production is either obtained free of charge, as is the case for the stones for cracking, or is commonly-used household equipment.
- the extent of milling can be controlled by the processor when pestle and mortar are used.

Disadvantages

- the methods are time-consuming and labour-intensive and physically strenuous.
- there is long exposure of the processors to extreme heat during the roasting of the nuts.
- yields are low (estimated figures are 27 per cent and 41 per cent of extractable oil).

TRADITIONAL METHOD OF COCONUT OIL PREPARATION

Description

The traditional method of coconut oil production is given in table 4.2. This is the wet method. The first step in the preparation of coconut oil is the removal of the fibre from the fruit. This is traditionally done by means of a cutlass. On average it takes 3 minutes to remove the fibre from one nut. The coconuts are cracked and shelled either with cutlass or by hitting the fruit on a hard surface. One coconut is shelled in 3 minutes on average. The shelled coconut is then grated using a perforated metal grater (see fig. 4.2). On average it takes 2 hours to grate 10 coconuts. Water is next added to the grated coconut and the chaff is sieved off by using a metal pan or a wire mesh sieve. Boiling is done in 44-gallon drums, iron pots or other metal containers. A metal spoon or three-penny pan is used to scoop the oil as the boiling mixture cools. One to two hours are required in order to scoop a gallon of oil in this way.

Fig.4.2 Traditional method of coconut oil preparation

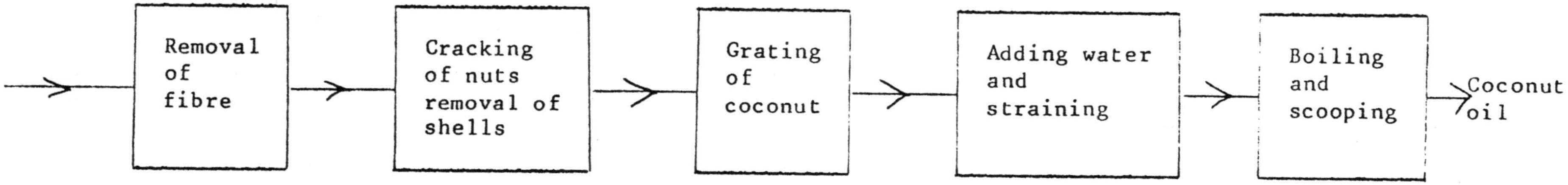

Technical performance

The average yield of coconut oil from the traditional method was estimated at 40 coconuts per gallon of oil produced. Allowing a percentage of oil by weight in coconuts as 34% and the average weight of one coconut as 1 kg,[12] the extraction efficiency by the traditional method can be calculated as 36%.[13]

Average firewood use in the preparation of coconut oil is 12 kg per gallon of oil produced.

Advantages

- no special equipment required; household equipment entirely used.
- the wet processing method gives a higher quality oil because the nuts are processed fresh and deterioration associated with drying coconuts (for dry-processing methods) is minimal.

Disadvantages

- lacerations of fingers during grating.
- certain operations expose the processor to danger e.g. removal of fibre by cutlass, and scooping of hot oil.

IMPROVED EQUIPMENT FOR VEGETABLE OIL PREPARATION

Improved technologies in palm, palm-kernel and coconut oil production are required to perform the following functions:
  - relieve the burden and reduce the time involved in traditional processing methods (for example, in palm fruit boiling and pressing, cracking of palm-kernels, grating of coconuts)
  - render the process more hygienic as compared to the traditional methods of preparation
  - increase the yield (extraction efficiency) of oil.

Methods for preparation of palm, palm-kernel and coconut oil using improved equipment are shown in tables 4.3 and 4.4.

Table 4.3: Methods of production of palm and palm kernel oils using improved equipment

Table 4.4: Method of coconut oil extraction using improved equipment

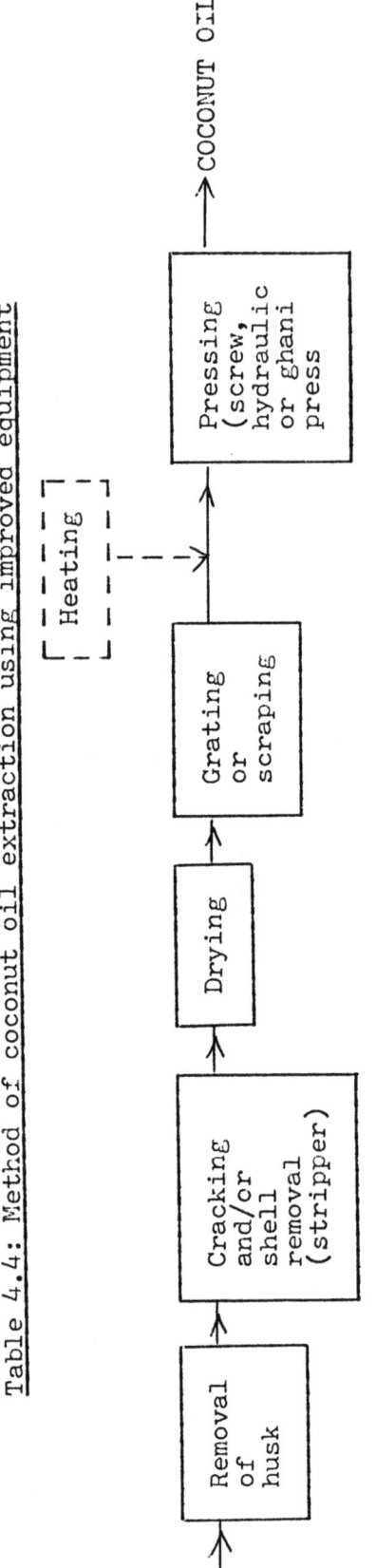

Hand-operated device for removing palm fruits from cob

Description and
design aspects

This device is shown in fig. 4.5. It consists of a drum and a number of rods supported at both ends by discs. Rotation of the handle causes the palm fruits to be removed from the cob by the action of the bars.

Materials and
parts

Sheet metal, wood for frame and discs, iron rods, bearings.

Manufacture

Sheet metal bending and cutting equipment, welding equipment basic carpentry and mechanical tools.

Special advantages

Eliminates the hazards of the traditional methods - accidents which are sometimes caused by cutlass, and pricking of the hands by the thorns in the cobs.

Disadvantage

Can be used with only given sizes of palm fruit bunches.

Supplier

Ceneema.

Fig.4.5 A device for removing palm fruits from the cob

Palm kernel crackers

Description and design aspects	The types of crackers which have been produced use centrifugal force to crack the palm nuts. This force is provided by means of a disc which is rotated inside a drum. A hand-operated cracker of this type is shown in fig. 4.6. It has a capacity of 150-200 kg per hour with 95% of kernels being shelled. The Siscoma cracker (fig. 4.7) is driven by a 3 hp petrol engine while the Agrico cracker is operated by a 5 hp diesel engine. In contrast to the other types of crackers the Agrico device rotates in a horizontal plane.
Materials and parts	Sheet metal, metal pipes or rods, heavy metal base.
Manufacture	Sheet metal bending and cutting equipment, welding equipment, basic mechanical tools.
Special advantages	Relieves the arduousness of shelling palm kernels as well as reduces considerable time required for this operation.
Disadvantages	Does not separate nuts from shells. This means than separation has to be done by hand - a time consuming operation.
Output	Siscoma cracker 300-400 kg/hr Agrico cracker 750 kghr
Suppliers	Agrico, Ltd. SISCOMA.

Fig. 4.6   A hand-operated palm kernel cracker

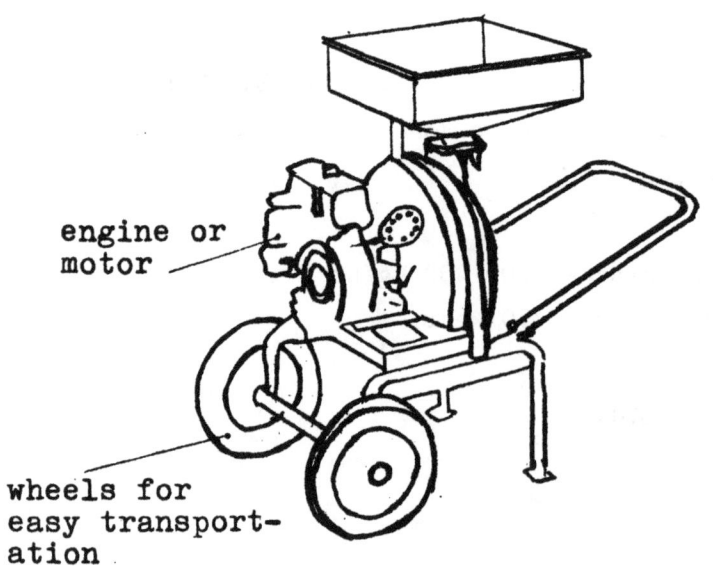

engine or
motor

wheels for
easy transport-
ation

Fig. 4.7   SISCOMA power-operated palm kernel cracker

CECOCO coconut cracker (dehusker)

Description and   This device is shown in Fig. 4.8. It is made mainly of
design aspects   wood and the coconuts are dehusked by cam action. The nut
                       is struck manually against the close toothed blades and
                       next the handle is turned around the coconut snaps into two
                       pieces to separate the core completely: one or two
                       subsequent operations are required.

Materials and   Wood, screws.
parts

Manufacture   Basic carpentry tools.

Special advantages Ease of manufacture.

Output   100-200 coconuts/hour.

Supplier   CECOCO.

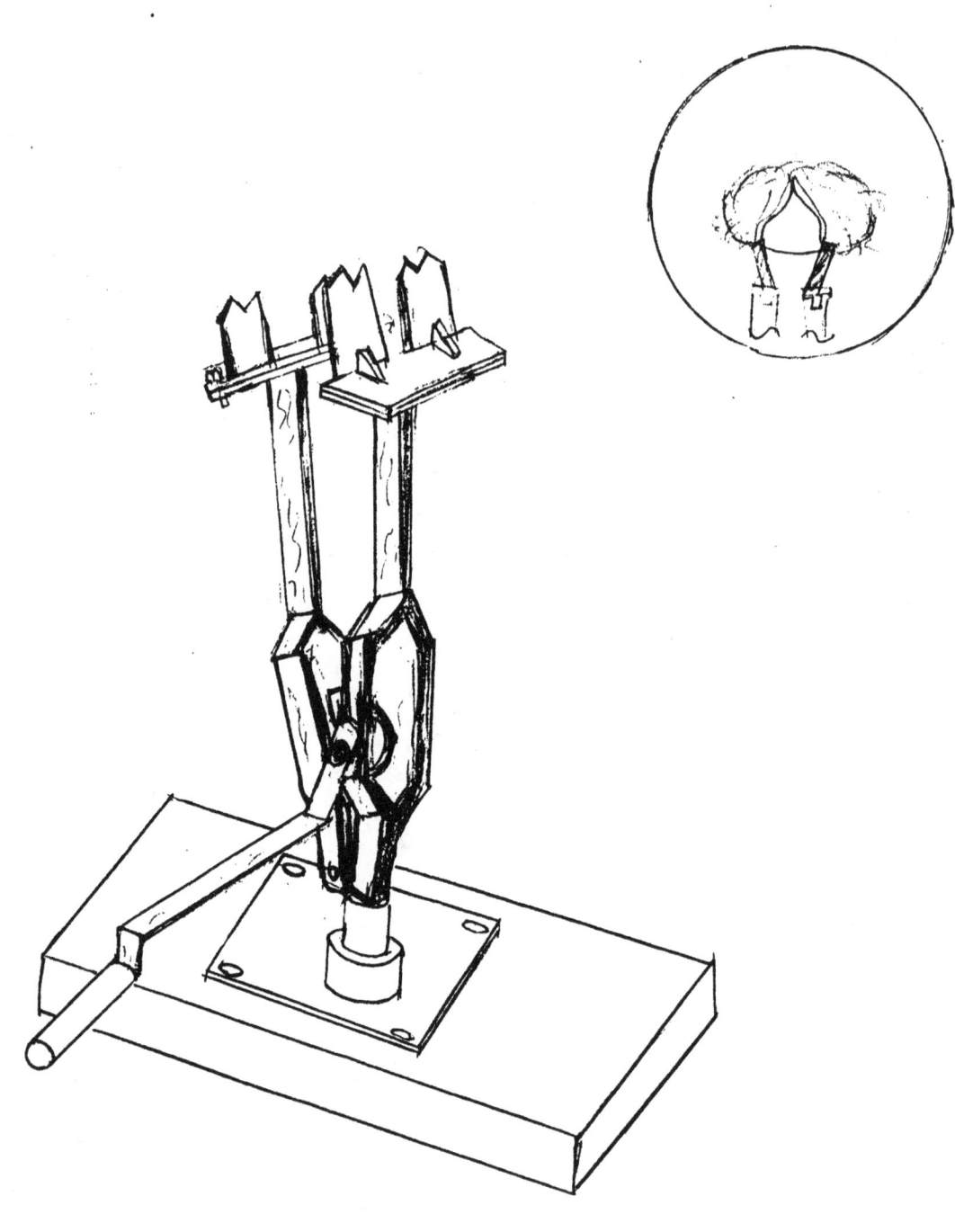

Fig. 4.8 A hand-operated coconut cracker

Coconut scrapers and graters

Simple hand-held coconut scrapers

Description and design aspects	The type of scraper is shown in Fig. 4.9. It is made out of metal plate with slits made as shown. The coconut is scraped with slitted edge of the device. Another type of hand-held scraper is shown in Fig. 4.10. It is manufactured by the TAEC in Sierra Leone. The coconut is scraped by means of sheet metal blades shown.
Materials	Metal plate, wooden handle for TAEC type.
Manufacture	Steel plate cutting, basic carpentry tools.
Special advantage	Low cost and ease of manufacture.
Suppliers	Tikonko Agricultural Extension Centre.

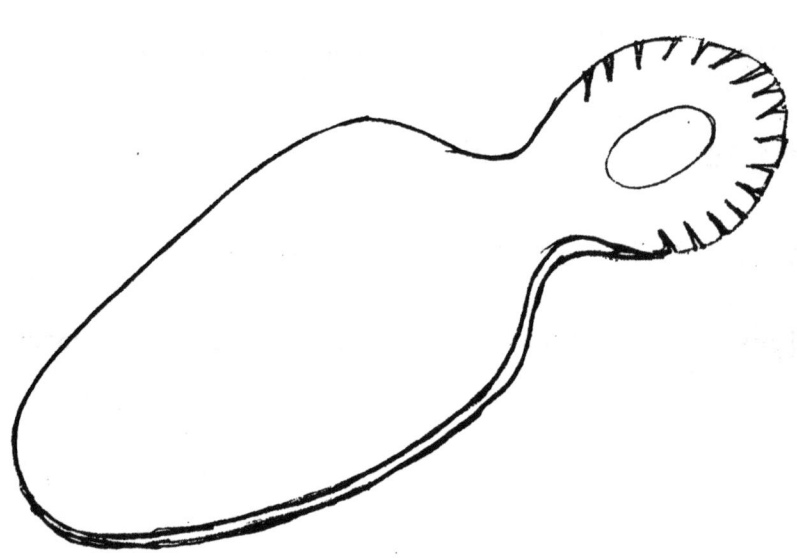

Fig. 4. 9 <u>A hand-held coconut scraper</u>

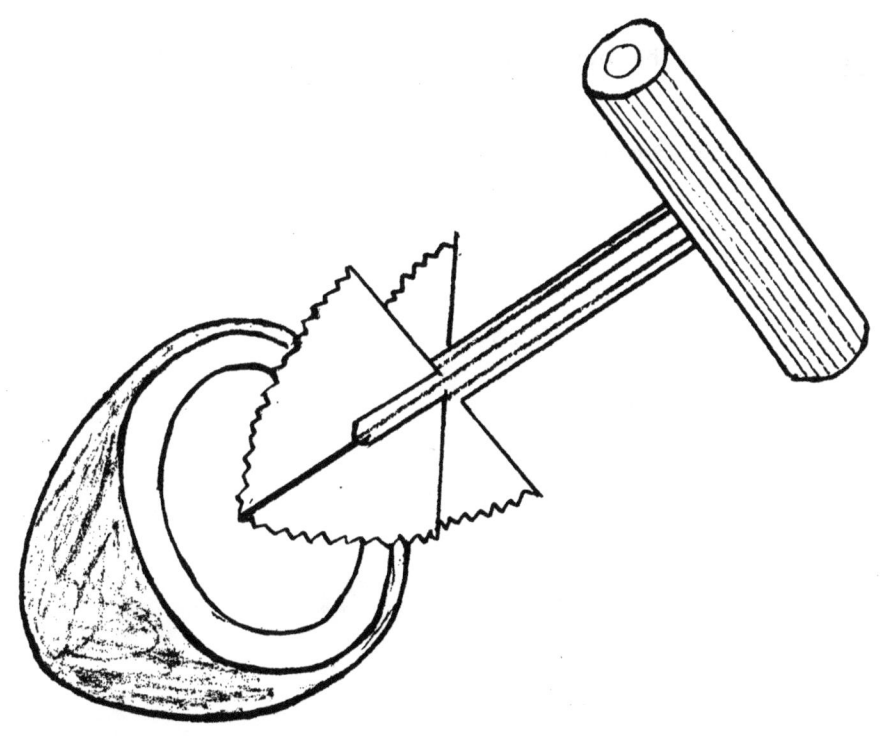

Fig. 4.10   TAEC hand-held coconut scraper

Simple threadle-operated coconut scraper

Description and
design aspects

In this device (Fig. 4.11) the coconut is scraped by means
of a group of rotating nail heads arranged as shown. A
flexible pole is used as a spring for the threadle
mechanism.

Materials

Flexible wooden pole (e.g. bamboo), nails, wood and strong
string or rope.

Manufacture

Can be owner made. Requires no specific skills.

Special advantages Low cost and ease of manufacture.

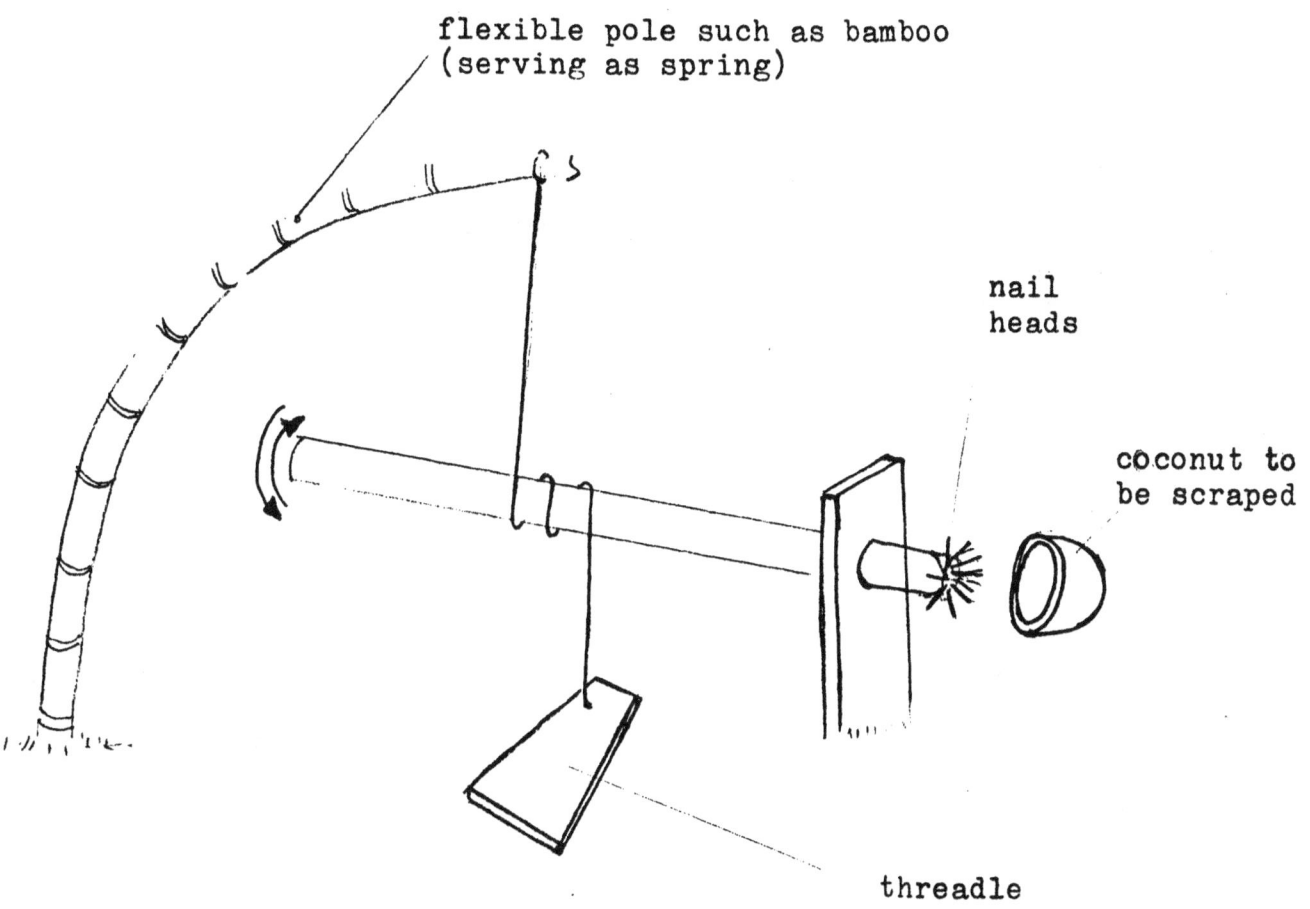

flexible pole such as bamboo
(serving as spring)

nail
heads

coconut to
be scraped

threadle

Fig.4. 11 Simple threadle-operated coconut scraper

Hand-operated coconut scraper

Description and design aspects	This type of scraper is shown in Fig. 4.12. The difference between this and hand-held variety described earlier is that scraping is done by means of rotation of the handle.
Materials and parts	Sheet metal blades, front axle and bearing of bicycle wheel, wooden handle, screw.
Manufacture	Welding equipment, basic mechanical tools.
Special advantage	Can be manufactured almost entirely by using scraps from old bicycles.

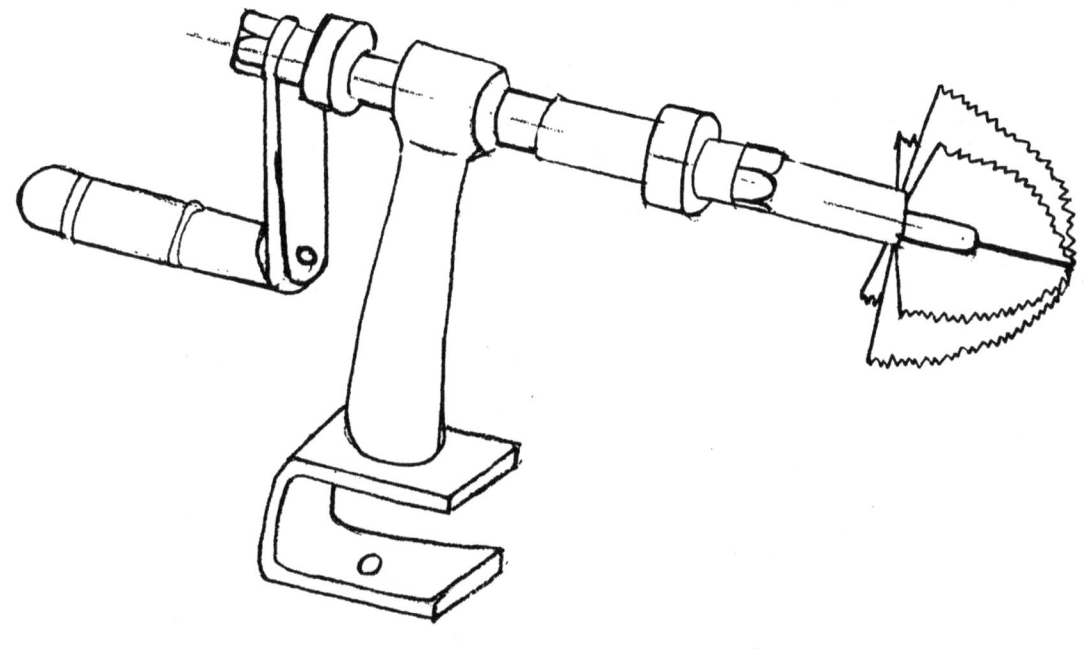

Fig. 4.12 <u>A hand-operated coconut scraper</u>

Coconut grater (engine-operated)

Description and
design aspects

In this device (manufactured in Djakou, Benin), the grater
is a grooved cylinder which rotates inside a prism as shown
in Fig. 4.13. The inclined surface holds the pieces in
position while rotation of the grooved cylinder causes
grating of the coconut.

Materials

Wood for body of machine and cylinder. Sheet metal for
grooves, angle iron for legs, (bearings), fan belt for
connection to engine.

Manufacture

Basic carpentry tools.

Special advantages

In some parts of West Africa where wood is plentiful its
use instead of metal reduces the cost of production.

Output

300 nuts in 4-5 hours.

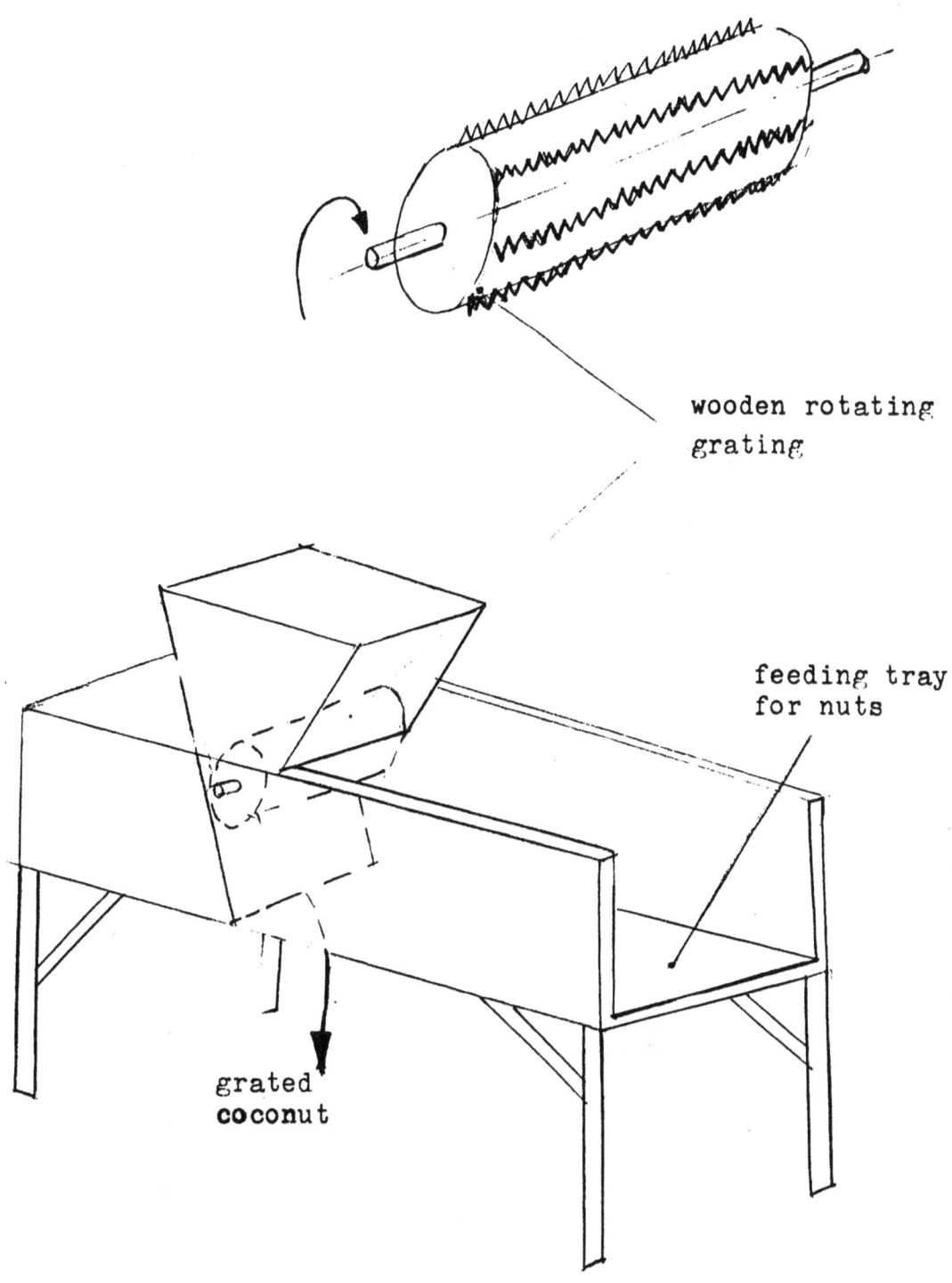

wooden rotating
grating

feeding tray
for nuts

grated
coconut

Fig. 4.13 A power-operated coconut grater

Palm kernel roaster

Description and
design aspects   Palm kernels can be roasted on an oil drum roaster (see
                   Fig. 4.14). Such a roaster consists of a drum which can be
                   hand-rotated over a fire. The nuts are placed in the drum
                   which is rotated thus allowing the nuts to roast. Loading
                   and unloading are done by means of a sliding door as shown
                   in the diagram.

Materials   Wire mesh, iron bars for support and shaft wooden handle.

Manufacture   Basic carpentry and metal working tools.

Special advantage The processor is at some distance from the heat.

sliding door

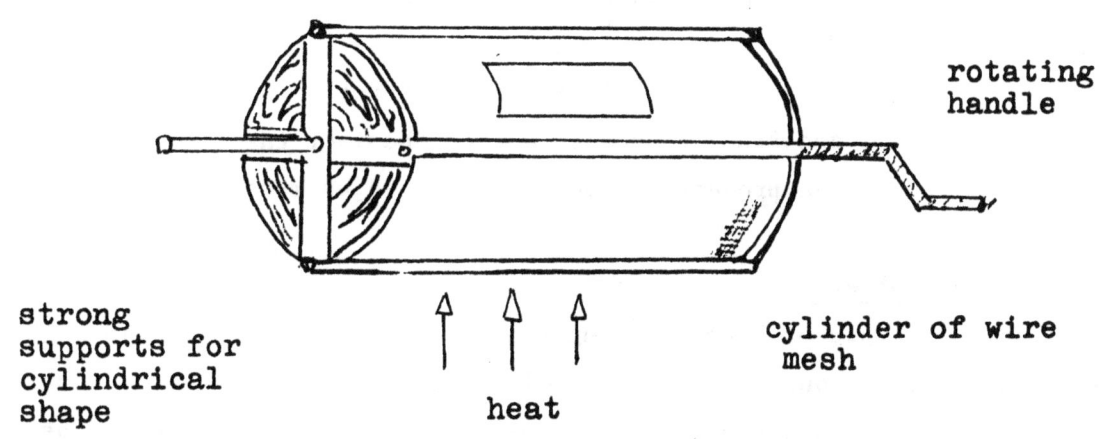

rotating
handle

strong
supports for
cylindrical
shape

heat

cylinder of wire
mesh

Fig. 4.14 <u>Basic features of a palm kernel roaster</u>

Coconut and palm kernel crushers

Description and
design aspects

Crushing of palm kernels can be done in adapted maize
mills. These are plate mills. Hammer and roller mills
could also be used for milling of palm kernels. Fig. 4.15
shows a cross section of a hammer mill which can be used
for this purpose. Hammer mills have only one rotating
shaft making 2000-3000 revolutions per minute. On this
shaft are mounted swinging or fixed beaters (hammers).
Size reduction is brought about by the impact of the
hammers as well as some cutting and rubbing action. The
product, sufficiently reduced, passes through a screen
which has either perforated plates or bars.

Hammer mills can be used for both preliminary crushing
and final reduction due to the fact that the fineness of
the product can be varied by adjustment.

Seed-crushing rollers

The principle of seed crushing rollers is shown in Fig. 4.16. The nuts
are fed and crushed between pairs of rollers as shown. Two grooved horizontal
rollers are turned in opposite directions and at different speeds. The
rollers are spring loaded to avoid damage due to hard foreign objects and the
pressure can be controlled by adjusting the spring. Roll clearance can be set
to suit the character of the seeds.

When roller mills are used for preliminary breaking of coconuts they
are known as breaker rolls. A special type of three-pair high roller mill is
shown in Fig. 4.17. The rollers are fluted and the fluting is progressively
reduced from coarse to fine.

Agrico nut disintegrator

The Agrico disintegrator manufactured by Agrico Ltd. is a hammer mill
which incorporates a variety of screens which grade the product so that the
fineness can be varied by changing the screens. It is driven by a diesel
engine or electric motor. Specifications of the types produced are as
follows:

Size	Diameter of chamber	Speed	H.P.
12	305 mm	5 000	7.5/10
17	432 mm	4 100	10/15
22	559 mm	3 300	15/20

Advantages of crushers described

- They save time and labour.
- They can be adjusted to give finer textures. Also grinding could be done in stages moving from coarse to smooth.

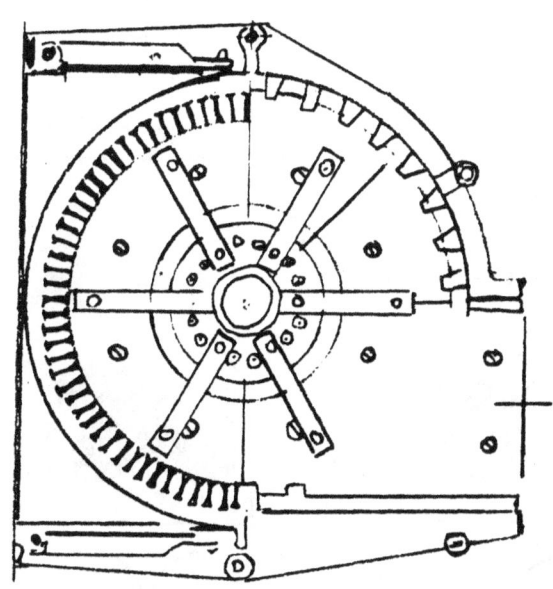

Fig. 4.15 Diagram of a Hammer Mill (Thieme, 1968)

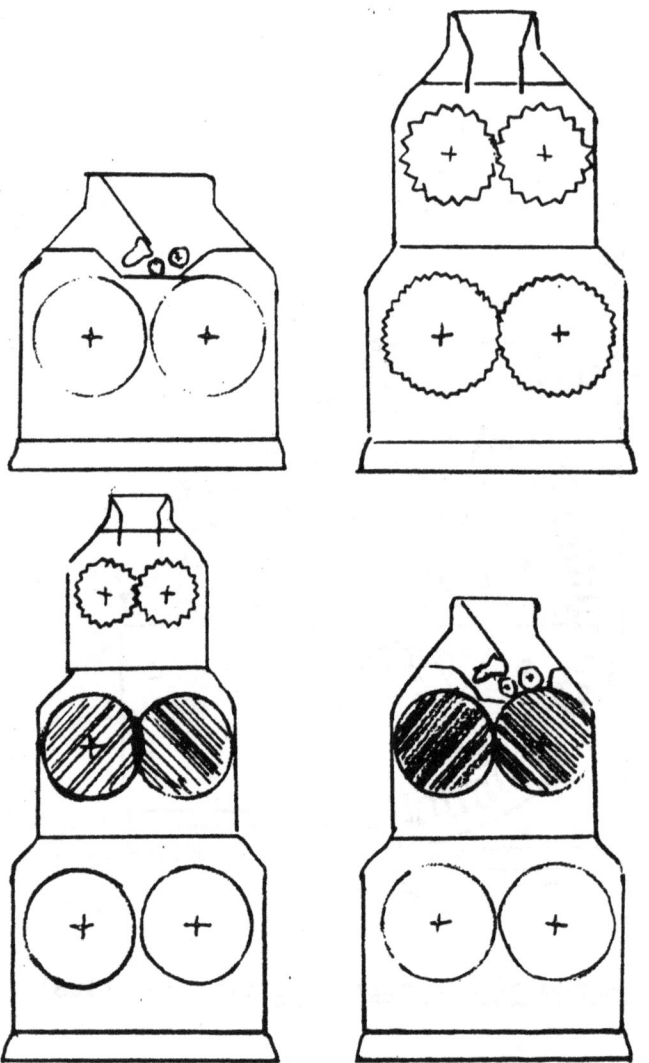

Fig. 4.16 Seed crushing rollers (Thieme, 1968)

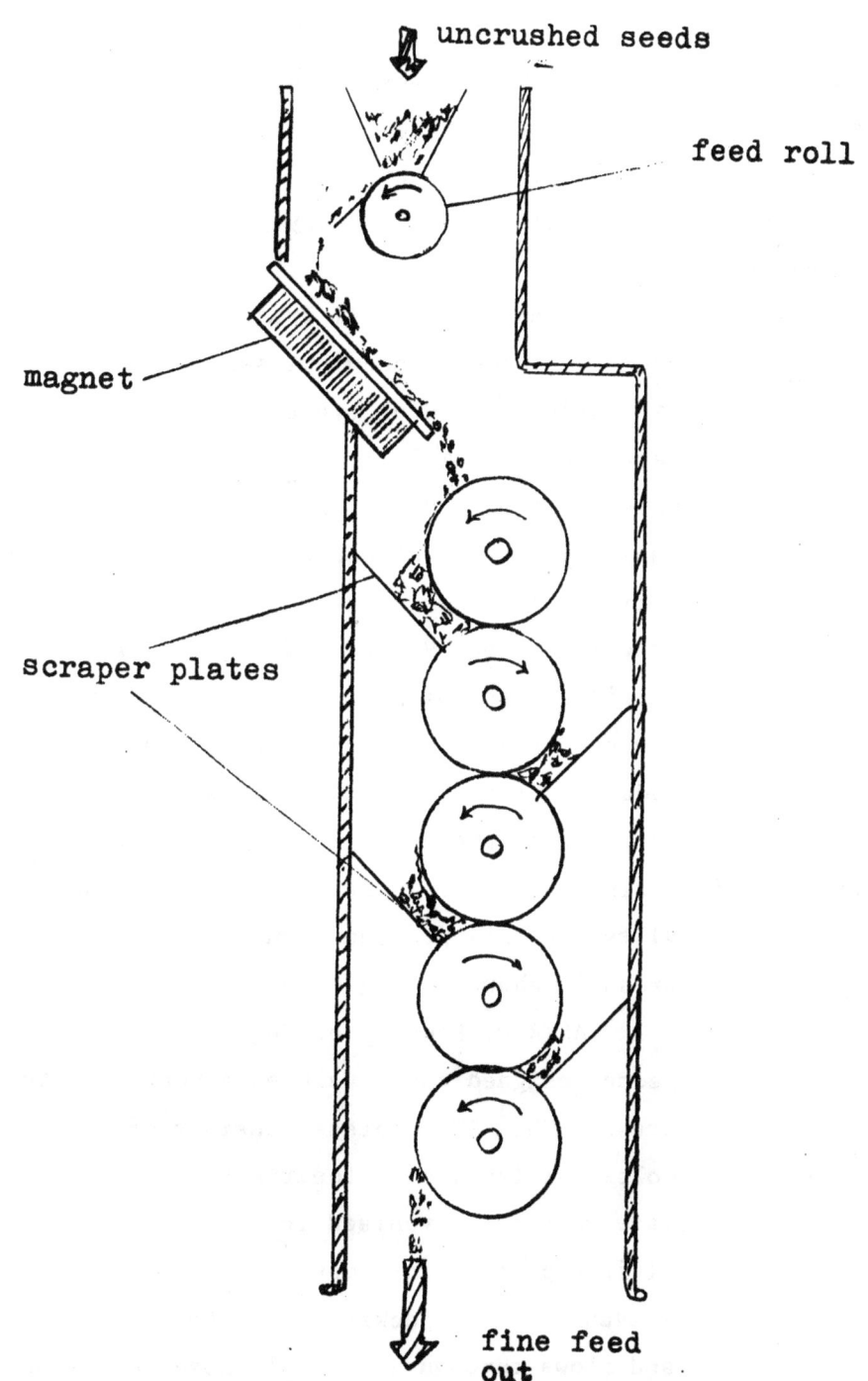

Fig. 4.17 Series of seed crushing rollers (Thieme, 1968)

Presses for vegetable oil extraction

The wedge, screw and hydraulic presses described in chapter 3 can also be used for oil extraction. In this case, unlike cassava processing, the extracted liquid is of primary interest and has to be adequately collected. The presses described are called 'batch' presses because the material is pressed in batches. In 'continuous' presses the cake is automatically ejected and fresh material can be fed in continuously.

Batch oil screw presses

Description and
design aspects

After pounding the palm fruits and separation of the pulp from the kernels screw presses can be employed for oil extraction. Several types of screw presses are in use in West Africa (fig.4.18 and fig.4.19). The TCC press[14] uses a pressure of $40kg/m^2$ to extract palm oil. Its capacity is 20kg of pounded boiled fruit and extraction efficiency, assuming a 20% yield of oil by weight of fruits ranges between 79% and 85%. These figures refer to the hybrid variety of palm fruits. When the traditional fruits are used the screw press's performance is considerably reduced due to the high viscosity of the oil and the clogging of the holes in the cylinder as the oil solidifies during pressing. Heating of the pulp during pressing can alleviate this problem. One suggestion for a heat-assisted press is shown in fig.4.20.

ASTRAD, Faculty of Engineering, University of Sierra Leone designed and developed a heat-assisted palm oil press. The ASTRAD press consists of two cylinders with holes drilled around their surfaces. The inner cylinder is made of thin galvanised iron sheet and the outer cylinder of iron plate. This outer cylinder is enclosed in a thin galvanised iron jacket. The steam is provided by a boiler and flows through a flexible hose to the outer cylinder. Design of the boiler and its position ensures that he boiler remains just slightly above atmospheric pressure and that this pressure can be withstood.

Materials and   See screw presses under cassava pressing.
parts and
manufacture

Suppliers   TCC Ghana, ASTRAD, CENEEMA, National Workshop.

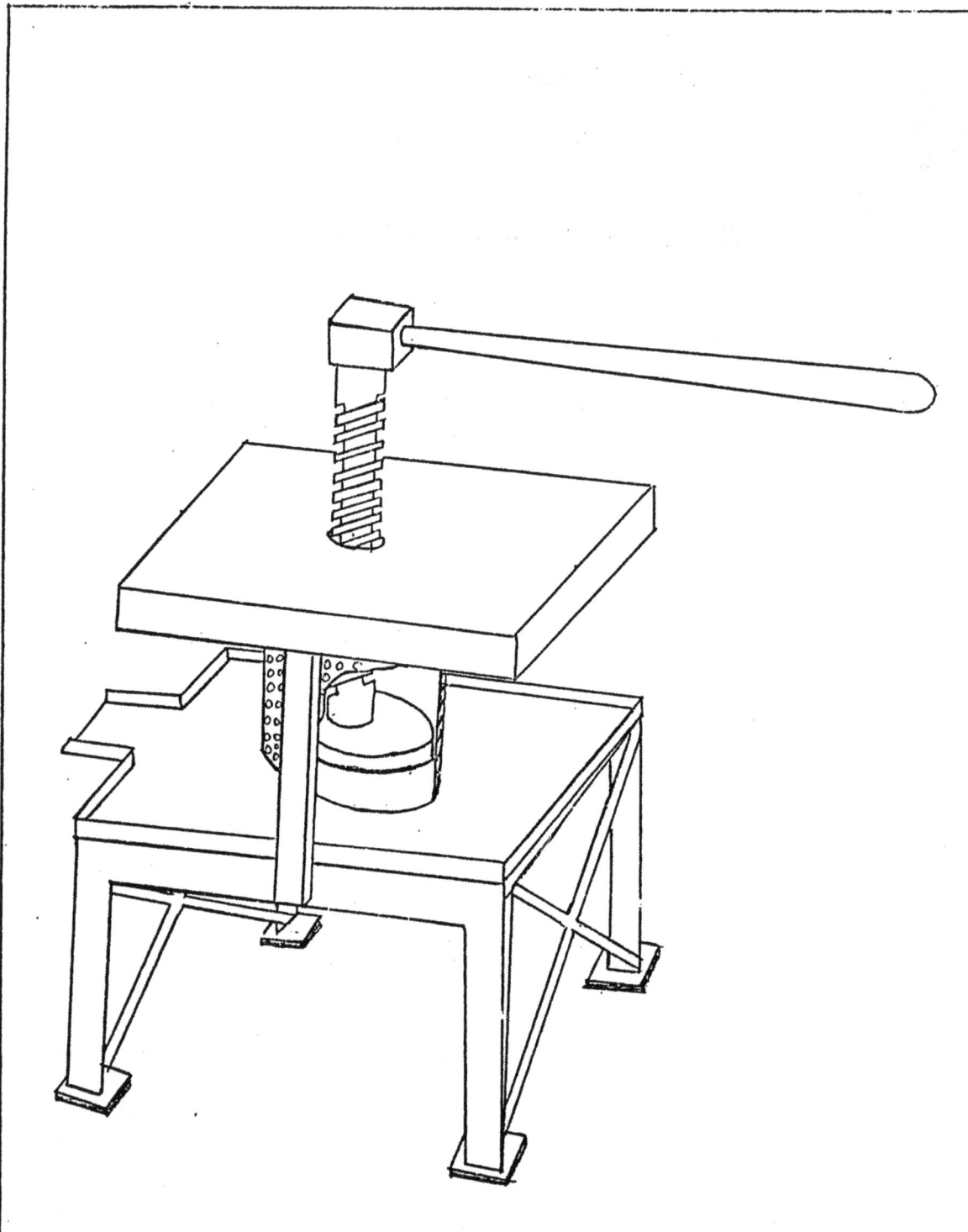

Fig. 4.18 One version of a palm oil press in use

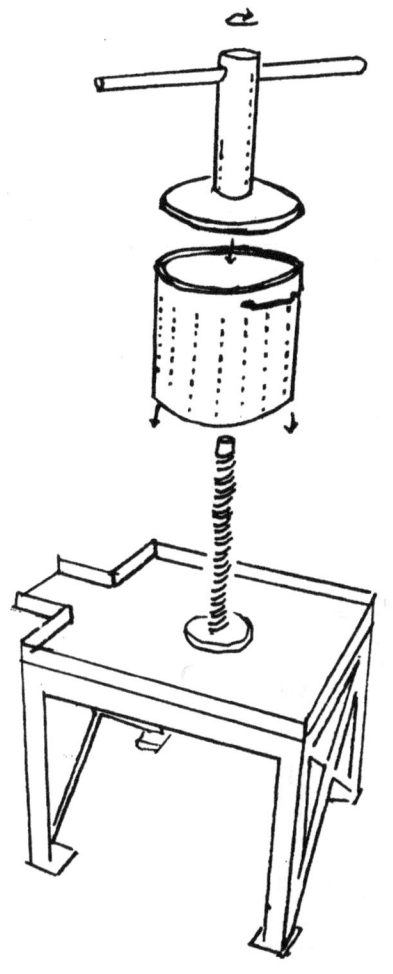

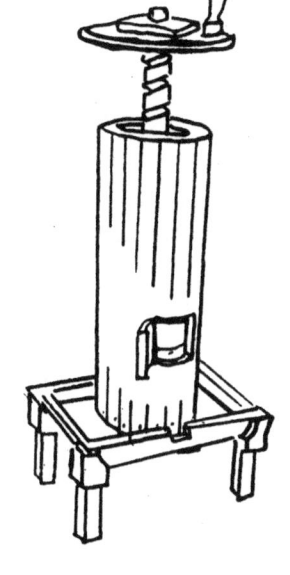

(a) TCC screw press
(Ghana)

(b) Wooden screw press
(CENEEMA, Cameroon)

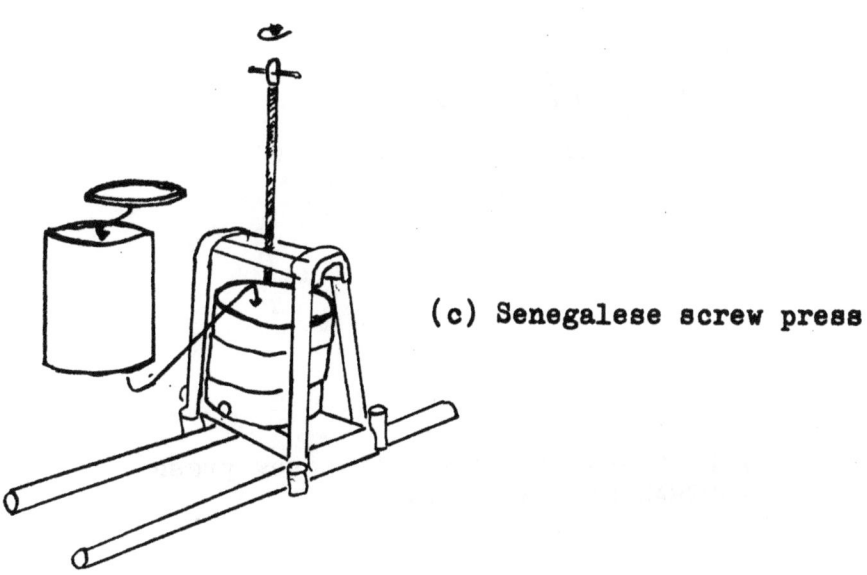

(c) Senegalese screw press

Fig. 4.19   Batch screw presses for oil extraction

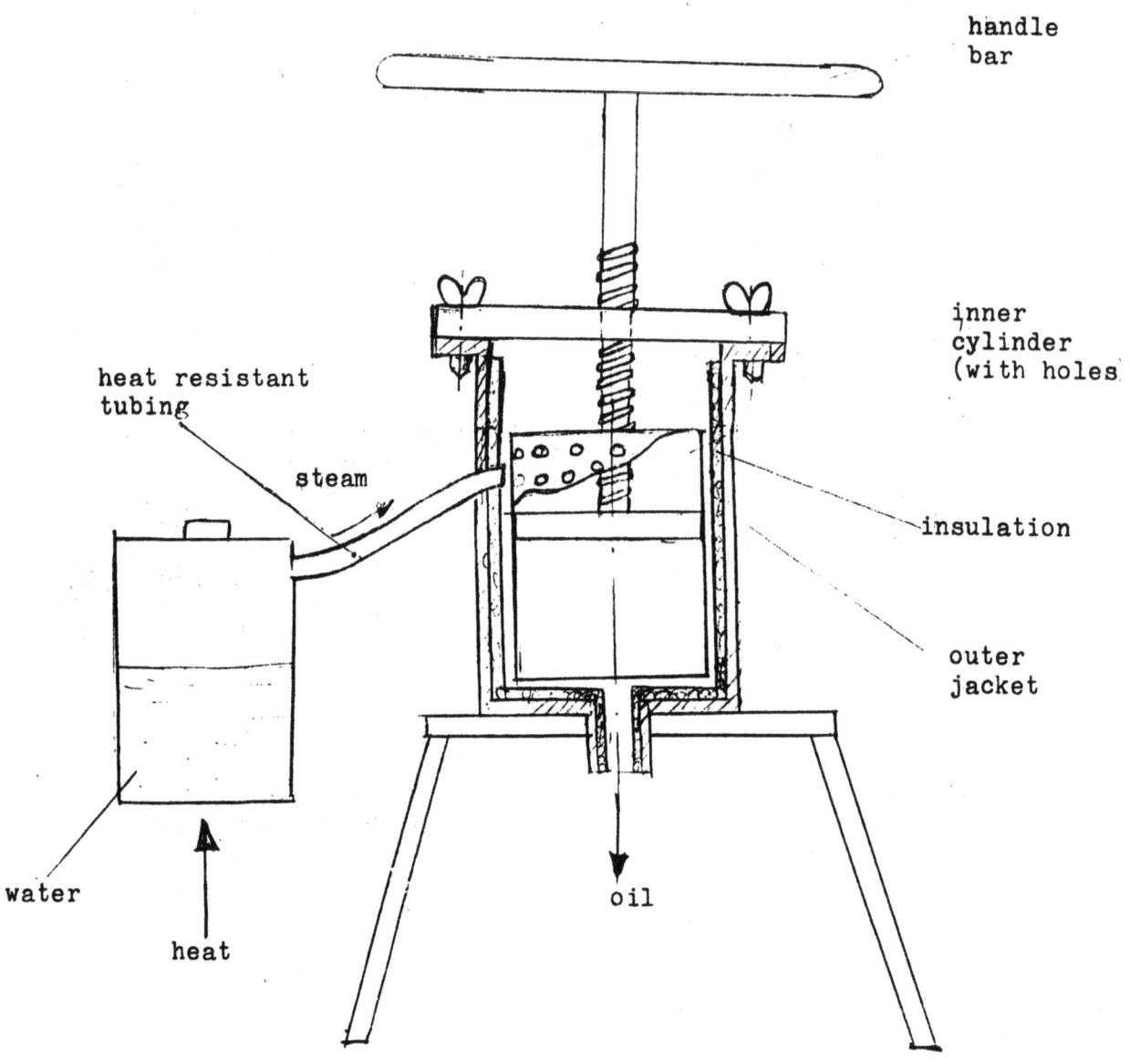

handle
bar

inner
cylinder
(with holes

heat resistant
tubing

steam

insulation

outer
jacket

water

heat

oil

Fig. 420 A heat-assisted palm oil screw press
         (ASTRAD Sierra Leone)

Continuous oil screw presses (Expellers)

Description and design aspects	This machine consists of a seed feeder, for feeding the oil seeds, a pressing box, a cage which surrounds the shaft carrying the worm and an adjustable cone for press-cake outlet. When the meal is fed the horizontal shaft rotates and causes the meal to push forward by its screw action, the internal pressure being regulated by adjustment of the cone. The oil flows out through perforations on the box and the cake is expelled through the opening around the cone. AGRICO Ltd. of Ghana manufactures one such expeller suitable for crushing groundnuts, copra, cotton seed, linseed palm kernels, castor and other oil seeds.
Materials and parts	High grade forged steel, gears, screw, castings.
Manufacture	Well-equipped workshop facilities (foundry, forging and machinery operations).
Special advantages	Does not need dismantling to discharge and recharge.
Disadvantages	High-cost and need for complicated manufacturing techniques.
Output	AGRICO oil expellers: 60-500kg/hr. Collin's press (no longer manufactured but used in francophone countries) 150 kg/hour.
Suppliers	Agrico, Ltd. Ceneema.

The Stump Press (Ghani)

Description and
design aspects

This type of press is in effect a mortar and pestle. The huge "pestle" can be hand-driven, animal-operated (known as chekkus), or driven by engine or motor (ghanis).

A simple type of ghani consists of a stone or wooden mortar 75 to 100 cm in height which is held firmly to the ground via a sunken rod. Inside the mortar a hole is made as an outlet for the oil. A pestle of hard wood about 150 cm long and 60-80 cm in circumference is placed inside the mortar. A cone-like construction holds the pestle obliquely in position. The pestle revolves while being forced inside the mortar by means of a lever about 5 m long which at its extremity is loaded with stones. The pestle is slowly turned round by means of the applied power at the end of the lever. It moves up and down at the same time thereby crushing the material in the mortar. The pressing is completed by heating the pestle. Fig.4.21 shows one version of a power-operated ghani.

Materials and
parts

Pulley (motor), wood (stone) mortar, wooden pestle, gears, iron casting (in case of iron mortar).

Manufacture

Woodworking lathe and tools, or carving tools (in case of stone mortar) machinery; foundry (in case of iron cast mortar).

Output

Power-operated ghani for coconut oil extraction 93% extraction efficiency. (60% out of the 64% of oil present in the nuts is extracted).

Information on
suppliers

Khadi & Village Industries Commission,
Gramodaya,
3, Irla Road,
Vile Park West,
BOMBAY 400 065,
India.

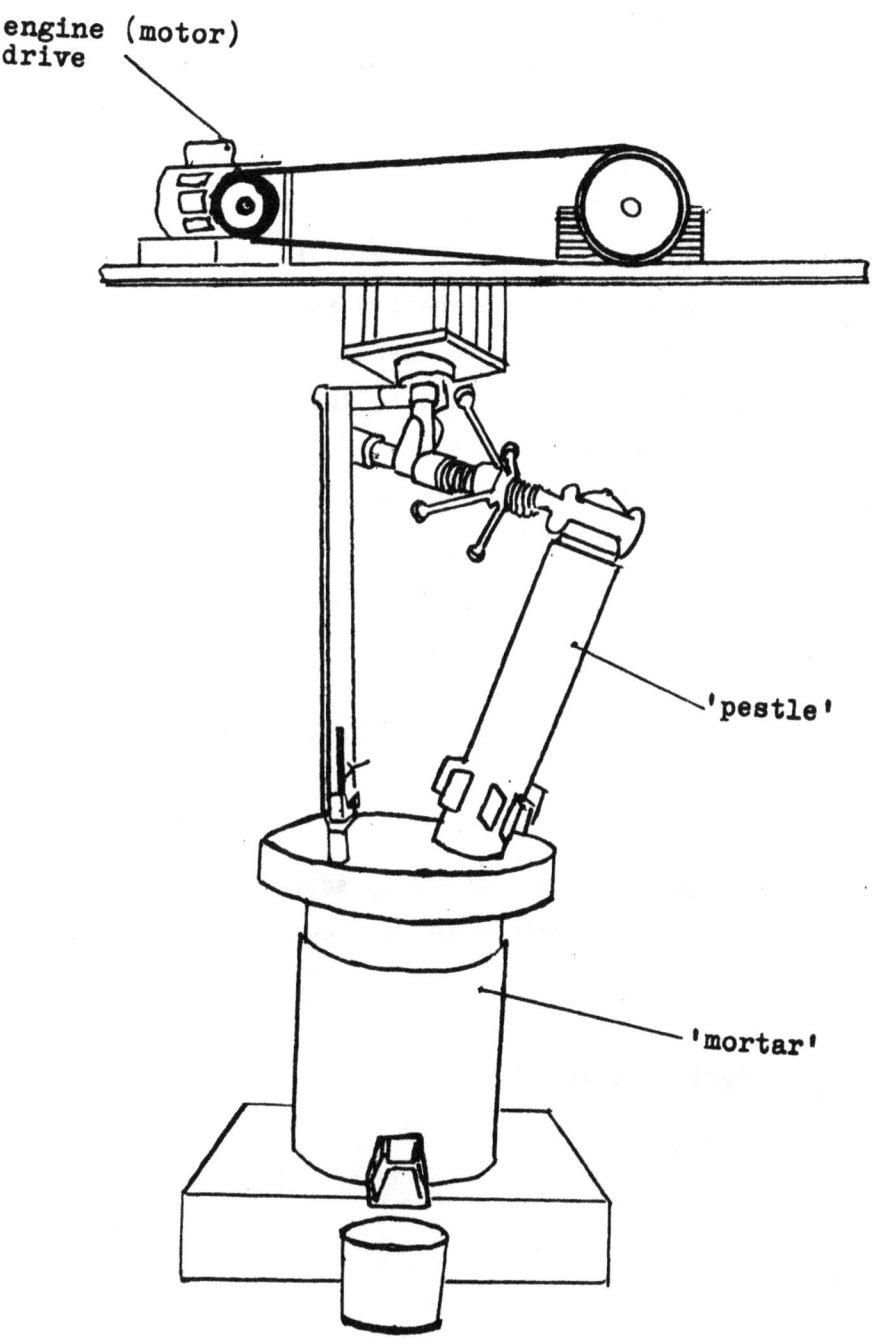

engine (motor)
drive

'pestle'

'mortar'

Fig. 4.21 A power operated ghani (Hoda,1977)

Hydraulic press for oil extraction

This is a press similar to the one described in Chapter 3. One hydraulic press gave extraction efficiencies of 90% working with heated pulp. However, manufacture of hydraulic presses is much more complicated than that of screw presses: they are also more expensive.

Oil clarifier

Description and design aspects	An oil clarifier is shown in fig.4.22. Water up to a certain level is preboiled in this tank and the pressed oil is introduced via the funnel at the top. During heating the lighter oil floats to the top and is let out through the upper tap into a container. The water and sludge are removed through the lower tap.
Materials and parts	Sheet steel, taps.
Manufacture	Sheet metal bending and cutting equipment, welding equipment.
Special advantage	Danger of burns caused by scooping hot oil in the traditional method is reduced. Low cost and ease of manufacture.
Supplier	Agrico, Ltd.

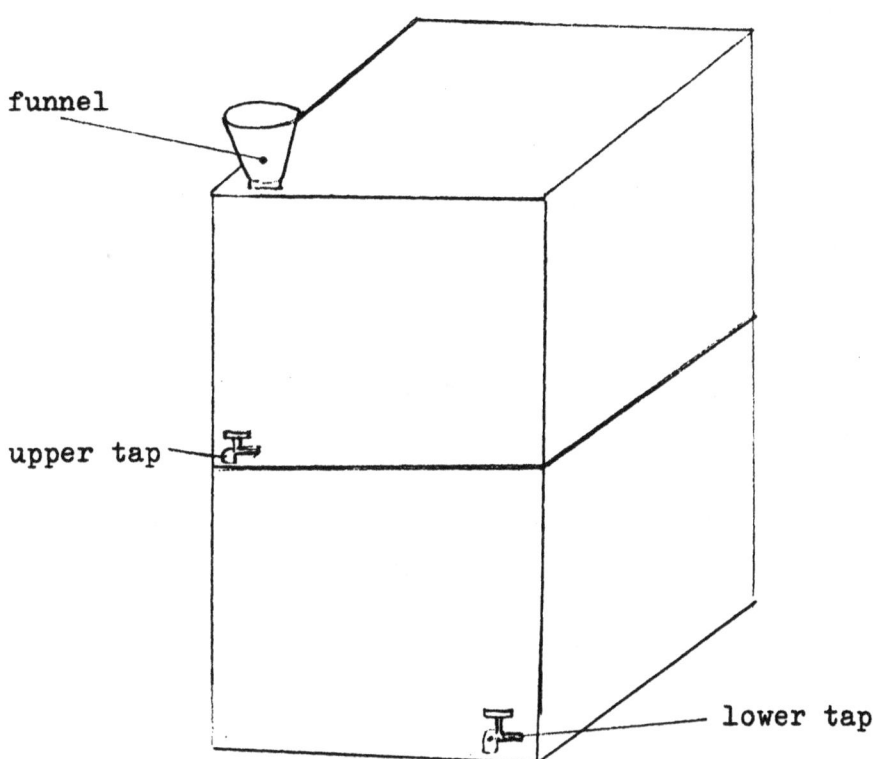

funnel

upper tap

lower tap

Fig.4.22 An oil clarifier

Agrico palm oil plant

This is a plant which consists of a steriliser which sterilises bunch fruit by steam produced in a boiler. This steriliser takes two hours to sterilise one ton of fruit.

The next step of stripping the fruit is done by a stripper. The fruit is removed from the bunches and stripped by beaters. The fruit falls into a horizontal conveyor tube and the empty bunch is thrown out of the machine. The machine can handle 2 tons of bunch-fruit per hour. It is operated by 10 hp diesel engine or electric motor.

After stripping the fruit is pounded by another machine. In this machine the beater mechanism is mounted on self-aligned and self-lubricated ball bearings. This machine is run by a 10 hp diesel engine or motor.

The oil is pressed out by means of a hand-operated hydraulic press.

The mixture of palm fruit cake and the kernels can be separated in a fibre separator operated by a 10 hp diesel engine or motor. The breakers disintegrate the cake and push the fibre out of the machine through bars. The nuts are conveyed to the other end of the hopper through a conveyor.

The oil is clarified using an oil clarifier.

Table 4.2 Comparison of some figures of merit of Traditional and Improved Technologies for Vegetable Oil Preparation

Operation	Figures of Merit	Method	Value of Figures of Merit	Comments
Boiling of palm fruits	Capacity of boiler (kg of palm fruits)	Traditional: oil drum	360 kg	
		Agrico palm fruit steriliser	1 tonne	
	Time required for boiling above capacity of palm fruits (hours)	Traditional: oil drum and 3-stone fire	5-10 hours	
		Agrico palm fruit steriliser	2 hours	
Stripping palm fruits from bunch	Time required to strip one tonne of fruit	Traditional: cutlass or other tools (per indiv.)	10-40 hours	
		Agrico palm fruit stripper	30 minutes	
Pounding to separate palm fibres from kernels	Time required to pound one tonne of palm fruits	Traditional: mortar and pestle	5-8 hours	Capacity of mortar 30 kg of palm fruits. Each batch takes 10-15 minutes
		Traditional: trampling in pit	90-150 minutes	Capacity of pit 300 kg of fruits. Each batch takes 30-50 minutes
		Agrico palm pounding machine	40 minutes	Continuous process in this equipment
Extraction of palm oil	Time required to extract oil from one tonne of fruit	Traditional: pit (scooping)	13-26 hours	It is estimated that 1 gallon of oil is scooped in 1-2 hours
		Screw press (20 kg capacity). Pressure 40 kg/cm	10 hours	Each batch of 20 kg of fruit is pressed in 12 minutes. Figures are for hybrid fruits
	Extraction efficiency	Traditional: pit	30%	This assumes a 20% by weight oil component of fruits (as can be extracted using the solvent method)
		screw press	75-83%	
		hydraulic press	90%	
Palm kernel cracking	Time required to crack open 10 kg of kernel	Traditional method using stones	3.3-6.0 hours	
		Centrifugal Palm kernel cracker	1.5-2 minutes	
Shelling of coconuts	Time required to crack one coconut	Traditional method using cutlass	3 minutes	
		CECOCO coconut cracker (dehusker)	0.3-0.6 minutes	

NOTES TO CHAPTER 4

1   The traditional variety has an endocarp which is between 2.5 to 4 mm thick while the hybrid variety has endocarps of between 0.5 to 2.5 mm (Larousse Agricole, 1952).

2   The 'iron pot' is a heavy cast-iron pan usually of 4 or 8-gallon capacity.

3   Bunches of the hybrid variety are much bigger and contain more fruits.

4   While in Ghana a standard pit which can hold only one person was used, in Sierra Leone the sizes of pits varied. The larger pits could hold more than one processor.

5   For a pit 0.8 m wide, 1.5 m long and 0.8 m high, with two men working and 20 bunches of fruit, the process took 30 minutes.

6   Larousse Agricole 1952. Figures for weight of average palm bunches in Africa are 10-25 kg. Bunches can, however, weigh up to 50 kg. Taking a middle figure of 20 kg per bunch, and allowing for the fact that 75 per cent of the bunch consists of fruits the weight of fruits from a bunch can be estimated at 15 kg.

7   These figures are arrived at by taking 63-75 per cent by weight of fruit per bunch; 75-80 per cent by weight of pulp per fruit for the hybrid variety; 60-65 per cent by weight of pulp per fruit for the traditional variety and 50 per cent by weight of oil in the pulp for both varieties. Agrico Ltd. of Ghana gives a range of 14-24 per cent of oil in bunches of fruit. By using solvent extraction method for the hybrid an average of 20% by weight of oil is extracted (Appropriate Technology 5 February 1979).

8   Boiling times of about 10 hours on the average in Ghana, as compared to 6 in Sierra Leone.

9   These were reported figures. The larger might refer to cases where cracking is combined with other household chores.

10   The 'three-penny' pan is a small aluminium or enamel pan of 1 litre capacity.

11   One gallon (4.45 litres) of palm-kernel oil is taken to weigh 4.45 kg, assuming a specific gravity of oil as 1.0 (this figure is between 0.9-0.99).

12   Encyclopaedia Britannica.

13   This assumes a specific gravity of 0.9 for coconut oil.

14   See Intermediate Technology Vol.5 No.4 for more information and detailed test results.

Chapter 5
MAIZE PROCESSING

INTRODUCTION

Maize (zea mays) is the staple food in some countries in West Africa. Processing of maize involves shelling from the cob, soaking and/or milling (see fig.5.1).

TRADITIONAL METHODS OF PROCESSING MAIZE

Description

Traditionally maize is processed into maize flour or into a type of dough (called kenkey in Ghana) or porridge.

The initial preparation involves the removal of the maize from the cob (shelling). Maize is shelled mainly with the bare hands and by rubbing one cob against another. This method yields an output of 4-7 kg per hour. Another method of shelling is by putting it in a sack and hitting the sack with a piece of wood. 13 kg of maize can be shelled in one hour in this way, but the breakage rate is high.

Milling of maize is done using a mortar and pestle or grinding stones. An individual can pound 13 kg in one hour.

Kenkey preparation

In Ghana, the maize is further processed into kenkey. To prepare kenkey, the maize is soaked for one to three days before milling, after which it is allowed to ferment for another one to three days. The dough is then cooked, mainly in cast iron pots with an average fluid capacity of 8 gallons (see fig.5.2). During cooking the dough is stirred with a long wooden spoon. The three-stone[1] method is mainly used for this purpose.

The cooked dough is put into a metal bowl and is mixed using a wooden spoon, or the bare hands, together with an equal quantity of uncooked dough. Mixing lasts for an average of 40 minutes after which the dough is made into balls with the bare hands or a wooden spoon. It takes an average of 30 minutes to produce 50 balls of kenkey. After being made into balls maize husks are used to wrap each ball and they are subsequently placed in the iron pot for boiling. Boiling takes an average of 30 minutes, after which the kenkey is ready for consumption or sale.

The average yield of kenkey from maize is 2:1 by volume. Average quantity of fuel used is 3 kg of firewood to process 3.5 kg of maize into kenkey.

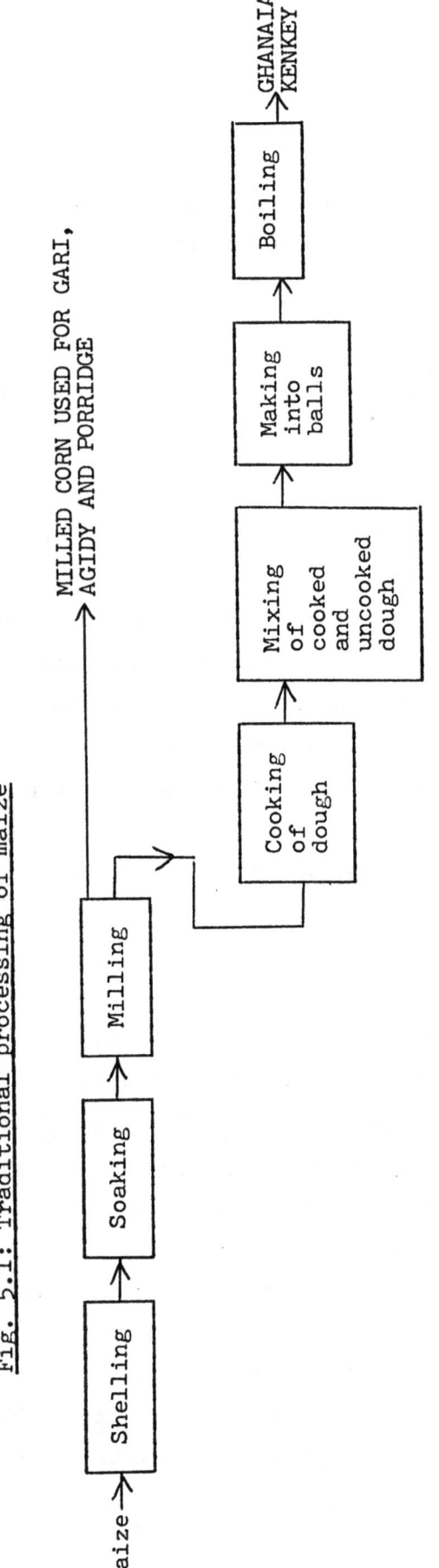

Fig. 5.1: Traditional processing of maize

Fig. 5.2 <u>The traditional 'iron' pot used in kenkey
preparation</u> (note the tyre rims used to
replace the 'three stones')

Other maize products

Other maize products are agidi (fermented maize dough made from finely ground maize) and ogi (porridge made from ground fermented maize). The operations required for their preparation are common - shelling, milling and fermenting.

TECHNICAL PERFORMANCE OF TRADITIONAL METHODS

Operation	Output
Shelling of maize using bare hands or by rubbing cobs against each other	4-7 kg/hr
Putting in sack and hitting sack	13 kg/hr
Milling of maize using mortar and pestle	13 kg/hr

Kenkey preparation

	Time required
Soaking of maize	1-3 days
Preliminary cooking of dough in 8 gallon pan	1-3 hours
Final cooking of 'packaged' dough	30 minutes

Firewood use = 3 kg/3.5 kg of maize processed.

Advantages

- the equipment used is cheap.
- the fineness of milling can be controlled by the processor.
- shelling by hand can be done while conversing.

Disadvantages

- it is time consuming.
- It is characterised by high physical strain both in the milling of maize and the stirring of the dough.

Improved equipment

In comparison with the traditional methods of maize processing, improved equipment for this activity is required to:
- decrease shelling time for maize
- relieve the strain involved in milling using mortar and pestle
- relieve the strain in stirring the thick maize dough for kenkey preparation
- same time used for these operations

Maize shellers

The hand-held maize shellers

Description and
design aspects

This type of sheller is made of wood and can be used to shell cobs when they are hard and dry. To use it the sheller is held in the right hand and the cob is introduced as shown (fig.5.3).

Materials and
parts

Wood.

Manufacture

Basic carpentry tools. Hand drill (see fig.5.3(b) and (c).

Special advantages

Cheap and simple to construct.

Disadvantage

The main disadvantage of this sheller is that only standard sizes of maize cobs can be shelled with it.

Supplier

Tikonko Agricultural Extension Centre.

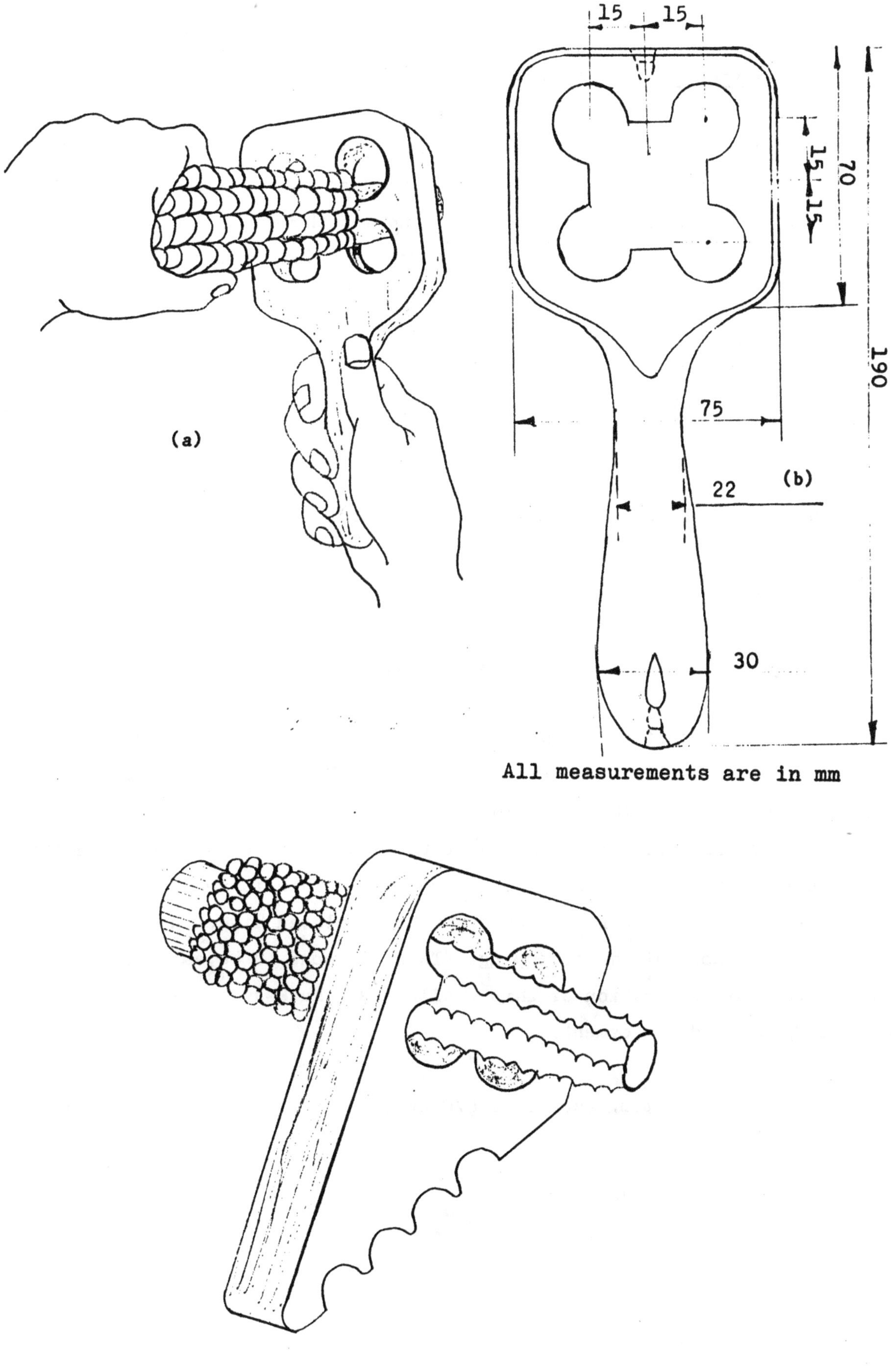

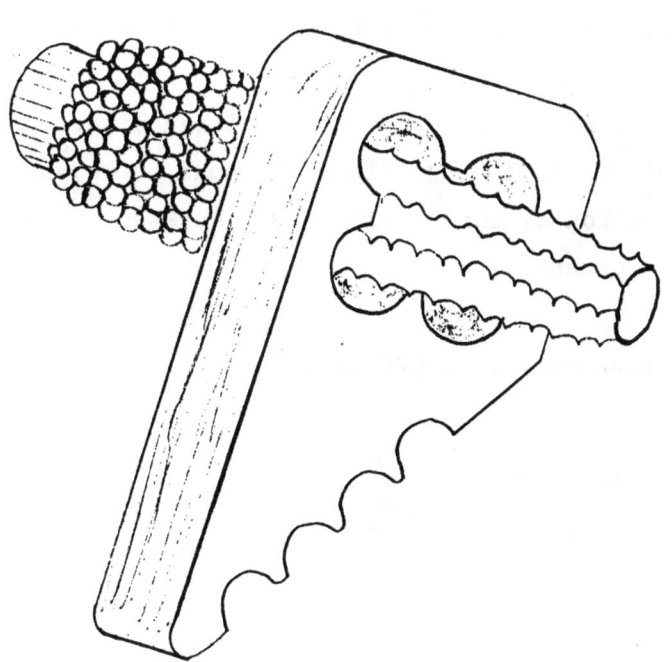

All measurements are in mm

Fig. 5.3 Hand-held maize shellers

Cylindrical hand-held maize sheller

<u>Description and design aspects</u>	This type of sheller is in the form of a short length of tube which has internal ribs as shown in fig.5.4(a). This device is held in one hand and the maize cob is introduced by the other with a twisting action. The rows of grains are engaged and stripped off by the internal ribs and fall out through the other end of the tube.
<u>Materials and parts</u>	Aluminium casting (or steel tube with welded ribs).
<u>Manufacture</u>	Foundry (or welding equipment).
<u>Specific advantage</u>	Low cost.
<u>Disadvantage</u>	Can only shell one size of maize cob.

A development of this type of sheller is shown in fig.5.4(b). The material of this sheller is polyvinyl chloride (PVC). A short length of 2" diameter is cut from a PVC pipe. The ribs (also of PVC) are glued on using a PVC solvent (trade name faigit) at $90°$ intervals. A slit is made along the tube to allow for different sizes of maize cobs. This is rendered possible by the material. One of the four internal ribs is placed higher up in the tube and it performs most of the stripping. This is found to be easier. The tools required for the preparation of this sheller is a hacksaw, a small clamp or vice, sandpaper and PVC cement.

<u>Output</u>   The stripping rate of a PVC type is 5-7 seconds for a single cob.

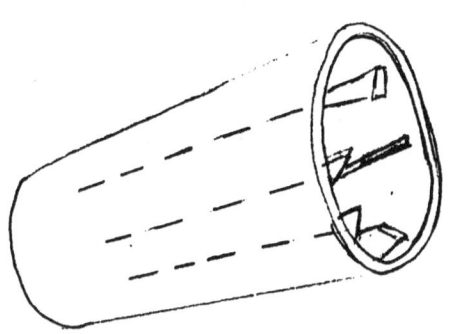

Fig. 5.4a <u>Maize sheller</u> (Cameroon)

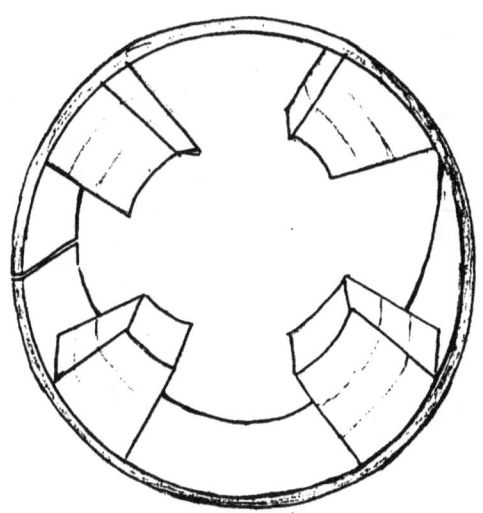

Fig. 5.4b <u>A P.V.C. hand-held maize sheller</u>

A simple maize shelling device

Description and design aspects	This type of sheller is shown in Fig.5.5. The maize cob is rubbed against the raised 'U' nails which are arranged in two parallel rows 2 cm apart. The distance between nails within the rows is 2.5 cm. This releases the grain which drops onto the floor.
Materials and parts	Wood and 'U' nails.
Manufacture	Simple carpenter's tools by village artisan.
Special advantages	Cheap and caters for various sizes of cobs.
Disadvantages	Care must be taken in use to prevent laceration of the fingers.

Output An estimated three times that of traditional method.[2]

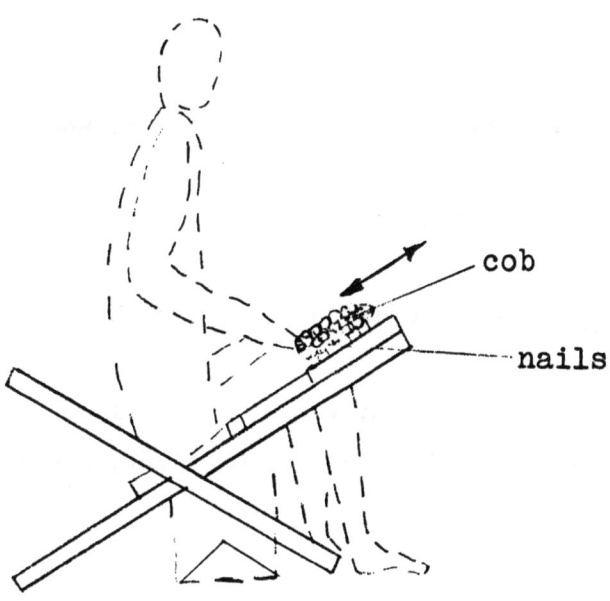

cob

nails

Fig.5.5 A simple maize-shelling device

A hand-operated rotating drum maize sheller

Description and
design aspects

This maize sheller is small, about the size of a kitchen
meat mincer and handles maize up to 25 cm in length. It
consists of a drum which can be rotated by hand (fig.5.6).
On the surface of the drum hob nails are driven at random
spaced 20-25 mm apart centre to centre. They should not be
in straight even rows. The maize is rested on a sloping
board.

Materials and
parts

Solid wooden drum D = 70 mm,   = 80 mm, boards, hob nails,
screws, spindle, metal rods, washer and split pin.

Manufacture

Simple carpentry tools.

Special advantages Easy to construct and can shell cobs of varying sizes.

For details, contact VITA; Volunteers In Technical Assistance,
3706 Rhode Island Avenue, Mt. Ranier, Maryland, U.S.A. 20822.

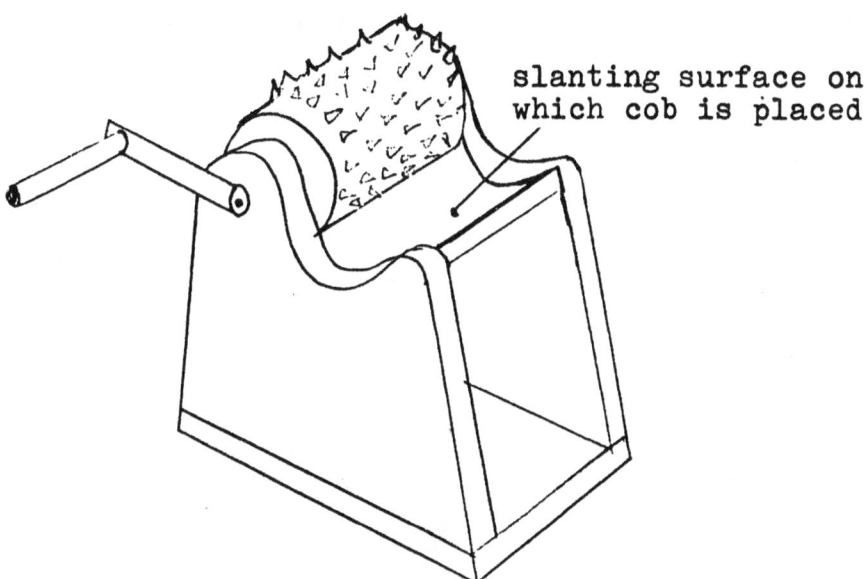

slanting surface on
which cob is placed

Fig.5.6 A hand-operated rotating drum sheller

Hand-operated rotating disc sheller

Description and design aspects	This consists of a wooden disc about 60 cm in diameter. Fencing staples are nailed on one side of the disc as shown in fig.5.7. The cobs are fed along a wooden chute adjacent to the disc, to a spring-loaded pressure plate which holds the cob against the stapled surface of the rotating disc. The maize kernels are shelled by the action of rotation of the disc and falls into a container placed below. The empty cobs are automatically ejected.
Materials and parts	Wooden boards, fencing staples, metal pipes.
Manufacture	Basic carpentry tools.
Special advantages	Low cost and simplicity in design and manufacture.
Disadvantage	For small cobs, spring-loaded pressure plate must be adjusted.

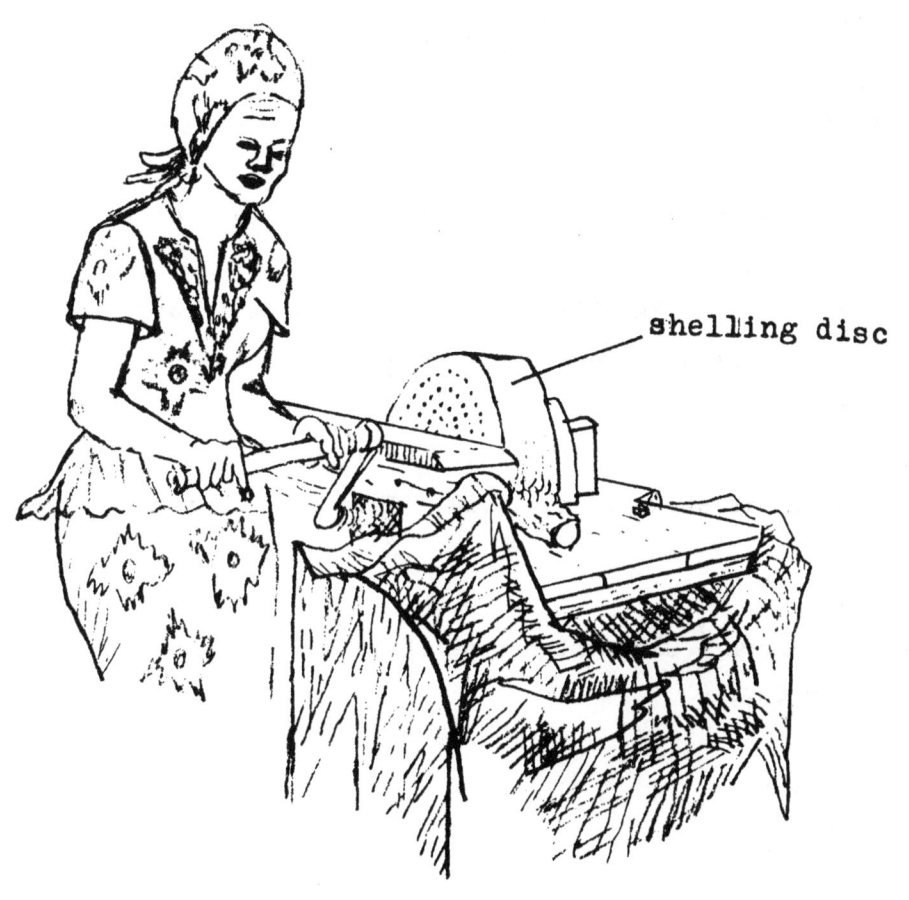

shelling disc

Fig.5.7 Hand-operated rotating disc sheller

Other maize shellers

SISCOMA of Senegal manufactures a maize sheller which can be hand or engine/motor-driven. Fig.5.8 shows this type of sheller. Its output is 80-100 kg of grain per hour (small model) and 150-200 kg per hour (large model).

Another type of sheller manufactured by Brown & Clapperton Ltd. in Malawi is shown in fig.5.9. This compact hand-operated type can be fitted to the side of a container. It allows maize to drop into this container and the cobs are ejected at the side. The tension is adjustable to suit the diameter of the maize cobs. There are a few varieties of this type of sheller and outputs range between 30-150 kg per hour.

The Agrico maize sheller (fig.5.10), is run by a 5 hp diesel engine/motor. The grains are cleaned by means of a winnowing fan. The output of the AGRICO machine is 1500-1800 kg of grain per hour.

The Faculté des Sciences Techniques, Conakry, Guinea has also developed a maize sheller which is shown in fig.5.10. This type is manufactured mainly from sheet metal.

Other suppliers of Brown & Clapperton type (fig. 5.9):
    Allied Trading Co.,
    CECOCO
    COSSUL & CO PVT LTD.,
    DANDEKAR BROTHERS
    R. HUNT & CO. LTD.,
    UBUNGO FARM IMPLEMENTS
    RAJASTHAN STATE AGRO INDUSTRIES CO LTD

Other suppliers of Agrico type:
    INTERNATIONAL MFG CO (REGD)
    ALLIED TRADING CO
    DANDEKAR BROTHERS
    MOHINDER & CO ALLIED INDUSTRIES

Other supplier of SISCOMA type:
    RANSOMES, SINS & JEFFERIES LTD.

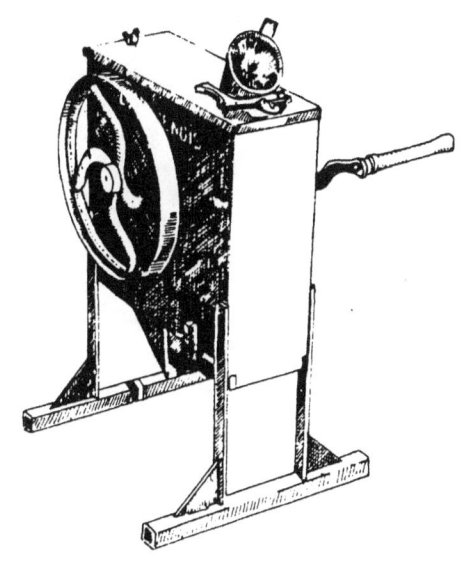

Fig. 5.8 <u>SISCOMA maize sheller</u> (Ellman et al 1981)

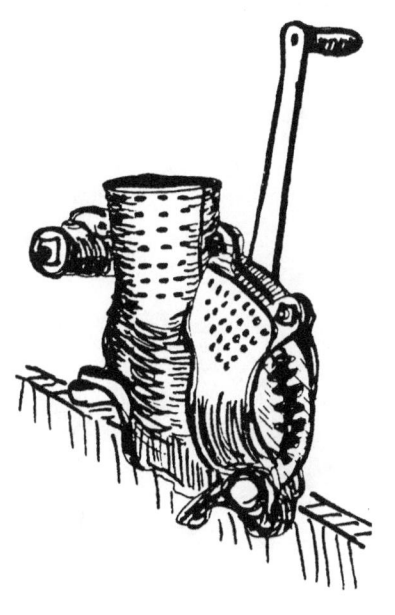

Fig. 5.9 <u>Brown and
          Clapperton maize
          sheller</u>
          (Ellman et al
          1981)

<u>Fig.5.10 The Agrico maize sheller</u>

(Agrico, 1977)

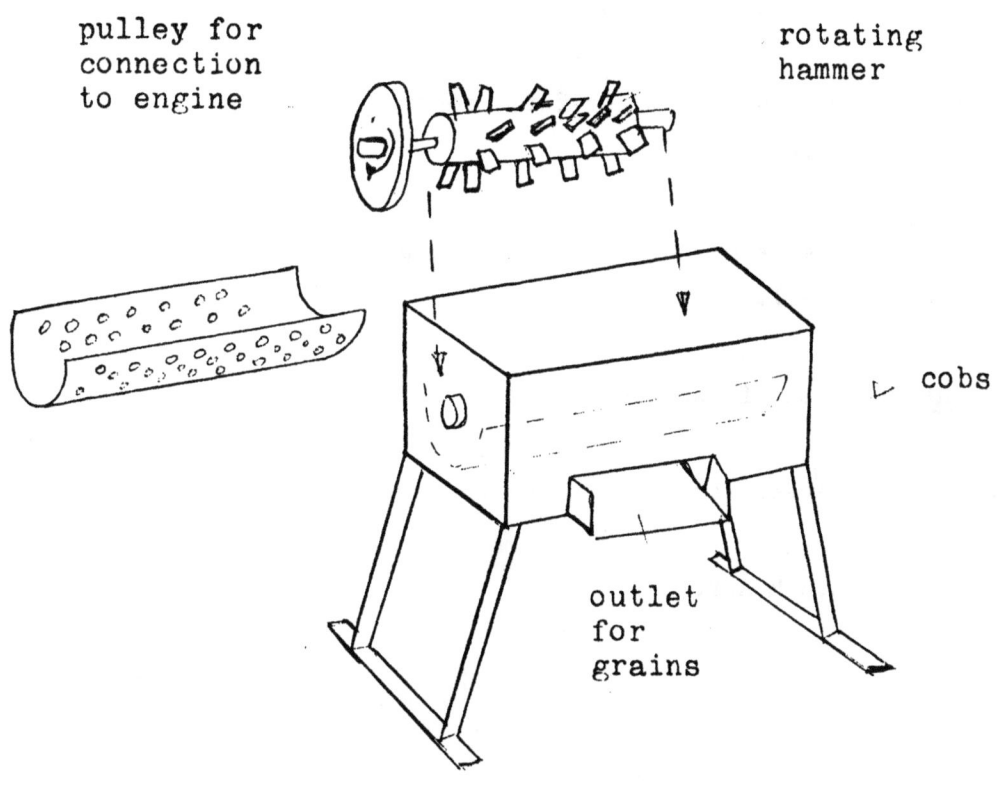

pulley for
connection
to engine

rotating
hammer

cobs

outlet
for
grains

Fig.5.11 <u>Guinean type maize sheller</u>

(La Faculté de Sciences Tecniques, Conakry, Guinea)

Maize mills

Concrete hand mill (Buhrstone type)

Description and   This type of mill is shown in fig.5.12. It operates like a
design aspects   millstone. Fine milling is obtained by several runs of the
                        maize. The forms for the concrete slabs can be made from
                        scrap pieces of iron, or from pieces of 20 litre round
                        tins. The concrete is allowed to cure for 3-4 weeks before
                        use. The equipment should be put on a mat or box or piece
                        of plastic to collect the ground grain.

Materials and   Old 20   drum for form, concrete (or wood) for handle and
parts   bolts.

Manufacture   Simple masonry tools (or carpenters in the case of wooden
                        type).

Special advantages Ease of manufacture and low cost.

Disadvantages   Several runs are required to produce a fine maize meal.

Supplier   S.A.M.A.P.

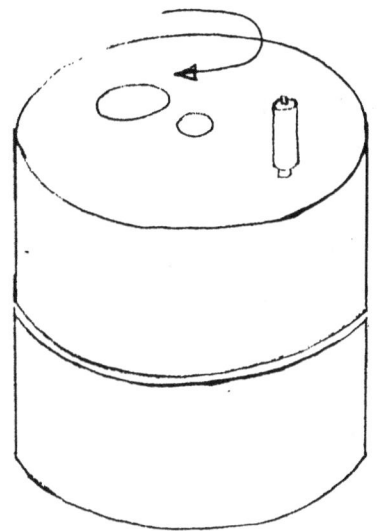

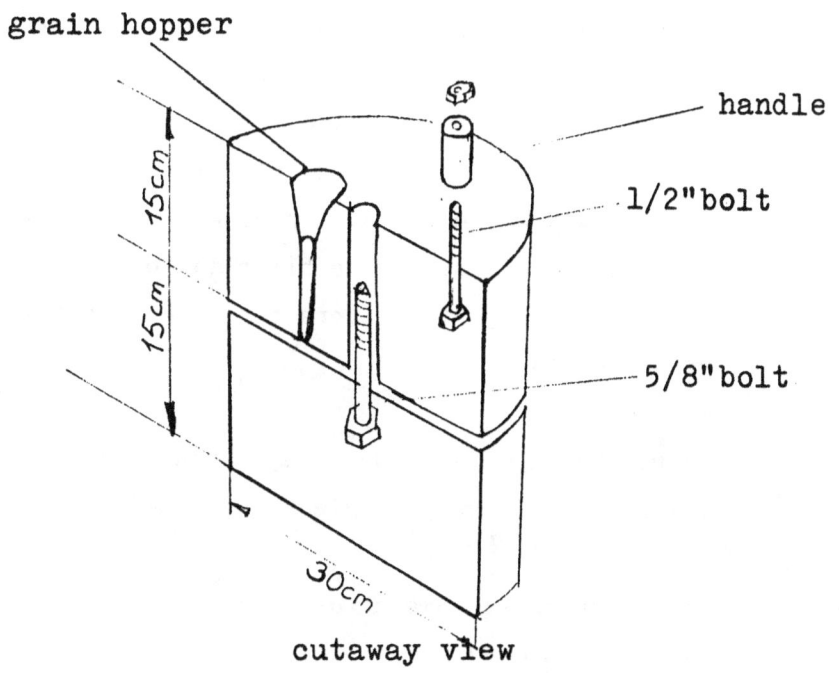

grain hopper

handle

1/2"bolt

5/8"bolt

15cm

15cm

30cm

cutaway view

Fig.5.12 A concrete hand mill

Animal-driven power gear maize mill (Buhrstone type)

Description and design aspects	The animal-drawn gear required to drive this meal works on the principle of a bicycle which transforms slow leg movement into a speedy rotation of wheels. The animals (horses, cows, camels, bullocks, donkeys, etc.) are hitched to the outer ends of wooden bars 4 metres long. These bars are bolted to the large input gear. The animals are required to walk in circles making approximately 3 tours per minute. With a gear ratio of 24:1 the output speed on the shaft of the mill will be 72 rpm. By assembling a number of gears a speed multiplication of 50 can be achieved. Examples of animal gear are shown in fig.5.12.

The grinding mill itself is a buhrstone type. It consists of two circular grindstones of 500 mm diameter. One is fixed and the second stone which is attached to the shaft connected to the gear from the drive mechanism rotates at a speed of 600 rpm. The grain is fed through a hopper drops into the space between the two stones and is thus crushed. The crushed grain is removed by centrifugal force and a forced draught produced by fan blades.

The fineness of the flour can be adjusted by an adjustment nut which alters the spacing between the two grinding stones.

Materials and parts	Gears, sheet metal, concrete, (wood or cellular quartz), shaft, ball bearing, angle iron, steel bar.
Manufacture	Gear-cutting equipment (or imported gears), sheet metal cutting and bending equipment, metal working lathe, milling machine, welding set, drill press, metal working tools.
Special advantages	Useful in rural areas where fuel or electricity for operation of power mills is scarce or expensive.
Disadvantages	Requires sophisticated manufacturing operations for fabricating gears.

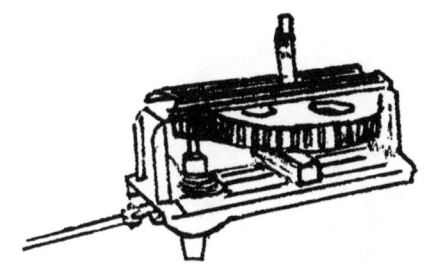

Fig.5.13 Animal-driven power gears

Pedal operated grinding mill (fig.5.14)

Description and
design aspects
In this type of mill, a bicycle provides the power for operation. An ordinary bicycle which can be quickly connected and disconnected is used. The back wheel turns a rotor at about 5,000 rpm which breaks up the grains. A wire mesh controls the fineness of the final product.

Materials and
parts
Ball bearings, wire mesh, 3 mm sheet steel 1.25" or 2.5" steel bars (8 inches long), 6 mm flat and angle iron.

Manufacture
Small metal working lathe, milling machine, welding set, drill press, metal working hand tools.

Special advantages Can be used in households possessing bicycles which can be detached after use with mill and used normally.

Disadvantages
Not intended for continual intensive use. Mainly intended to meet daily family needs.

For details, contact Tropical Products Institute (TPI), London.

Fig.5.14 A pedal-operated grinding mill

Plate-type hand-operated mills (Dunia mill)

Description and design aspects	These are small capacity plate mills which consist of a hopper through which maize is fed to a grinding chamber where two opposing 15 cm diameter grooved milling plates are housed. The handle is mounted on the rim of a flywheel mounted on the grinding shaft. By altering the distance between the plates by means of a screw, the fineness of the product can be changed (Fig.5.15).
Materials and parts	Steel sheet, ball bearings, steel bars, cast iron plates.
Manufacture	Welding set, milling machine, sheet metal bending machine, drill press and metal working hand tools.
Special advantages	Ease of manufacture (basically welding).
Disadvantages	Not suitable for fine grinding of grain.
Output	20 kg of grain/hour.
Suppliers	ETS A GAUBERT A.B.C. HANSEN COMP. A/S NDUME PRODUCTS LTD RENSON ET CIE

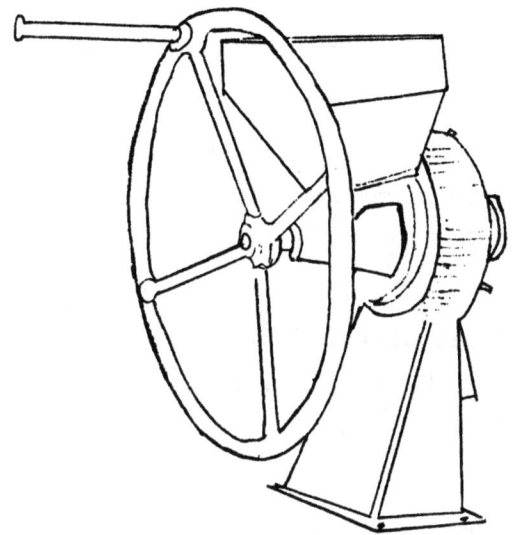

Fig.5.15 The Dunia hand-operated mill

Two-man operated plate mills

**Description and
design aspects**

These are stone or plate mills. Fineness of the products
can be adjusted by changing the space between the plates
and in some varieties various plates are available for
different materials.

The plates (stones) are rotated in opposite
directions and the grain is crushed by the resultant
grinding action.

**Materials and
parts**

Sheet steel, ball bearings, steel bars, iron cast or welded
fly wheel, and stand metal plates (or stones), screws
(bearings).

Manufacture

Forging facilities, sheet metal bending and cutting,
welding, machining.

Disadvantages

Requires two people to operate two rotating parts.

Output

With 140 mm plates - 7-9 kg/hr
With 190 mm plates - 16-18 kg/hr.

Supplier

R. Hunt.

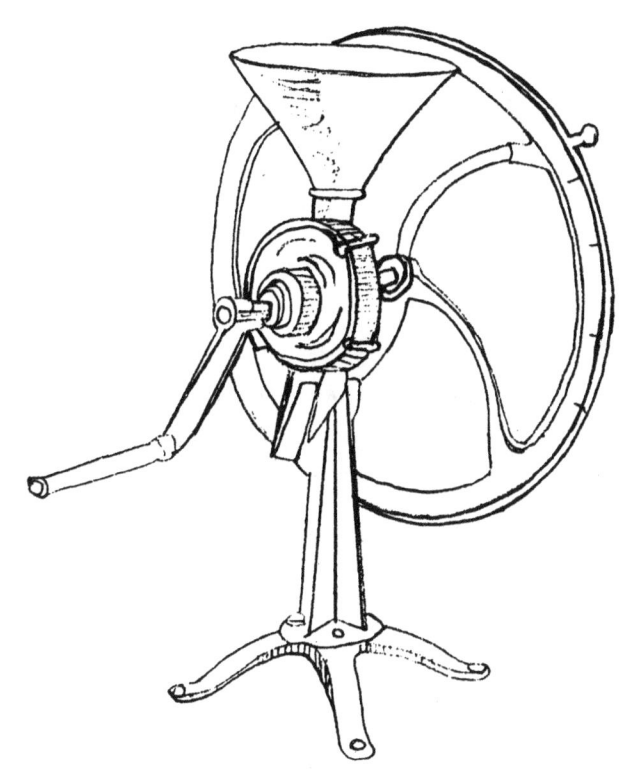

Fig. 5.15(a)   <u>Two-man operated plate mills</u>

Agrico power-operated mill (plate type)

Description and design aspects
These mills are fitted with cast iron plates which are easily replaceable. Adjustment of the distance between the plates can regulate the fineness of the final product (see Fig.5.16).

Materials and parts
Same as for plate mill described earlier except for belt and pulley mechanism for connection to engine/motor, engine or motor.

Manufacture
Same as for plate mill.

Output

Model	Size of mill	BHP	Size of pulley	Output/hour
1A	25 cm	5	25 x 8 cm	200 kg
2A	30 cm	7	30 x 10 cm	300 kg

Fig.5.16 Agrico plate mill

Power-operated hammer mills

Description and
design aspects

These are impact mills in which the grains are milled by
means of hammers revolving rapidly in a vertical plane
within a steel casting. In a typical mill there are 72
hammers about 15 cm long, 12 mm thick and 37.5 mm wide. At
the top of the chamber is a gauze net which sieves the
pounded grains. Its size determines the fineness of the
product.

Different types of hammer mills are shown in
fig.5.17. These mills are manufactured in a variety of
sizes with different capacities.

Table 5.2 shows characteristics of some of these
mills which are manufactured in East Africa. In these
types (except for the Atom mill) the grain is fed into the
central mill housing where the hammers crush them. A fan
blows them into an overhead screened hopper.

Suppliers

(See next page).

Table 5.2 Basic features of hammer mills manufactured in
East Africa

Make and type	Design features	Horse power rating of motor/ engine	Capacity
Kusinja maize mill (Brown & Clapperton Ltd. (Malawi)		10 hp 20 hp	150 kg/hr 400 kg/hr
Manik grinding mill (Manik Engineers, Tanzania	Constructed from heavy welded steel. Steel bearings. 16 reversible hammers with 4 different faces. Hammers replaceable. Bottom of chamber consists of milling screen and fan housing leading to a discharge pipe and cyclone chamber	8-12 hp 15-40 hp MGM 5 30-60 hp MGM 10	90-180 kg/hr 250-640 kg/hr 550-1100 kg/hr
Atom maize mill (Brown & Clapperton, Malawi)	Small size. Reversible hammers, screens and sealed bearings	7-8 hp	180 kg/hr
United maize mill (United Engineering Works Tanzania)	Casing of durable heavy steel. Sealed bearing units, steel shaft. Reversible and replaceable steel hammers	NM 25 NM 50 NM 75 NM 100	70-270 kg/hr 270-600 kg/hr 400-900 kg/hr 450-1000 kg/hr
Ndume hammer mills	Reversible and replaceable hammers. Models ND30 and GM40 have screens which allow over-sized particles to fall back into milling chamber. GM40 can be driven by tractor	12-25 hp (ND20) 16-100 hp (ND30) 25-100 hp Tractor 45 hp GM40	200-550 kg/hr 750-950 kg/hr 900 kg/hr

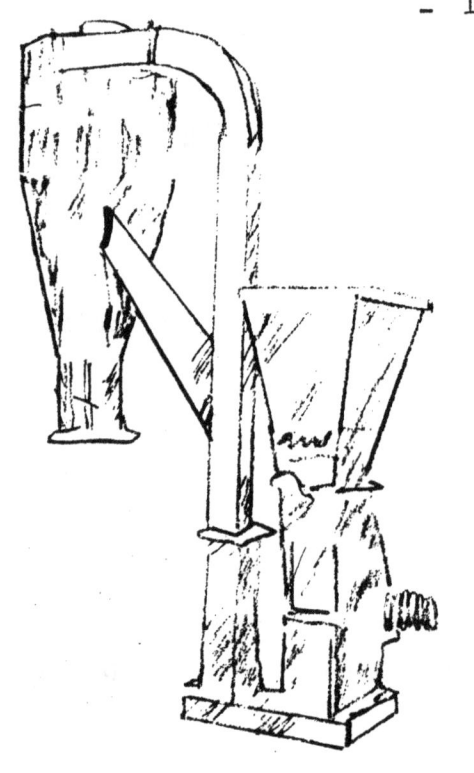

(a) Kusinga mill

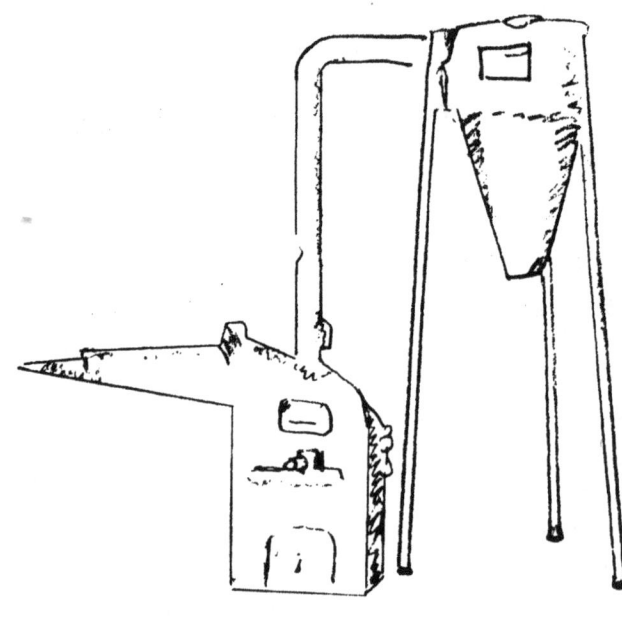

(b) Manik mill

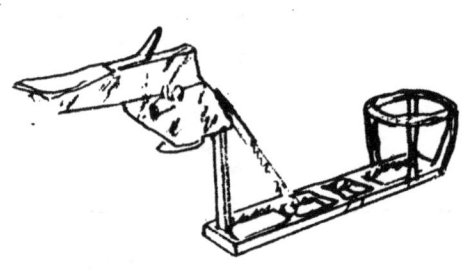

(c) Atom mill

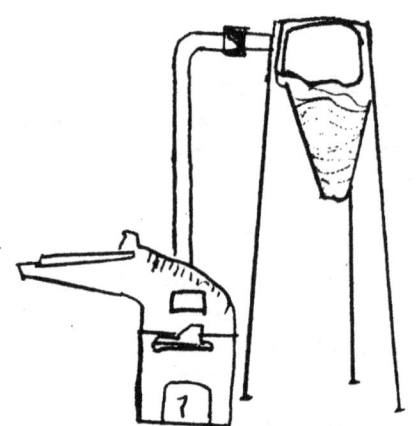

(d) United maize mill

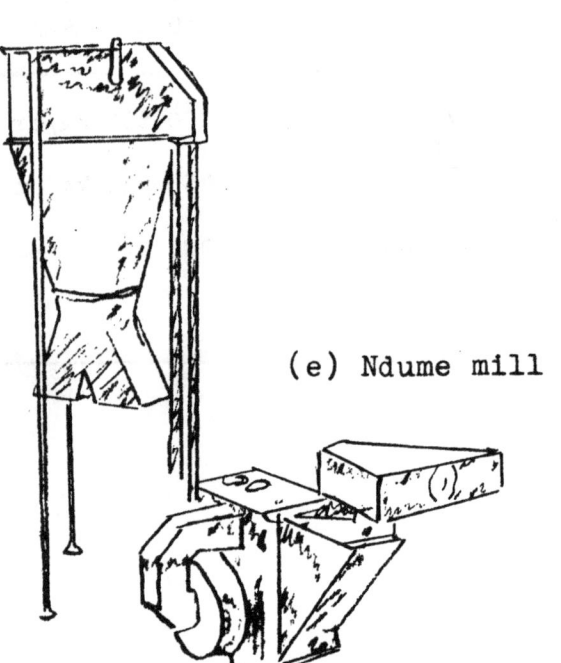

(e) Ndume mill

Fig. 5.17 <u>Power-operated hammer mills used in East Africa</u>

COMPARATIVE PERFORMANCE OF IMPROVED AND TRADITIONAL TECHNOLOGIES

Table 5.3: Comparison of some figures of merit of
traditional and improved technologies for
maize processing

Operation	Technology	Figure of merit (output)
Shelling of maize	Using bare hands or by rubbing cob against each other	4-7 kg/hour
	Putting in sack and hitting	13 kg/hr (high breakage rate)
	Cylindrical hand-held maize shellers	5-7 seconds for a single cob
	Other hand-held shellers	12-20 kg/hr
	Power-operated shellers (SISCOMA type)	80-100 kg/hr
	Power-operated sheller (Brown & Clapperton type)	30-150 kg/hr
	Power-operated sheller (Agrico type)	1 500-1 800 kg/hr
Milling of maize	Mortar and pestle	13 kg/hr
	Hand-operated mill (Dunma)	20 kg/hr
	Two-man plate mills	7-18 kg/hr
	Power-operated plate mills	200-300 kg/hr
	Power-operated hammer mills	150-1 100 kg/hr

NOTES TO CHAPTER 5

1   For the large kenkey pots, an improvisation of this method is the use of
the rims of car tyres to support the heavy weight of the pot, as can be
seen in fig. 6.2. These rims are partially buried in the ground.

2   Appropriate Technology, Vol. 2, No. 1.

Chapter 6
RICE PROCESSING

INTRODUCTION

Rice (oryza sativa) is the staple food in some countries (Mali, Guinea, Senegal, Gambia, Sierra Leone and Liberia) as well as some parts of countries like Ghana and Nigeria.

The rice grain consists of a hard outer husk (hull) which is covered with needlelike hairs and has a high silica content and a kernel covered with bran layers. Next to the bran is the 'aleurone' layer which is rich in nutrients and which encloses the starchy core of the kernel.

Parboiling hardens the grain to prevent damage during milling and also allows the rich nutrients of the aleurone layer to penetrate the starchy kernel. Milling or dehusking removes the outer husk of the rice. Steps in rice processing are shown in Fig. 6.1.

TRADITIONAL METHODS

Description

Traditionally, rice is removed from its stalk either by hitting the stalks on a hard surface or by trampling them. When the bunches are hit, it takes an average 1.5 hours to thresh 1 bushel.[1] When trampling is done this time is 1.8 hours.

Parboiling is usually done in 44-gallon drums and in other metal and earthenware containers. The total capacity for parboiling rice in the areas studied in Siera Leone was 1-5 bushels[2] of rice. The three-stone fire is used for parboiling. The rice is soaked in water and allowed to warm up, after which it is removed from the fire and allowed to soak for one day. The next day the water is changed and the rice is again heated until steam emerges. Heating is then stopped and the rice is ready for drying. Average fuel wood use per bushel of rice parboiled is 7 kilograms.

After parboiling the rice is sundried. Sun drying is done mainly on mats or on bare tarred surfaces. Sun drying times reported are on an average 2 days in the rainy season and 1 day in the dry season.

Dehusking of rice is the next operation. A pestle and mortar was used by all of these processors. The average reported weight in one round of pounding of the mortar was 9.0 kg of uncleaned rice, although the most common weight was 2.6 kg. Winnowing is done by using a flat tray made of the bark of a tree. The rice and loose husks are tossed into the air from the tray and, the rice being heavier, falls first on the tray. The husks and bran are

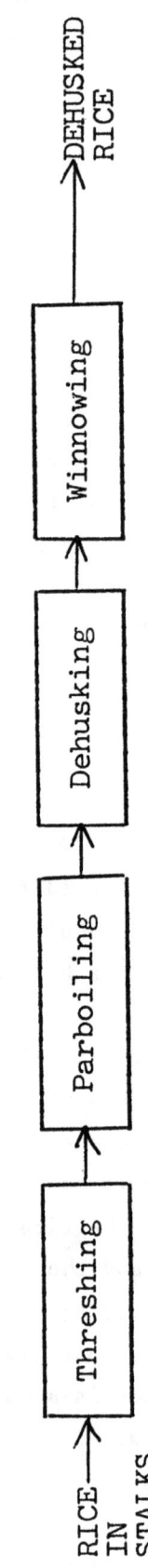

Fig. 6.1: Traditional operations involved in rice processing

allowed to fall to the ground. In order to dehusk the rice, the operations of pounding and winnowing are done alternatively until the rice is fully dehusked. Using the above methods of pounding and winnowing, an individual can dehusk and winnow 5-10 kg of rice in one hour.

Fig.6.2 suggests that the larger the mortar size, the less time is required to dehusk a unit weight of rice. Thus time could be saved by using larger mortars.

Performance

Table 6.1: Performance of traditional methods of rice processing

Operation	Figure of merit	Value
Threshing rice (hitting stalks on hard surface)	Quantity threshed in 1 hour	19 kg/hr
Threshing rice by trampling	Quantity threshed in 1 hour	16 kg/hr
Parboiling	Capacity of parboiling container	1-5 bushels
	Firewood use in parboiling	7 kg/bushel of rice parboiled
Open sun drying	Number of days required	1-2 days
Dehusking and winnowing	Quantity dehusked and winnowed in 1 hour	5-10 kg/hr

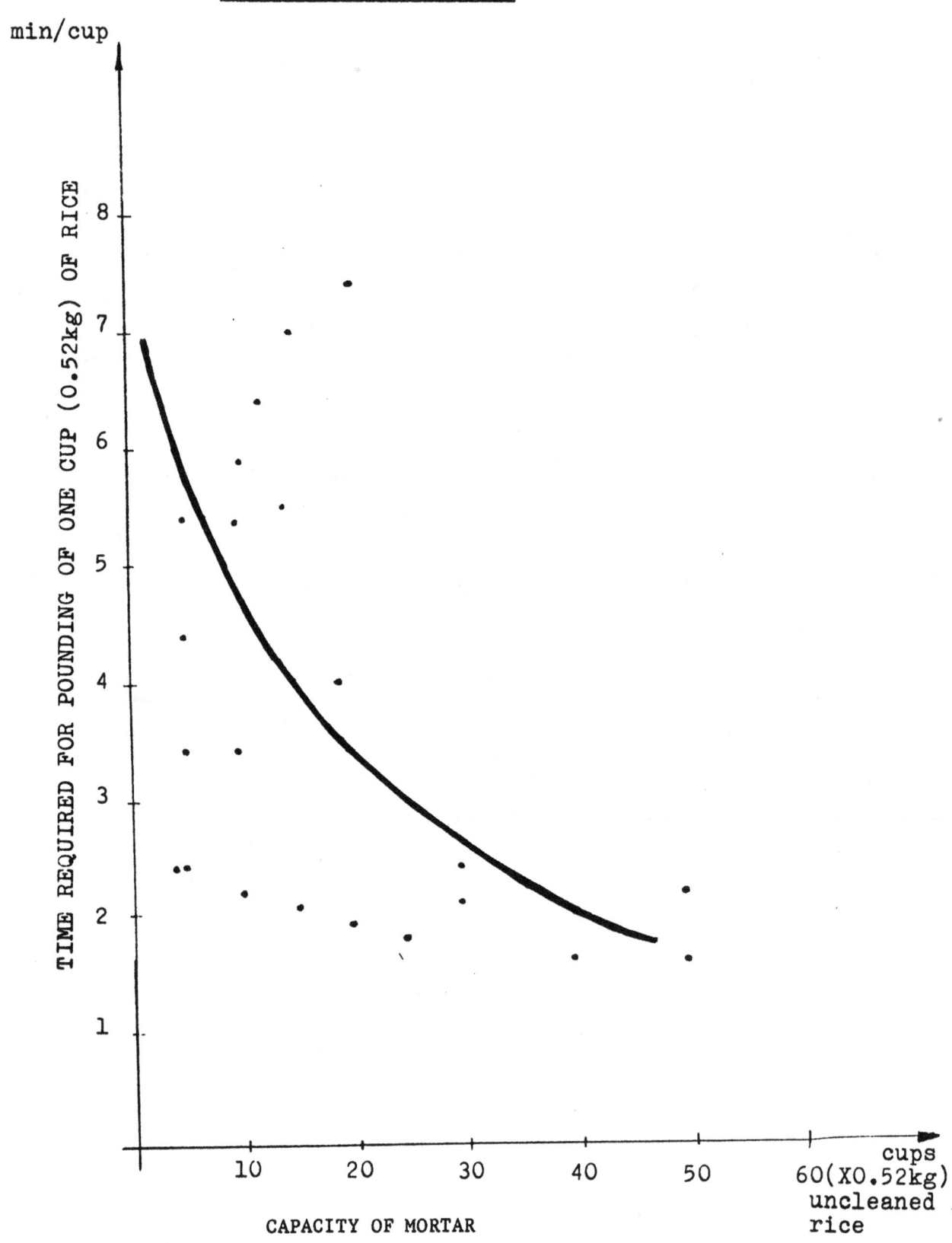

Fig.6.2 Relationship between time required for pounding rice
using mortar and pestle
and the mortar's capacity

Advantages

- they involve little cost in terms of equipment
- rice can be processed in small quantities for daily use. Rice stored in unprocessed form is less liable to be attacked by insects.

Disadvantages

- they are strenuous and time consuming
- sun drying on the ground can lead to contamination
- handling of hot rice during parboiling results in burns[3]

IMPROVED EQUIPMENT

Improved technologies of rice processing should possess the following advantages over the traditional processing methods in use:
- relieve the strain involved in threshing, parboiling, sundrying, dehusking and winnowing of rice
- reduce the time spent in these operations
- reduce the injuries caused by threshing rice by foot, and the hand blisters caused by hand pounding
- make parboiling safer
- reduce fuel used in parboiling
- more hygienic methods of sundrying
- reduce wastage caused by (i) unthreshed grains remaining in the stalks and (ii) breakage of grains during winnowing
- reduce percentage breakage of rice during processing

Rice threshers

The stone thresher

Description and design aspects	This type of thresher is shown in fig.6.3. A threshing roller is pulled round in circles over the rice stalks and this separates the rice from the stalks.
Materials and parts	Iron rods (wood), stone and concrete nuts and bolts.
Manufacture	Simple tools (masonry, carpentry and metal working), cylindrical form.
Specific advantage	Low cost
Disadvantages	Laborious to manufacture. Grains could be broken during threshing.

A modified version of this type of thresher is manufactured by Agrimal Ltd. of Malawi (fig.6.4). In this version the roller is mounted in an oblong box and is operated by means of a foot threadle. Output from this type is 200 kg per hour.

Suppliers	Dandekar Brothers.
	Agrimal Ltd.

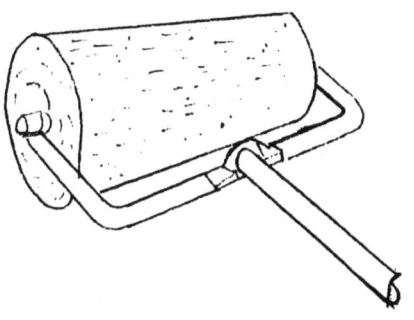

Fig.6.3 Stone roller threshers

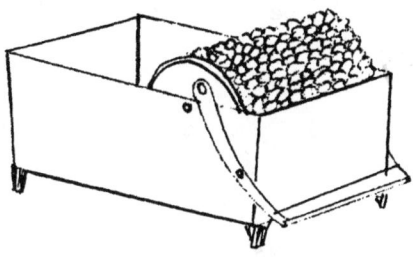

Fig.6.4 A threadle-operated roller thresher

Single cylinder type rotary threshers (fig.6.5-6.10)

Description and design aspects	This type of thresher consists of a cylinder (wooden or metalic) on which are fixed wire loops ('teeth') or spokes. When this cylinder which is suspended on a shaft via bearings rotates the bundle of stalks of rice are held firmly in the hand against the rotating cylinder. Beating and twisting of the bundle ensures that the grain is combed out of the stalks. The threshed grains fall to a mat or a special container for collection.
Materials and parts	Wood, iron rods, bicycle pedals, bearings, steel wires.
Manufacture	Welding equipment, drill press and simple hand tools.
Special advantages	These threshers are operated by foot thus enabling one operator to use her hands for feeding the device. They are faster than the traditional method. Wastage is minimised as stalks can be refed. This equipment can be adapted for use with engines or motors.
Disadvantages	The version which incorporates pedalling, might be unsuitable for some areas in West Africa where customs stipulate that it is indecent for women to sit astride.
Outputs	See table 6.1
Suppliers	American Spring and Pressing Works, PVT Ltd. Cossul & Co. Ltd. (see overleaf).

Table 6.1 Types of rotary threshers

Type	Threshing rate
Cecoco light food thresher (Japan)	115 kg/hr
Melanisian Council of Churches type	45-50 kg/hr
Tikonko Agricultural Extension Centre type	75 kg/hr
SISCOMA type	150 kg/hr (pedal driven) 250 kg/hr (motor driven)
Agro paddy thresher (Agrico Ltd. Ghana)	110-140 kg/hr
Agro multicrop thresher (engine driven) 5-7 hp	500 kg/hr

Fig.6.5 CECOCO Rice thresher

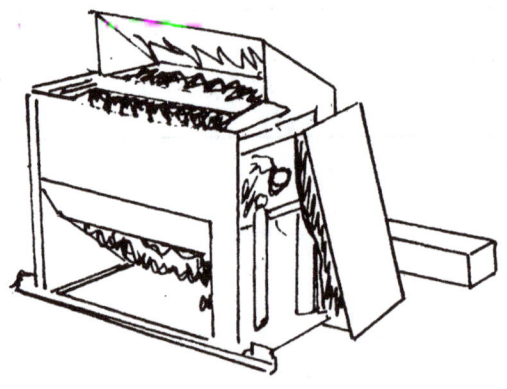

Fig.6.6 SISCOMA rice thresher

Fig. 6.7 <u>TAEC thresher</u>

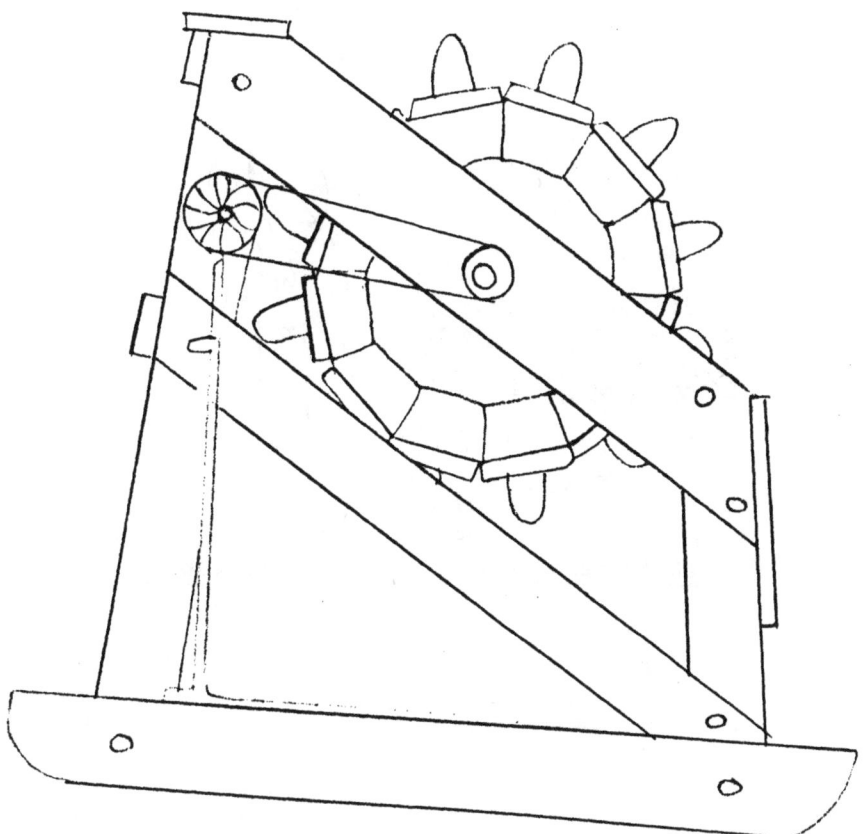

Fig. 6.8 <u>Malenesian Council of churches type thresher</u>

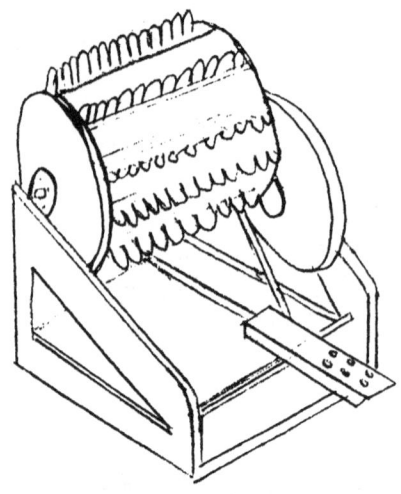

Fig.6.9 VITA threadle-operated thresher

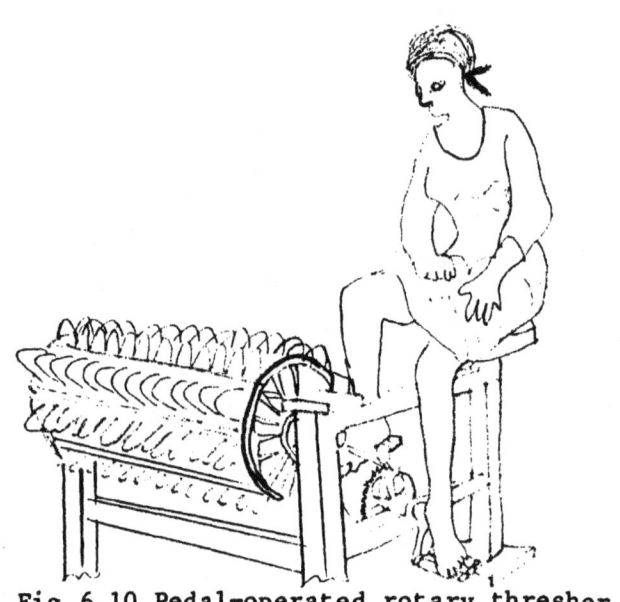

Fig.6.10 Pedal-operated rotary thresher

Two cylinder-type rotary thresher

Description and
design aspects

This Japanese type thresher consists of two rollers with raised portions as shown in the diagram (see fig.6.11). The rice stalks are introduced between the rollers as they rotate by means of a pedal mechanism. The threshed rice is collected in a bag.

Materials and
parts

Drums, wood, sheet metal, pedals and bearings.

Manufacture

Welding equipment, drill press, metal cutting tool and other basic hand tools.

Output

80-85 kg/hr.

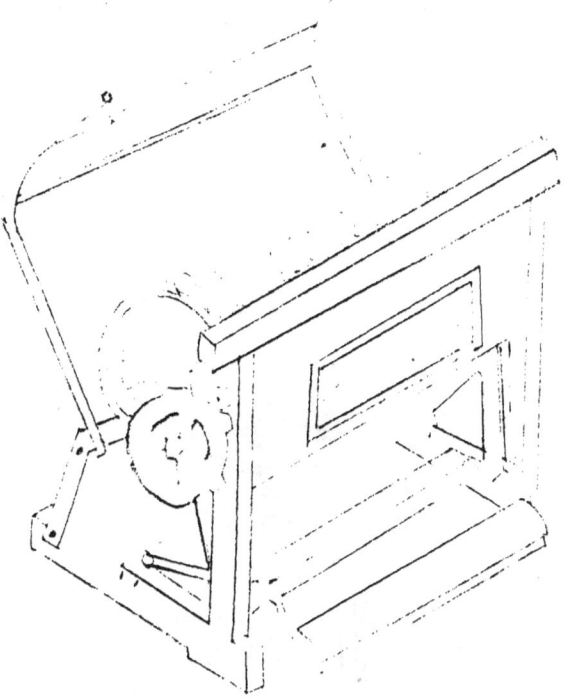

Fig.6.11 A two cylinder type thresher (Hoda, 1977)

Animal driven rice threshers

Description and design aspects

In using these types of threshers, the harvest is spread on a threshing floor and the device is drawn over the stalks round and round, separating the grains in the process. Fig.6.12 shows the 'Rasulia'[4] thresher of this type.

Materials and parts

Wood (for frame and seals), bearings, flat iron or steel strips (1.5" x 2"), draught ropes.

Manufacture

Basic carpentry tools, metal cutting tool, drill press.

Special advantages

Useful where draught animals are available. Does not require collecting the stalks in bundles.

The Olpcid thresher made in India works on the same principle. Grooved discs are used to thresh the grain as the device is moved along. The output of such a thresher is 30-85 kg/hr.

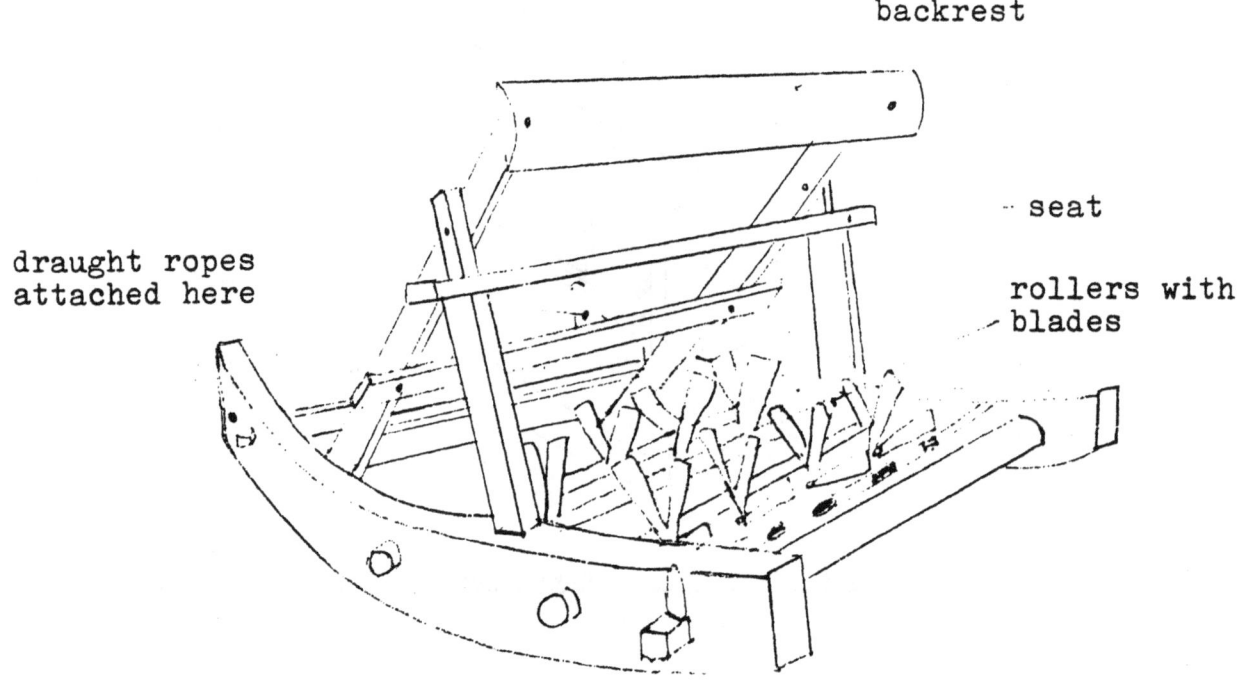

Fig.6.12 The Rasulia animal-driven thresher

Use of animal driven power-gear for rice threshing

Description and design aspects	The threshing unit consists of a longitudinal drum 1800 mm long and 230 mm in diameter rotated at about 1100 to 1250 rpm. The drum which has 6 beater bars along its circumference is partially encircled by a wire grid. The gap between the grid and the drum is arranged so that it is 22-24 mm at the top and 4-5 mm at the bottom. When the stalks are introduced between the grid and the rotating drum they are forced down into the narrowing gap and the beaters knock off the grains from ths stalks. A foot pedal enables the machine to be stopped by the operator.
	The animal-gear used to rotate the drum is described fully in Chapter 5. (Animal-driven power gear maize mills).
Materials and parts	Wood, sheet metal, wire rod, iron castings, pulley, gears, pedal.
Manufacture	Foundry facilities, welding, sheet metal bending and cutting, milling machine, forging.
Special advantages	Can be used with tractor or engine/motor.
Disadvantage	Manufacture is not as simple as other devices described earlier.
Output	300 kg/hr maximum.

Rice parboiling

Oil drum rice parboiling unit

**Description and
design aspects**

An improved rice parboiling unit consists of an old 44
gallon drum. At about 1/3rd of the height from the bottom
of the drum, cross rods are welded and on them is placed a
sieve made from mild steel sheet of 16 swg. This sieve is
the same diameter as the drum's internal diameter.

A small door is provided on the middle drum portion
for the purpose of inspection of the rice to ensure
adequate parboiling and for the removal of the rice after
processing (see fig.6.13).

To economise fuel consumption, a special oven has been
designed for use with this parboiling drum. The drum is
placed on the first fine grate and the excess heat can be
utilised for other purposes.

The rice to be processed is soaked with water and
placed in the upper chamber of the oil drum. When the
water in the lower chamber boils the steam passes through
the sieve to parboil the rice.

**Materials and
parts**

20 l drum, sheet metal, hinges.

Manufacture

Simple metal working tools. Masonry tools (for stove).

Special advantages

Separation of the water from the rice ensures that the rice
is not over cooked during parboiling.
There is access to the rice being processed and the rice
can be easily removed without risk of burns to the
processor.
Fuel use is reduced as compared to traditional methods of
parboiling.

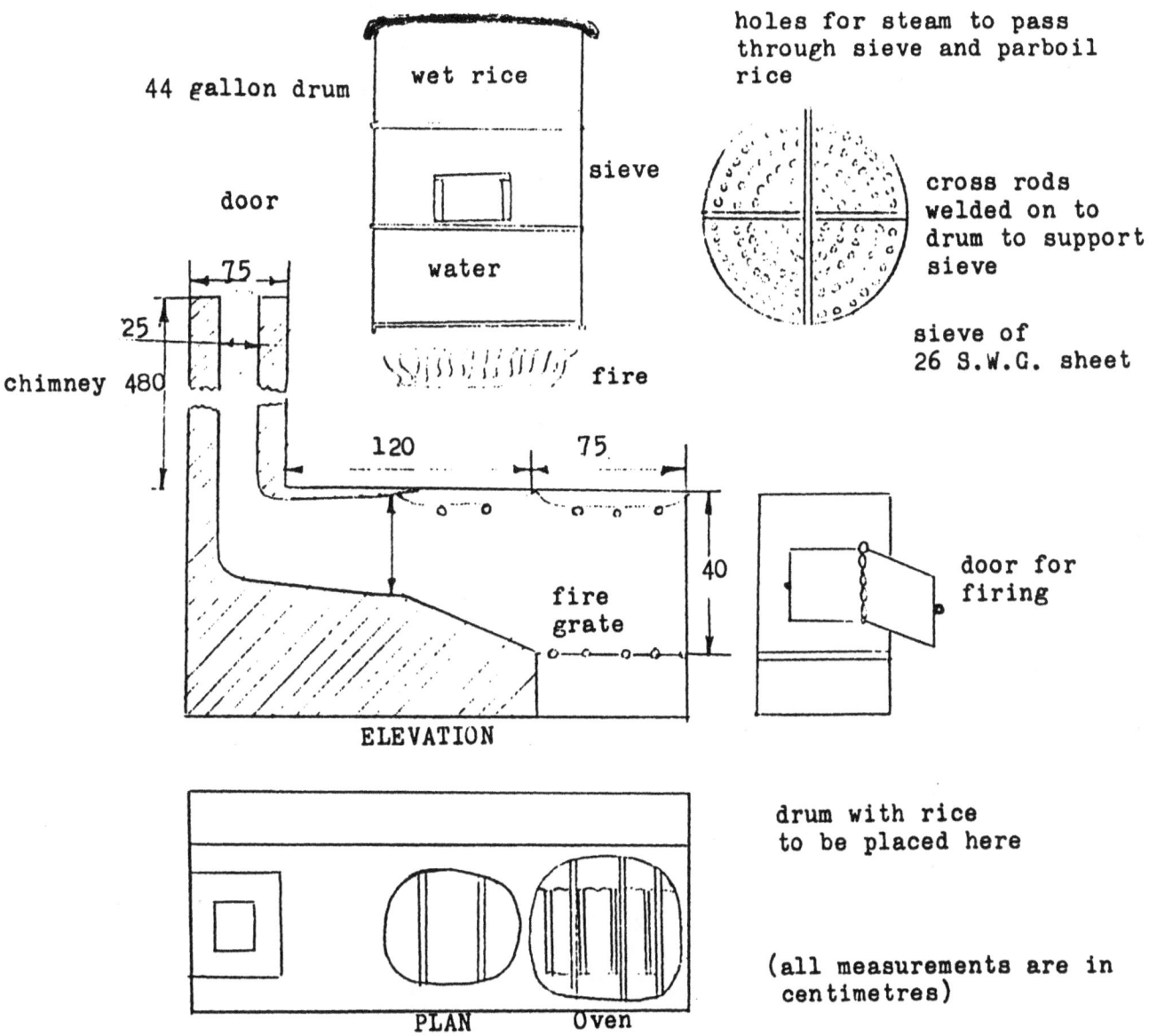

44 gallon drum

door

wet rice

sieve

water

fire

chimney 480

75

25

120

75

40

fire grate

ELEVATION

holes for steam to pass through sieve and parboil rice

cross rods welded on to drum to support sieve

sieve of 26 S.W.G. sheet

door for firing

drum with rice to be placed here

(all measurements are in centimetres)

PLAN   Oven

Fig.6.13 An oil drum parboiling unit

(Hoda, 1977)

Suggested small-scale solar parboiling plant

The uses of solar collectors such as those used in water heating or solar cooking could be extended to rice parboiling provided steam production is sufficient. Since parboiling requires comparatively low temperatures (90-100°C) this method would appear to be feasible. The steam could be fed into a parboiling chamber containing the rice. The method would eliminate the use of fuel although there is additional cost of the solar collector.

Rice dehullers

The cone-type hand-operated rice huller

Description and design aspects

This type of grinder is a modification of the concrete hand mill described in Chapter 5 for maize milling. In this case the mating surface slope to the centre at an angle of 15°. The huller consists of two parts. The bottom part (the body) is made of concrete poured over an iron frame consisting of a ring of 36 cm diameter to which three legs are welded, while three spokes slope down to a centre bearing. This bearing keeps the top cone centred during hulling. A tin ring is placed at the centre to allow the dehusked grain to fall out. The top part (the cone) consists of a turning handle in a concrete frame. The rod for the handle is fitted into the centre bearing of the bottom part (see fig.6.14). The outside lower edge of the cone is tapered to prevent rice from being ejected during husking. The sloped surface in the body is lined with two layers of rubber (thick inner tube). The first layer is fastened to the concrete by means of glue while rubber cement is used for the second layer.

Materials and parts

Iron rods, 1:3 concrete mix for lower part. 1:2 concrete truck inner tubes, metal pipe or tube, tin ring, welding equipment.

Manufacture

The welded iron frame is sunk into the ground which is sloped to become the form for the underside of the body. A ring from galvanised sheet forms the outside. Concrete of 1:3 mix is poured into the form and the surface is trowelled smooth for easy adhesion to the rubber. Several days after the top cone is cast inside the body in order to match the surfaces. A piece of newspaper or a thin strip of mud prevents the surfaces from sticking together. The edge of the cone is formed by a strip of metal 1 cm wide. The diameter is 3 mm less than that of the inside of the

body. The top of the cone is sloped 15°. The concrete
for the cone should be 1:2 mix. The concrete must be kept
moist at all times during the curing. Curing should last
for about a week after which the rubber is glued on the
surface of the body.

<u>Special advantages</u>	Ease of operation.
	Cheap and easy to manufacture.
	Suitable for dehusking rice for family use.
<u>Disadvantages</u>	Only small quantities of rice can be dehusked at a time.
	Short life (one unit shows perceptible wear after dehusking 60 kg of rice).
<u>Output</u>	4-6 kg/hr with 2.5-8.5% broken grains.

leg

spoke

tin ring

central
bearing to house
handle

to central
bearing of
body

(a) Handle

(b) Iron frame for
lower part (body)
of dehuller

(c) Galvanised steel form
(36 cm diameter)

Fig .6.14 Cone-type hand-operated rice dehuller

Tree-trunk rice dehuller

Description and
design aspects

This tupe of dehuller consists of a hollowed out log which
is supported on a conical shaped stump as shown
(fig.6.15). This trunk rotates when the handle bars are
rotated in both directions. The rice is hulled by rubbing
action of the two pieces of wood and the dehusked rice and
hulls spill out into the mat.

Materials and
parts

Tree trunk, bolts and nuts, mat.

Manufacture

Basic wood-working tools.

Special advantages Cheap and easy to manufacture.

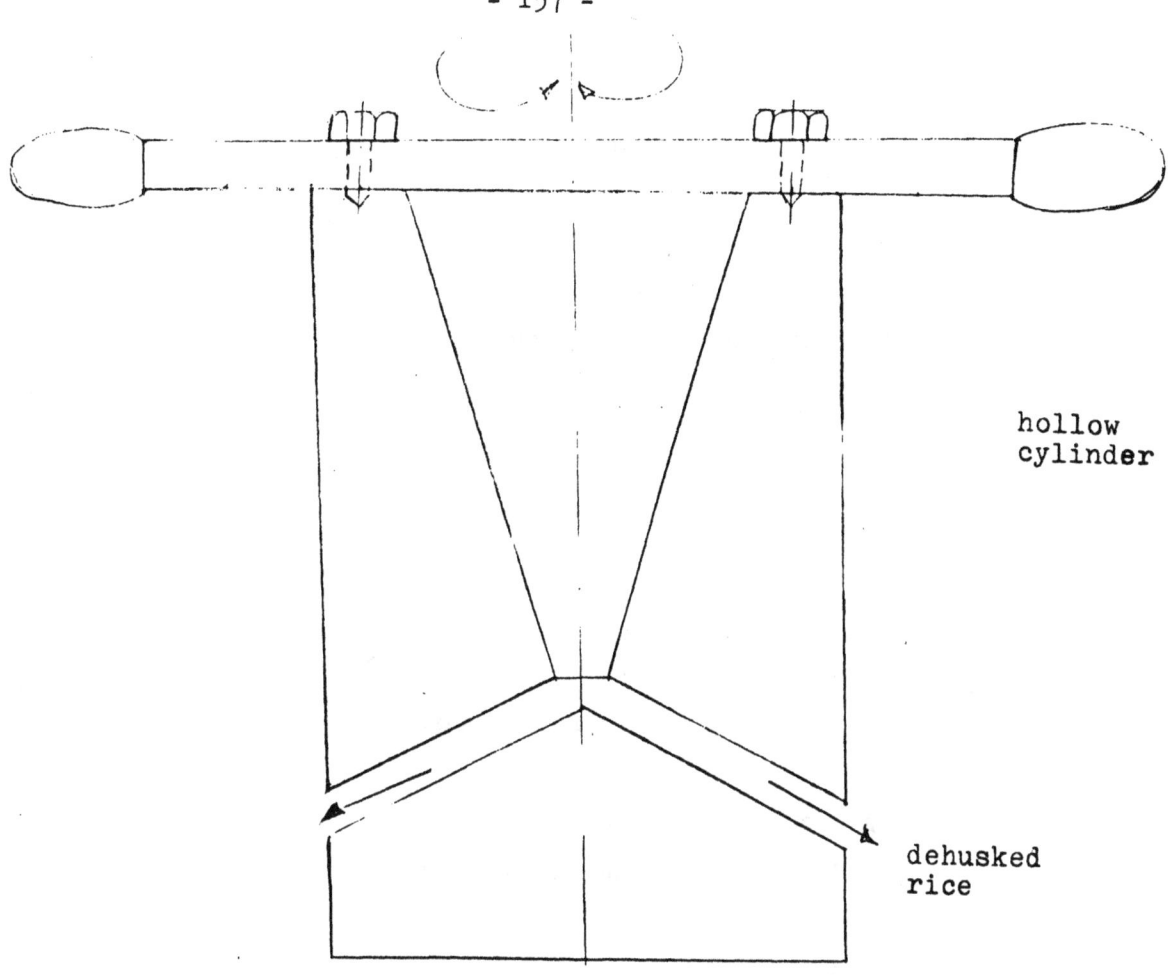

hollow
cylinder

dehusked
rice

Fig. 6.15 Tree trunk rice dehuller

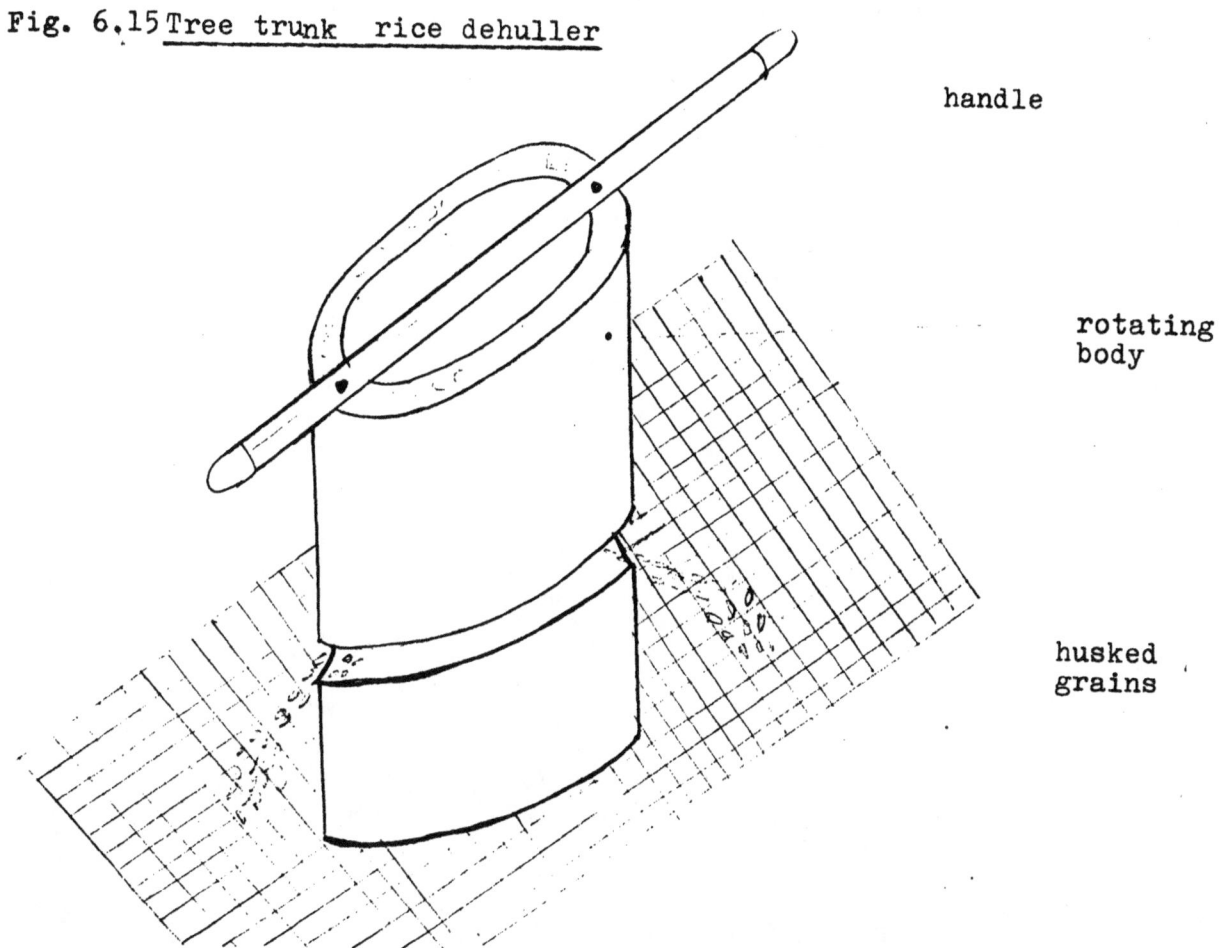

handle

rotating
body

husked
grains

A hand-operated dehuller (Engelberg type)

Description and design aspects

This type of dehuller consists of a grooved metal roller rotating in a hollow cylinder (Fig.6.16 and 6.17). A perforated plate allows dust to escape. The machine has three adjustments controlling the feed, discharge and the hulling knife.

Materials and parts

Iron castings, bolts, wooden handle, bolts and nuts, bearings.

Special advantages

Durability.
Can be opened easily for cleaning.

Disadvantages

High percentage of broken grains.
Grinds bran and significant amount of rice into the hull.

Output

14 kg/hr.

Supplier

J. Cordon & Co. Ltd.

Fig. 6.16   Small hand-operated dehuller

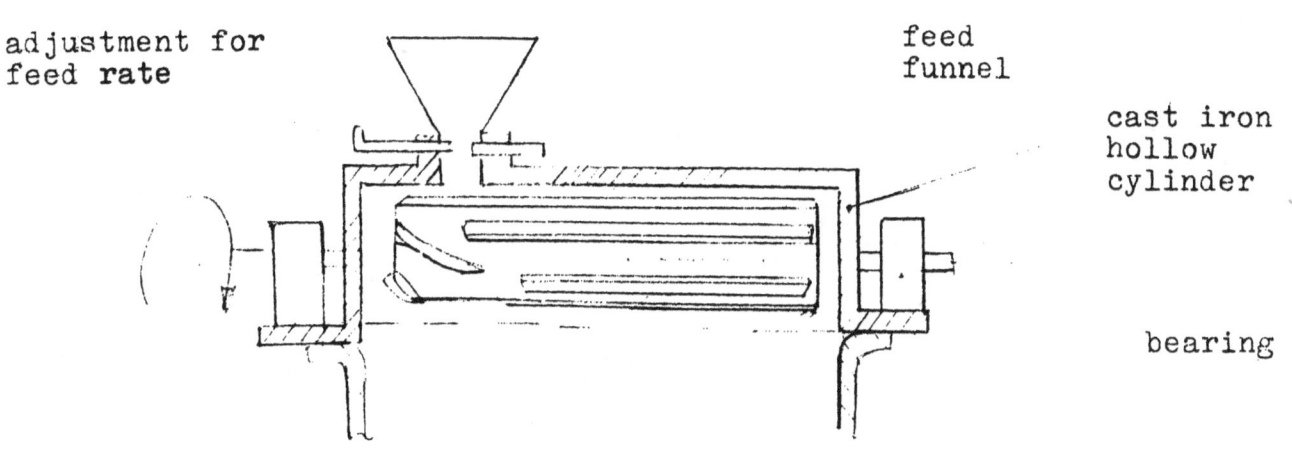

adjustment for
feed rate

feed
funnel

cast iron
hollow
cylinder

bearing

grooved
steel roller

Fig. 6.17 Principle of the Engelberg type dehuller

Two-man hand-operated rice dehuller (Rubber roller type)

Description and design aspects	This type of dehuller is shown in fig.6.18. It is a rubber roller type which consists of two rubber rollers rotating in opposite directions. The rice is introduced in the small space between the rollers and the husks are removed by the sheer forces produced by the rollers (fig.6.19). As the handle bars are moved forwards and backwards, a gearing system enables the rollers to rotate at speeds of 3500 to 4000 rpm.
Materials and parts	Wood, sheet steel, hinges, rubber rollers, gears, bearings.
Manufacture	Woodworking tools, welding equipment.
Special advantages	Does not cause damage to the grains.
Disadvantages	Rollers wear out and have to be replaced.
Output	250 kg/hr at 90% or more hulling efficiency.
Supplier	CECOCO.

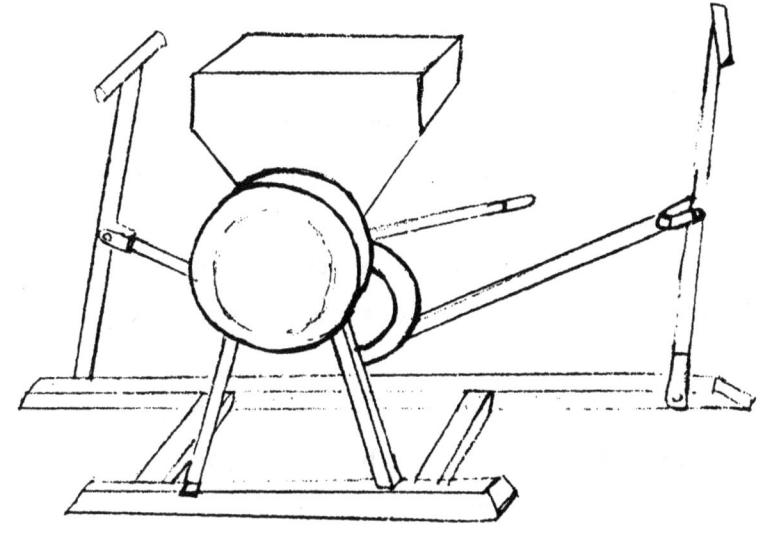

Fig. 6.18   Two-man hand-operated rice dehuller

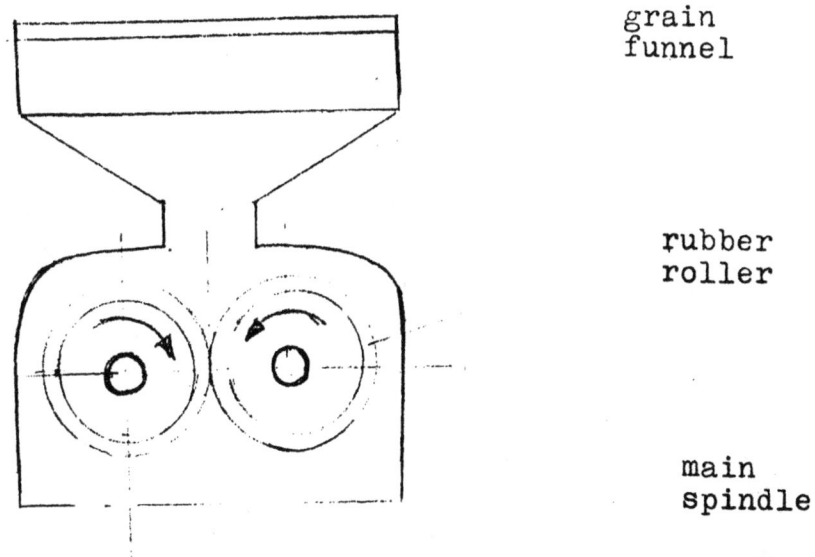

grain
funnel

rubber
roller

main
spindle

Fig. 6.19 The principle of the rubber roller dehuller

Rural customs mills (power-operated)

These mills are of the disc type, the steel roller (Engelberg) type and the rubber roller type. They are usually engine or motor driven.

The disc type or 'cono' mills consist of discs of stones or cast iron coated on their opposite surfaces with emery and cement. They consist of one or more under-runner disc units for dehusking and a number of vertical cone polishers for removal of the bran.

The Engelberg mill is the steel roller type. Although it is low cost, its high breakage rate and high power consumption makes it unattractive as compared to other types of mills.

The rubber-roller (Japanese type) mills have a high recovery rate. One development of this type of dehuller is the belt type. In this type the shelling surfaces consist of a wide rubber belt of uniform thickness along its length (see fig.6.20). The grain in dehusked as it moves past the shelling roller.

Comparative performances of these types of dehuskers are given in table 6.

These dehuskers incorporate aspirator mechanisms for separating the grains from the husks.

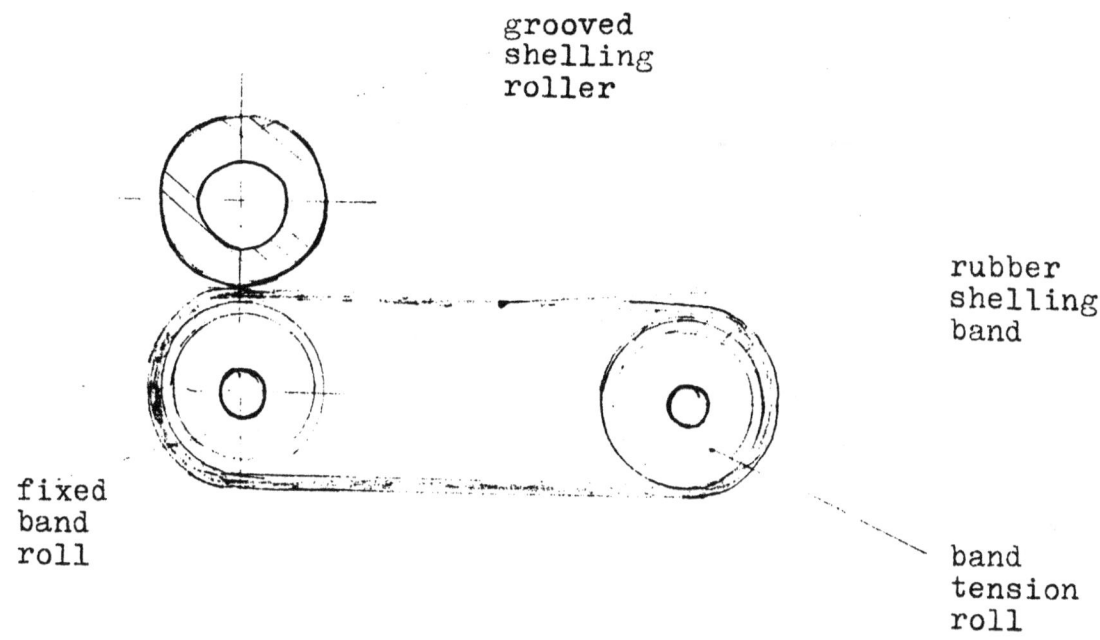

grooved
shelling
roller

rubber
shelling
band

fixed
band
roll

band
tension
roll

Fig. 6.20 <u>Principle of the belt type dehusker</u>

Table 6.2: Performance of commercial rice mills

Mill type	Output	Milling	% breakage (parboiled rice)
Engelberg	300 kg/hr	63%	16-18%
Cono	300-1000 kg/hr	67%	-
Rubber roller	300-5000 kg/hr	70%	3%
Belt type	1000 kg/hr	-	-

Rice Winnowers

Fan Winnower

Description and design aspects	This type of winnower is shown in fig. 6.21. The mixture of grains and husks is held near the rotating fan and the lighter husk is blown away. The fan can be hand, pedal or power driven.
Materials and parts	Steel sheets for fan blades, steel rods for frame. A bicycle parts, wood for frame pulley, bearings.
Manufacture	Forging for production of fans, carpentry and mechanical tools, welding equipment.
Supplier	Cossul & Co. PVT Ltd.

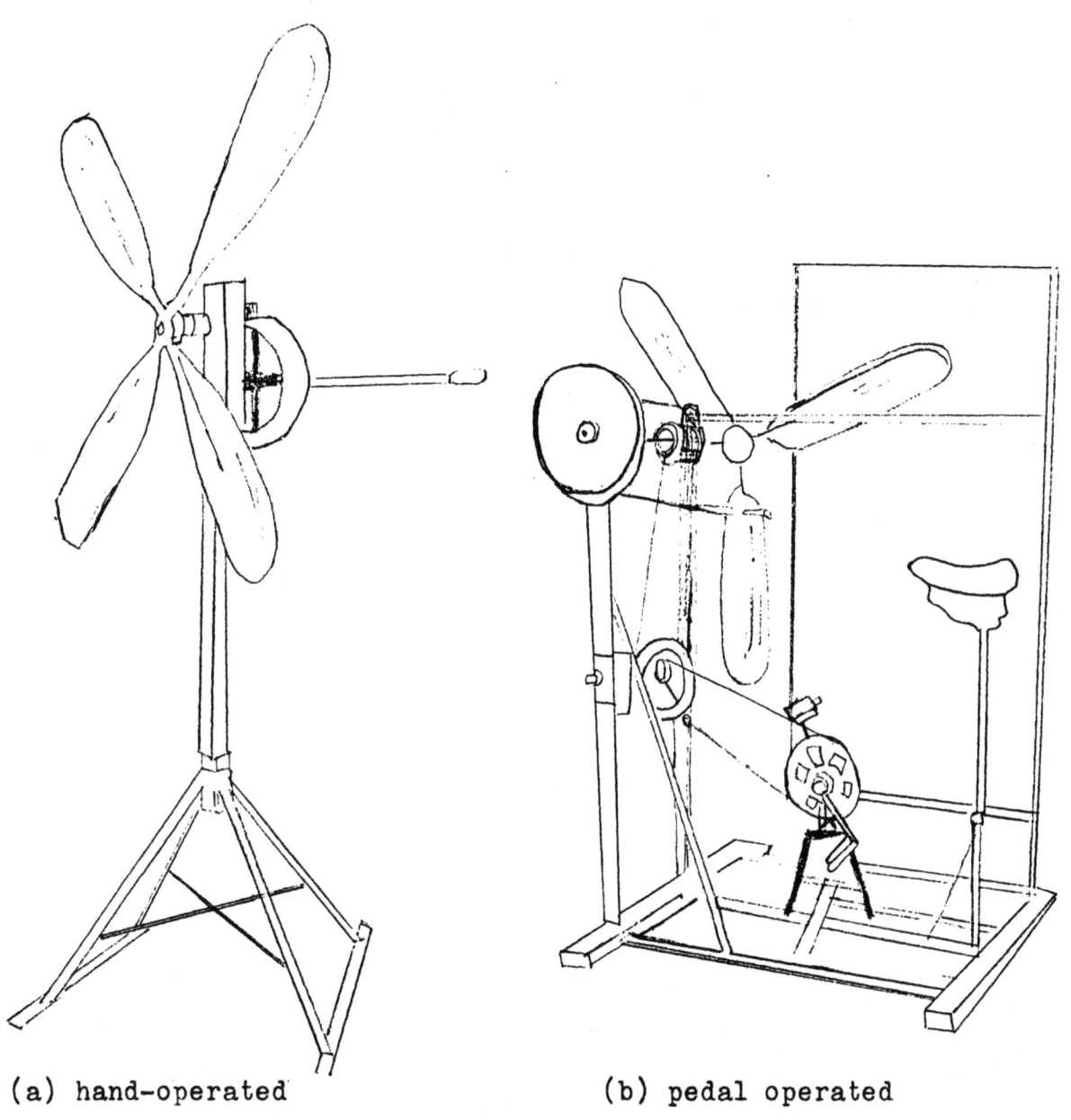

(a) hand-operated   (b) pedal operated

Fig.6.21 Fan winnower

Foot-operated winnower (TAEC type)

Description and design aspects	Thw winnower consists of a sloping 44 gallon drum with a fan at one end as shown in fig.6.22. The fan is turned by the threadle mechanism and the rice is introduced via the hopper. The lighter husk is blown away while the heavier grains slide down the drum and are collected as shown.
Materials and parts	44-gallon drum, sheet metal for fan blades, steel pipes from frame, pulleys, threadle mechanism.
Manufacture	Welding equipment, basic mechanical tools.
Special advantages	Low cost.
Output	600 kg/hr.

Fig.6.22 TAEC winnower

Hand operated winnower

Description and
design aspects

This type of winnower is shown in fig.6.23. It consists of hopper and a stack of four horizontal wire screens spaced about 80 mm apart. When the handle is turned at 45-60 rpm, these screens are shaken or vibrated sideways and the ingredients are either retained or fall through the different screens. The mesh on the screens vary from top to bottom the coarsest being on top. The chaff is retained by the topmost screen and the husks by the second. At the same time, a fan at the back of the machine blows off the light chaff and husks off these two screens which are tilted forwards. The two lower screens are slightly tilted to the rear to prevent the grains being affected by the moving air. By means of vibration the grains are made to flow back down the inclined screen into a collecting chamber. Any sand or dirt sifts through the third screen and drops on to the bottom one.

Materials and
parts

Wood framed wire net screens, wood and sheet metal crank shaft, gears, rods and rocking levers to produce vibration.

Manufacture

Carpentry tools, sheet metal cutting shears, screwdriver, drill for wood.

Output

600 kg/hr.

Supplier

SISCOMA.

Fig. 6.23 SISCOMA hand-operated winnower
(Ellman et al , 1981)

The Ceneema hand-operated winnower

Description and
design aspects

This type of winnower consists of a vertical drum
containing a fan at its upper end. The mixture of rice and
husks is introduced through the hopper (fig.6.24). When
the handle bar is turned the fan rotates and the husks are
blown away from the side of the equipment while the grains
drop to the bottom.

Materials and
parts

Sheet metal, angle iron.

Manufacture

Sheet metal bending and cutting equipment, welding.

Special advantages Low cost and ease of manufacture.

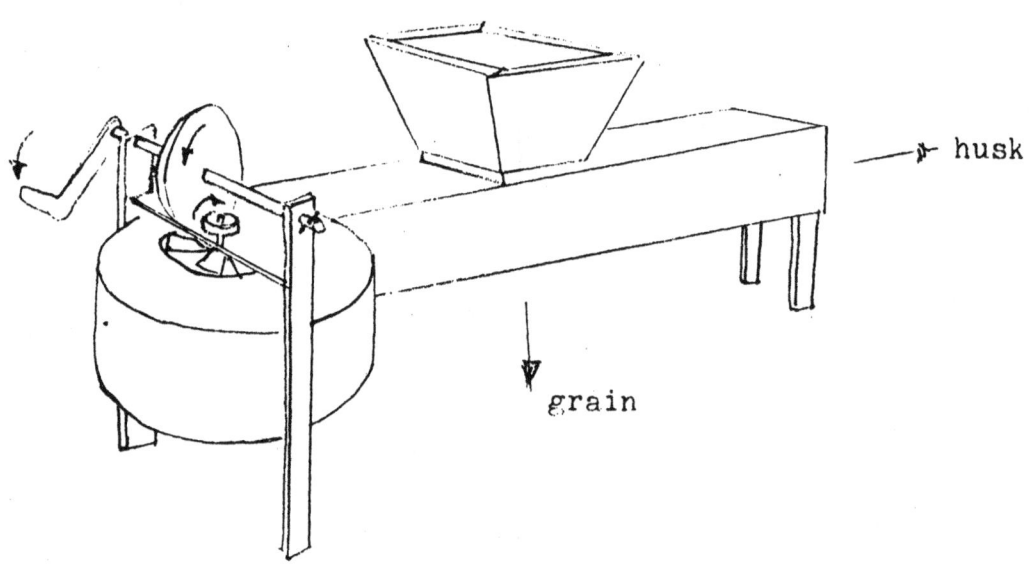

Fig.6.24 Ceneema rice winnower
(Cameroon)

COMPARATIVE PERFORMANCE OF IMPROVED AND TRADITIONAL TECHNOLOGIES

Table 6.3: Comparison of some figures of merit of traditional and improved technologies for rice processing

Operation	Technology	Figures of merit (output)
Threshing	Hitting stalks on hard surface	19 kg/hr
	Trampling	16 kg/hr
	Rotary threshers	45-500 kg/hr
	Two-cylinder type thresher	80-85 kg/hr
	Animal driven rice thresher	30-85 kg/hr
	Thresher operated from animal driven power gear	300 kg/hr
Dehusking	Mortar and pestle (dehusking and winnowing)	5-10 kg/hr
	Cone-type hand-operated dehuller	4-6 kg/hr
	Hand-operated dehuller (Engelberg type)	14 kg/hr
	Two-man hand-operated dehuller	250 kg/hr
	Power-operated rice mills	300-5 000 kg/hr
Winnowing	Hand/pedal operated winnowers	600 kg/hr

NOTES TO CHAPTER 6

1   1 bushel = 28 kg of rice.

2   Usually harvested rice is stored in stalks and only processed before
     cooking in order to minimise damage caused by insect attacks.

3   When huge containers are used, processors have to climb into them to
     remove the parboiled rice.

4   For design drawings, see ITDG "The 'Rasulia' Bladed Roller Thresher".

Chapter 7

FISH PRESERVATION AND PROCESSING

INTRODUCTION

The methods of fish preservation and processing commonly used in West Africa are salting, sundrying and smoking. Some fish are preserved by only one of these processes but combinations of two or all three of these are not usual.

TRADITIONAL METHODS

Fig.7.1 shows the stages in fish processing.

Description

Salting of fish

The action of salt on fish is to extract the moisture from it. This forms a brine solution with the salt which then enters the cell walls of the fish by the process of osmosis. By this same process, water passes out of the cells although the coloidal proteins remain. The cells of bacteria are also dehydrated and, as a result, collapse, thus retarding bacterial action. As little as 4 per cent salt in the tissues slows down bacterial and enzyme spoilage, and if this is increased to 20 per cent good preservation results.

In West Africa salting is traditionally not used as an end in itself for preserving fish, but as a preliminary step in fish preservation, probably to suppress bacterial action before other methods of preservation such as frying, sun drying and smoking can be done, as well as to give flavour to the fish. From the quantity of salt added one can distinguish two types of salting which can be classified as "heavy" salting[1] and "light" salting.

Fig.7.1 Methods of fish processing in use by respondents

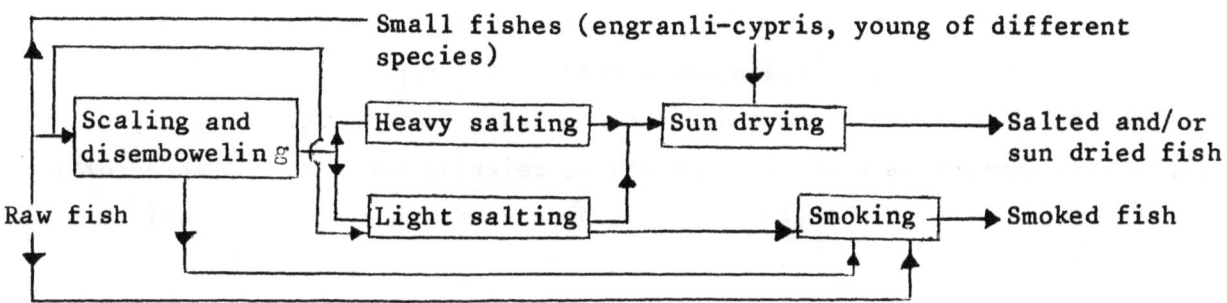

In the case of heavy salting the salting is the main method of preservation, with the subsequent methods only being used to complete the cure. Common types of fish preserved in this way are catfish (arius spp) and snappers (dentex angolensis), horse mackerel (scomber japanicus), shark (scolodien spp) and herrings (sardinella aurita or sardinella cameronensis).

Heavy salting usually precedes sun drying and in this case smoking is not done. The ratio by weight of salt to fish ranges between 1:2 and 1:20^2 in Sierra Leone and is approximately 1:8 in Ghana. The period for which the salt is left to act on the fish before further processing is started is known as the "rousing" time. This varied according to the quantity of salt used. For the ratio of salt to fish of 1:8, usual rousing time was reported to be 24 hours.

The fish is scaled and gutted and dry salt is added to it in the container. The salt is "rubbed" into the fish and it is left to stand throughout the rousing period. This method is known as "dry curing".

"Light" salting precedes smoking, or combined sun drying and smoking, in which cases the salt is mainly used to savour the fish rather than as a method of preservation. In this case both the quantity of salt used and the rousing times are small, as compared to heavy salting. The ratios by weight of salt to fish were recorded to be 1:20 and 1:100^2. In these cases the fish has to be processed almost immediately (usually one to two hours after applying the salt).

The containers used to salt fish are oil drums, wooden barrels, enamel-coated metal pans, cemented pits, plastic containers and earthenware containers. Enamel-coated metal pans are the most widely used. The use of enamel-coated pans is not satisfactory as any exposed metal surface in the pan leads to its rapid rusting and deterioration. Cemented pits seem to be the most appropriate container and, in the long run, the additional costs would be outweighed by the increased life of the container.

Open sundrying of fish

Sun drying is designed to remove moisture from the fish by evaporation. There are two phases in this process. In the first, water is evaporated from the surface of the fish and in the second, water rises from inside the flesh to the surface where it is again evaporated to the atmosphere.

The final moisture content of open sun dried fish is determined by atmospheric conditions such as temperature, relative humidity and speed of the current of the air. For a given set of these conditions the final moisture content is known as the 'equilibrium moisture content'. Products which are dried in the atmosphere can only be dried up to an equilibrium moisture content which is dictated by atmospheric conditions such as temperature and humidity. At this equilibrium point, a longer exposure to the atmosphere does not result in further reduction of the moisture content. It can be assumed that it is at the equilibrium moisture content that the processed fish can be expected to have maximum life under given atmospheric conditions[3].

In West Africa, sun drying is done by direct exposure to sunlight. The fish is spread on the bare ground, on mats, cemented drying floors, raised stands, wire mesh and on roof tops. The predominant methods used are mats on the ground, and raised stands. The further away from the ground the fish is dried, the more hygienic is the process, but this involves additional costs (in the case of stands) and the presence of a relatively flat-topped roof to hold the fish (in the case of roof-top drying). Raised platforms are the traditional "banda" in Sierra Leone (see fig.7.1) and make-shift stands consisting of a sheet of wood or metal supported by oil drums.

When sun-drying follows heavy salting the period required to sun dry the fish to the equilibrium moisture content of the atmosphere is less the longer the salt is allowed to act on the fish. Sun drying times in Sierra Leone[4] were reported to be between 2-14 days in the dry season, with an average spoilage rate of 11 per cent, and 7-21 days in the rainy season, with an average spoilage rate of 42 per cent. Due to the high spoilage rate in the rainy season this method of preservation is rarely used during this season.

In some areas (e.g. Ghana) sun drying is used mainly as a preliminary preservation method before smoking, mainly to conserve fuel. These are for small fishes known locally as "Keta schoolboys" (a collection of small fishes of different species). If no further processing is done, this fish can last on an average for 70 days after sun drying has been done before spoilage. Spoilage during drying was reported to be an average of 3 per cent in the dry season.

Smoking of fish

The action of smoking is to deposit phenotic and other compounds which have antimicrobial action on the surfaces of the fish, thus suppressing bacterial action. In hot smoking the heat also has the effect of reducing the moisture content of the fish.

The most common method of fish preservation in West Africa is smoking. Smoked fish is required in the traditional dishes and thus has a high demand in this area.

Smoking of fish is done on stands (open or closed)[5] or in special traditional smoking ovens. Also in some areas (Senegal) fish is 'smoked' on the ground under a pile of burning straw.

The traditional Ghanaian mud oven is shown in fig.7.3. While that in use in Sierra is shown in fig.7.4, other types of ovens in use are shown in figs.7.5 to fig.7.9.

fig.7.3 The traditional Ghanaian mud oven

Fig.7.4 The Sierra Leonean "Banda"

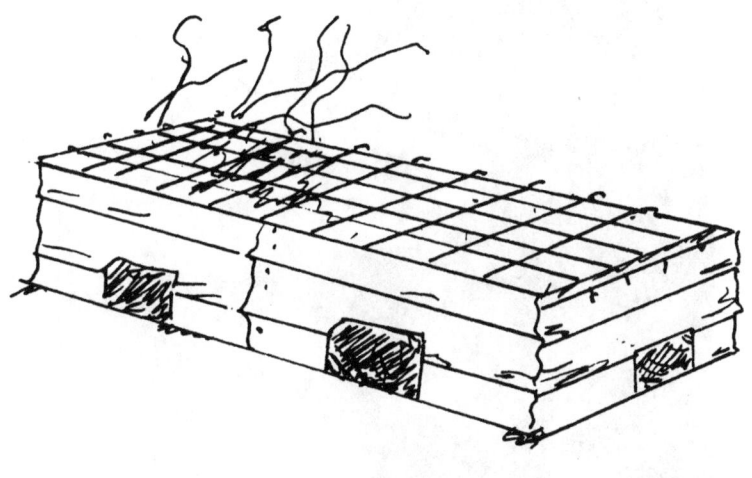

Fig.7.5 The "Fante" oven used in Goderich, Sierra Leone

Fig.7.6 A make shift cut oil drum oven

Fig.7.7(a) A roofed 'fante' oven

Fig.7.8 A rectangular mud oven

Fig.7.9 'Closed' stands. The covers for the sides are
made from opened 44-gallon drums

Technical performance

Fish smoking in Ghana: the traditional Ghanaian mud oven

This oven is cylindrical in shape with a firepit at the bottom (see fig.7.3). The main fuel used is firewood, although the use of some agricultural waste, whenever available, was reported by some respondents.

The size of the ovens in terms of the physical dimensions and capacity varied from processor to processor but the usual capacity seems to be approximately 60 kg of fish. Capacities as low as 20 kg and as high as 600 kg of fish were reported. Points corresponding to firewood use per unit weight of fish and the capacity (in kilogram weight of fish) of the ovens are shown in fig.7.10.

The variation of the values of fuel used at the same oven capacity can be explained by the fact that the physical dimensions, such as the over-all height of the ovens, the height between the fire pit and the fish, the diameter of the ovens and the height to which the fish is packed are not standard and vary from household to household. Within the variations of the physical dimensions which exist in the areas surveyed, one can deduce from these points and the geographical regression curve that the fuel use per unit weight of fish decreases the greater the oven capacity in terms of kilograms of fish. Savings in fuel can thus be attained by using larger ovens instead of a number of small ones.

Smoking times ranged from 1-48 hours, with an average of 6 hours. The lower smoking times of 1-4 hours refer mainly to fish which has been previously sun dried for more than one day. Some of the fish which was originally sun dried was smoked for longer periods at lower temperatures. The effect of lowering the smoking temperatures is an increase in the drying times. This, however, leads to savings in fuel since the closer the temperatures are to those of the surroundings, the lower the heat losses caused by convection. Fig.7.11 shows the relationship between fuel used per unit weight of fish smoked and the length of smoking. From the trend obtained it can be seen that fuel can be saved in the traditional Ghanaian oven by reducing the oven temperatures (rate of burning of fuel) thus increasing smoking times.

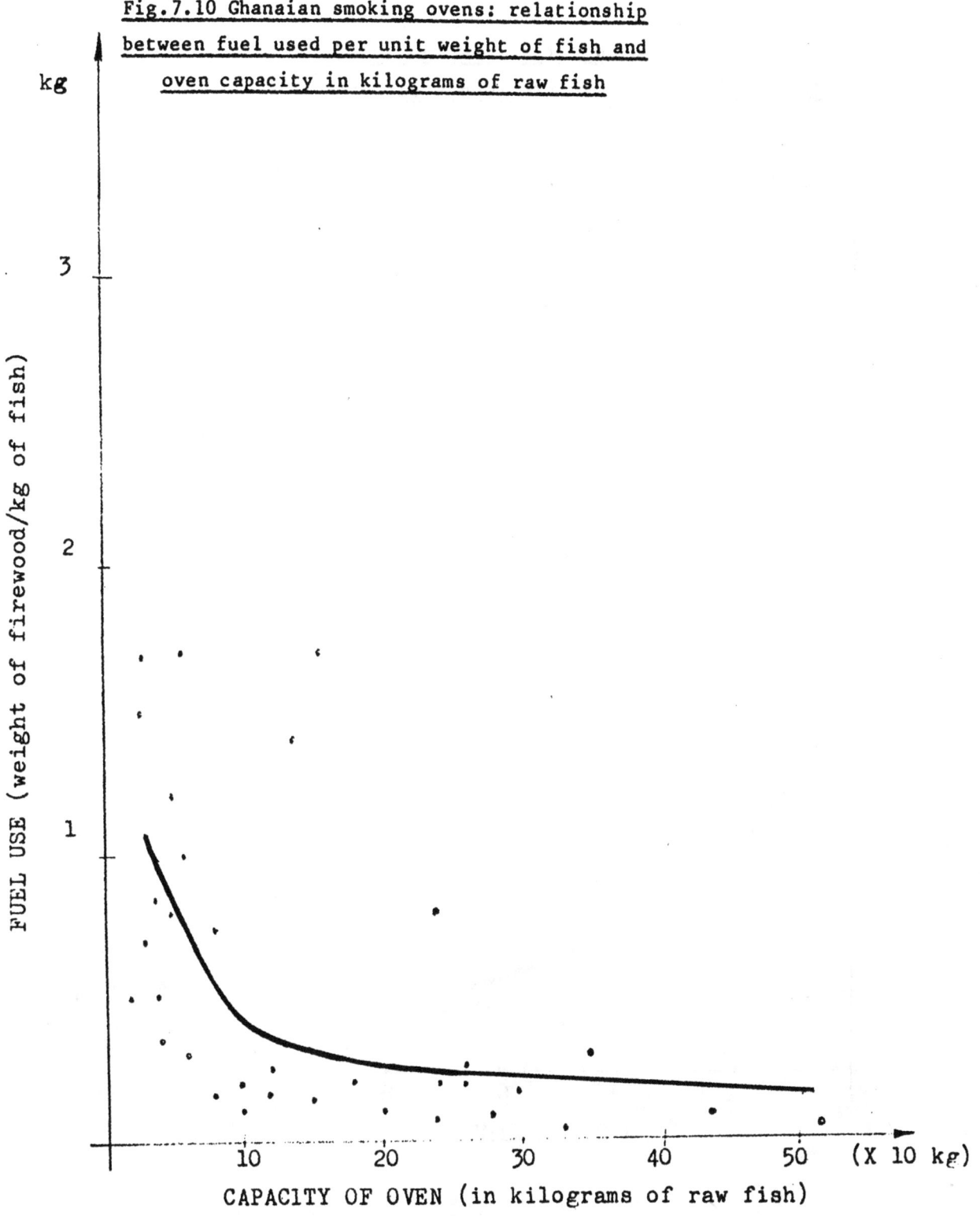

Fig.7.10 Ghanaian smoking ovens: relationship between fuel used per unit weight of fish and oven capacity in kilograms of raw fish

Fig.7.11 Ghanaian traditional mud oven:
Relationship between fuel used per unit weight of fish
and the smoking times for fish previously sundried

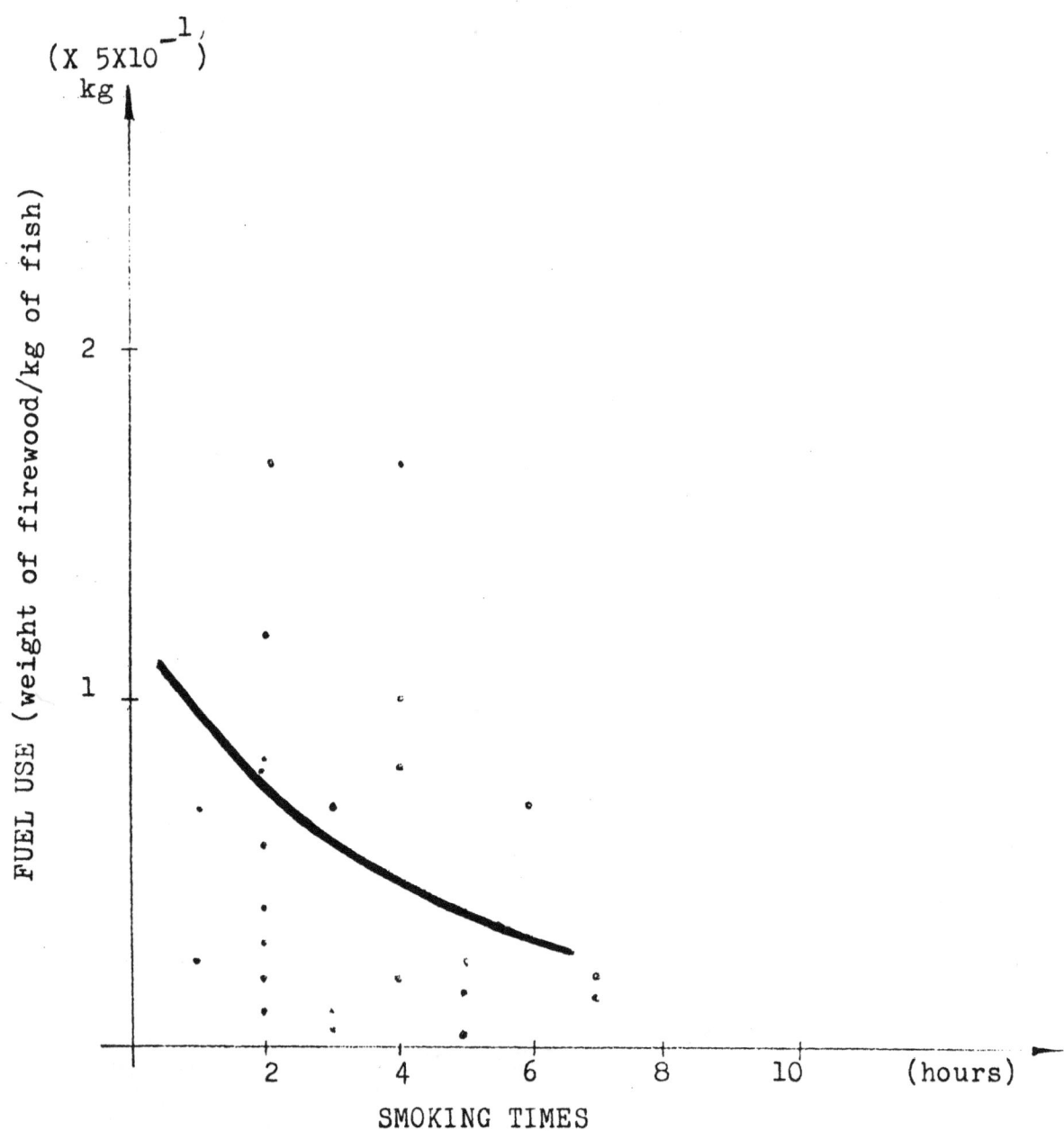

The higher smoking times (5-10 hours) refer to fish which has not been previously sun dried. The fish smoked for 40-48 hours is that which is to be transported to the northern parts of the country. Most of the processors initially sun dry the fish and smoke it for an average of two hours. Since the ovens themselves are used for storage (fig.7.12), the fish is left in the ovens is usually heated up every day for short periods, until it is sent away for marketing.

Fish processed in Ghanaian traditional mud ovens has a shelf life of between 1 and 95 weeks, depending on the extent to which the moisture is reduced by sun drying and smoking. The average shelf life recorded was approximately 24 weeks.

Fish smoking in Sierra Leone

In Sierra Leone stands are traditionally used to smoke fish (see figs.7.4 and 7.5). The sides of the traditional Sierra Leone stands, known as "banda", are usually covered with flattened oil drum pieces. In the rainy season these stands are situated indoors, usually in the kitchen, while in the dry season they are located out of doors. Some stands (usually the larger ones) are built in the form of "smoke houses". The sides of the stands are built with corrugated iron sheets on a wooden frame and the fishes are laid on wire nets which are spread over the top. The whole construction is covered with a roof suspended on wooden poles. This type is usually called the "fante oven".

The more sophisticated stands (fante ovens(are used in areas which specialise in the smoking of herrings (sardinella aurita or sardinella cameronensis) or bongas (ethmalosa spp). Capacities of 10-800 kg of fish were reported. Of these, 50 per cent were of capacities of 50 kg or less, 25 per cent were between 100 and 50 kg and 25 per cent greater than 100 kg. Fig.7.13 shows that the fuel (firewood) used per kilogram of fish processed is less the greater the capacity of the stands. Smoking times for this type of oven are between 3 and 16 hours (average 6.2 hours) and the life of the smoked fish, if no further processing is done is between two and three days. (One respondent, who reported an average smoking time of 16 hours, claimed the shelf life of her produce as 13 days.) This is explained by the fact that the final moisture content after 16 hours of smoking is low enough to enable preservation over a longer period.

The Sierra Leone traditional "banda" has capacities of between 20 and 100 kg of raw fish. Again, in this case, the fuel used per unit weight of fish was seen to decline the greater the capacity of the oven (see fig.7.14).

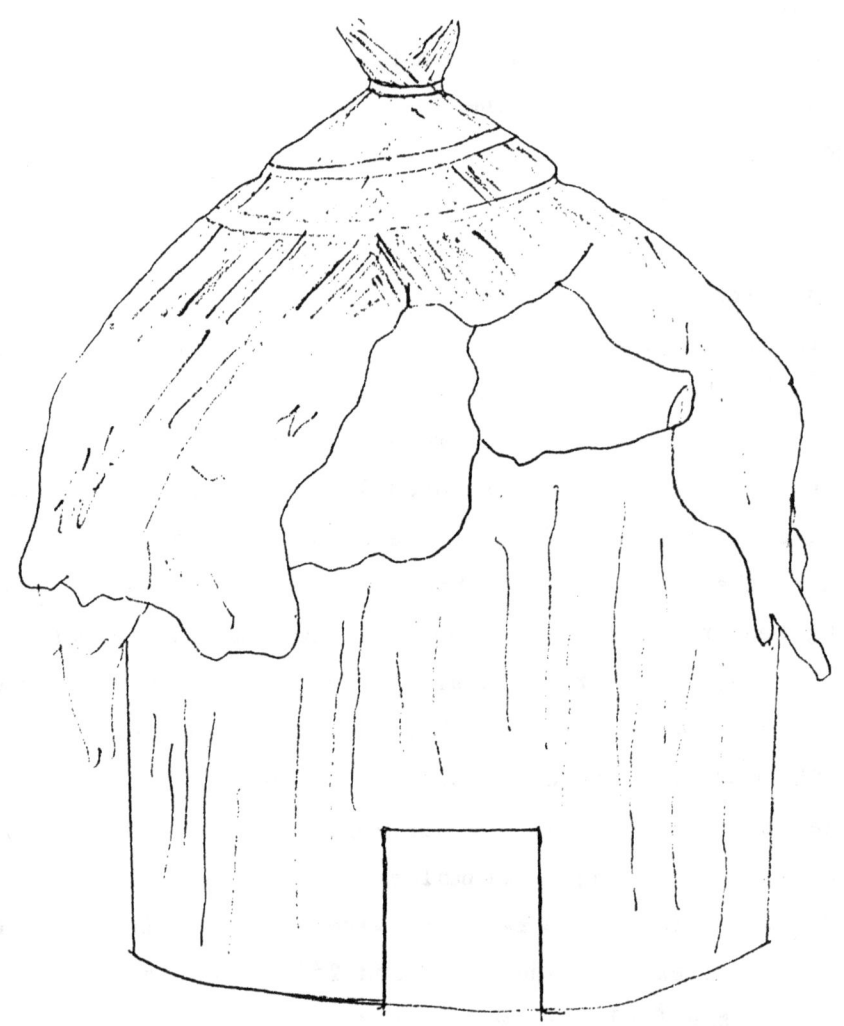

Fig. 7.12 <u>Use of Ghanaian mud oven for storage</u>

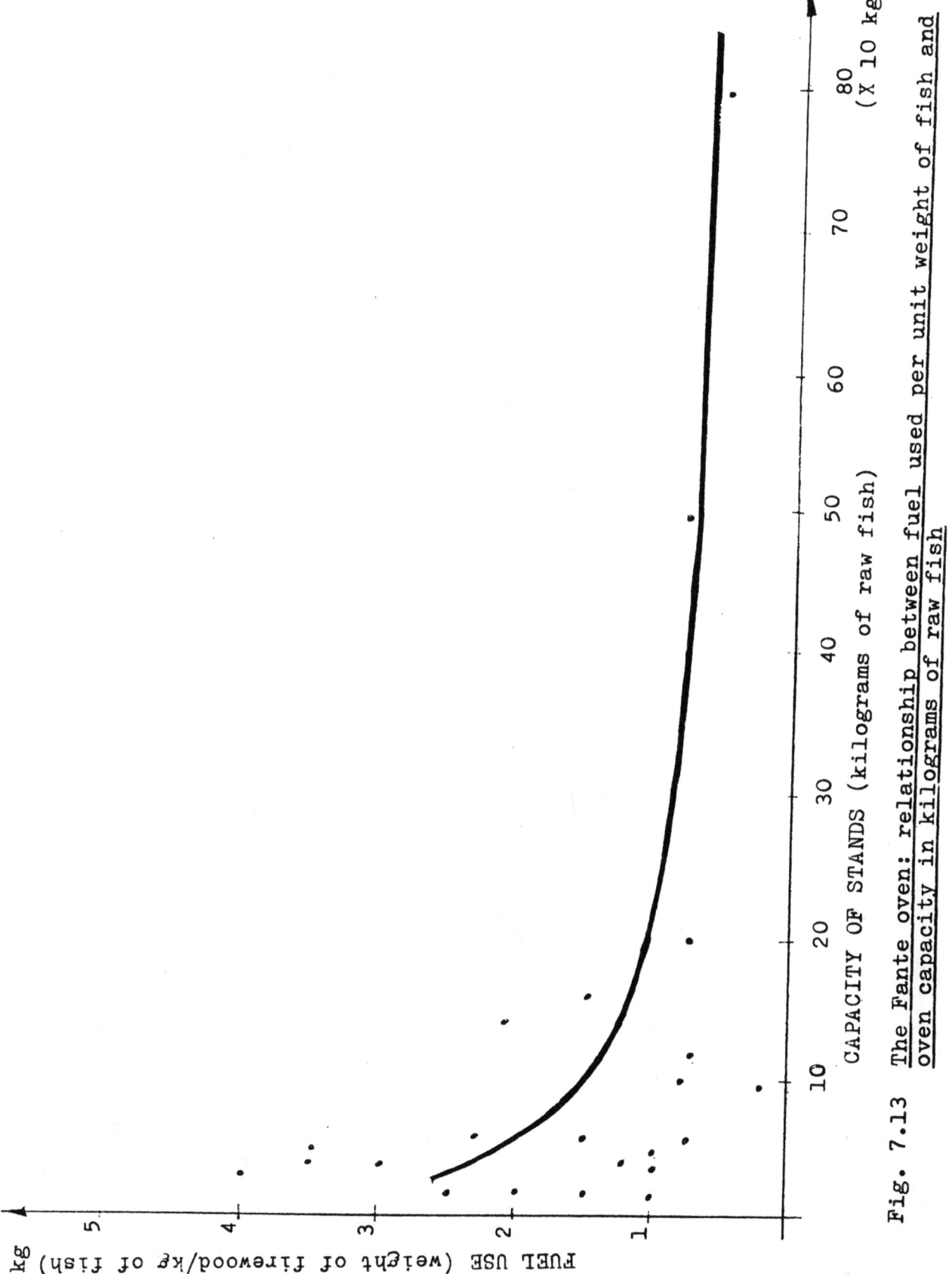

Fig. 7.13 The Fante oven: relationship between fuel used per unit weight of fish and oven capacity in kilograms of raw fish

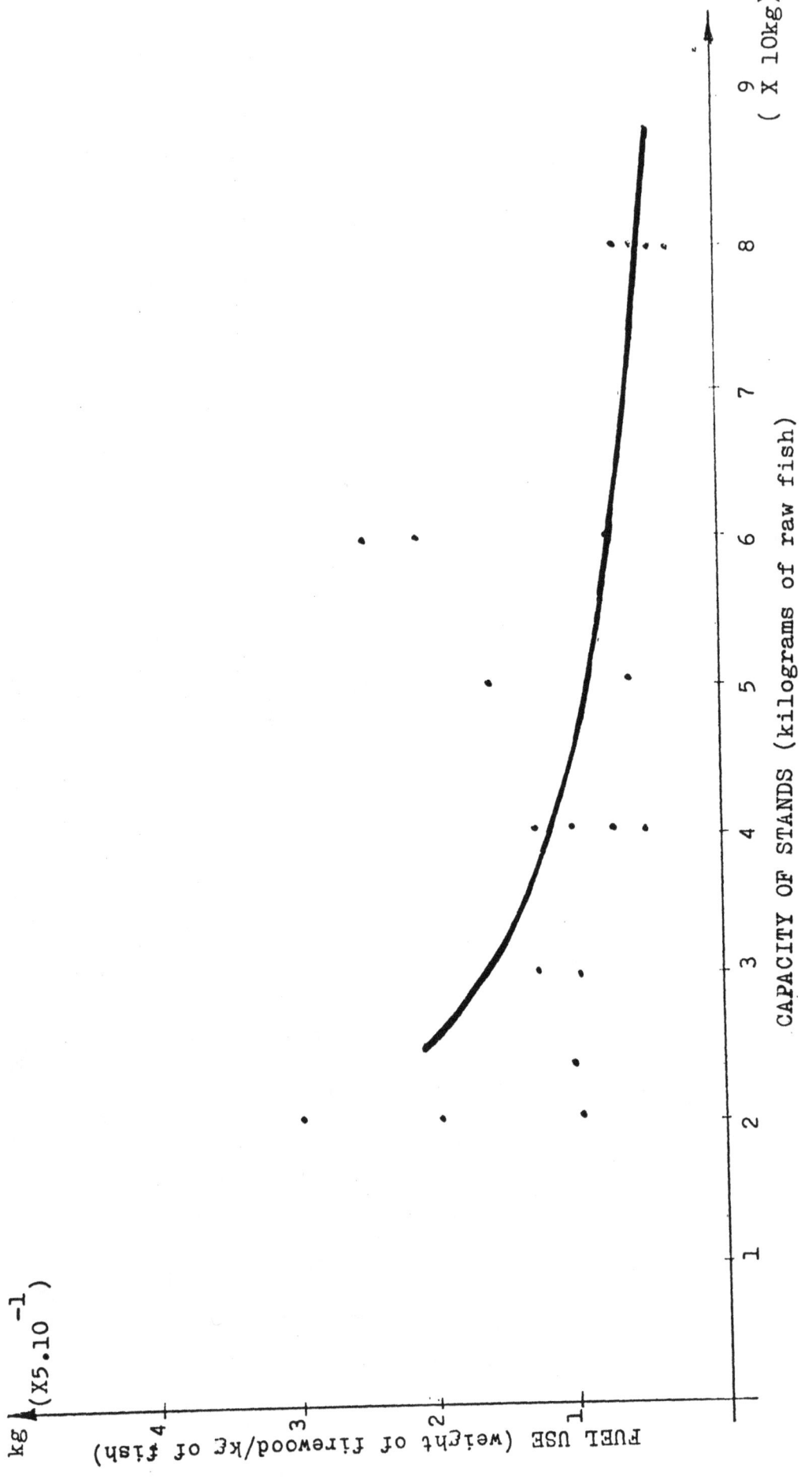

Fig. 7.13(a) Sierra Leone traditional banda: relationship between fuel use per unit weight of fish and oven capacity in kilograms of raw fish

Smoking times were recorded as 2-9 hours, the average being 5.5 hours, and the life of the smoked fish is between 1 and 8 days, the longer periods referring to the longer hours of smoking.

Advantages

- they are inexpensive since they are usually built of locally-available mud in the case of Ghana and Kenya and of bush sticks in Kenya and Sierra Leone[6].
- their construction can be done by the village artisans.
- the possibility of installation in the home means that the smoking of fish can be combined with other household activities.

Disadvantages

- long smoking times are required for smoking the fish to ensure a shelf life of over one week.
- fuel used for ovens of small capacities (not exceeding 60 kg of raw fish)[7] is high, ranging from between 0.15 to 0.85 kg of firewood per kilogram of raw fish in the case of ovens and 0.4 to 2.0 kg of firewood per kg of fish in the case of stands. (This assumes a standard firewood bunch weighing 5 kilograms).
- the small capacities of the ovens/stands[7] make it necessary to construct a number of them to cope with processing necessitated by big catches.
- the fish has to be turned over to ensure even smoking. This migh lead to breakage of the fish.
- the non-availability of methods of regulation of the smoke leads to scorching of the fish if due care and attention is lacking.
- since open smoking is used flies and other insects rest on the fish, especially at the final stages of smoking when there is not much heat. This reduces the shelf life of processed fish further.

Table 7.1 gives some characteristics of traditional ovens in use in Ghana and Sierra Leone.

Table 7.1 Characteristics of fish-smoking ovens in use
in Ghana and Sierra Leone

Oven type	Reported capacities (kg of raw fish)			Reported smoking times (hours)			Fuel Use kg of firewood/kg of fish		
	Mean	Mode	Range	Mean	Mode	Range	Mean	Mode	Range
1 Ghanaian traditional mud oven	160	60.0 (48%)	20-600	5.6	2.0 (35%)	1-48	0.25	0.125 (6%)	0.85
2 Traditional Sierra Leone Banda	60	40.0 (20%)	20-100	5.0	3.0 (29%)	1-8	1.2	0.5 (21%)	0.25-2.4
3 Fante oven in use in Sierra Leone	110	20.0 (25%)	10-800	6.0	4.0 (20%)	3-12	0.5	0.29 (12%)	0.09-1.8

Source: Rural Survey of Women. (see sources of data in Chapter 1).
N.B. Figures in brackets refer to the percentage of people reporting modal values.

IMPROVED TECHNOLOGY

Fish salting

The traditional method for salting fish in West Africa is the dry salting (dry cure) method. The setback of this method is that an initial period is required before the process of osmosis can start since, initially, the salt is in solid form. Also penetration of salt into the membranes of the fish is slow. Improved smoking methods have to:
- speed up the process of osmosis, thus minimising spoilage; and
- allow more salt to penetrate the tissues of the fish.

Wet cure

This method consists of immersing the scaled and gutted fish in a saturated brine solution. Its main advantage is that the presence of the salt in the solution from the moment of immersion means that penetration of the salt into the fish cells can start immediately. The disadvantage is that the brine solution is weakened as a result of absorption and thus might hinder further penetration of the salt in the solution.

Kench cure

This method consists of salting the scaled and gutted fish in piles, with alternate layers of salt and fish, and allowing the pickle which is formed to drain away slowly. This method has the disadvantage of requiring a relatively large amount of salt, but the excess salt can be reused. Rousing times can be indefinite as the large percentage of salt in the fish tissues which results guarantees a high degree of preservation.

Pickle salting

The only difference between this method and kench cure is that the fish is cured in watertight containers and instead of draining the pickle thus formed the fish is allowed to cure in it.

Combined method

The traditional method of heavy salting (the dry cure), in the way it is done results in large bacterial contents of processed fish. The percentage of spoilage is also quite high. In order to suppress bacterial activity altogether a combined method of salting and brining is recommended where salt is plentiful and inexpensive. The fish is salted before it is immersed in the brine solution. Fish preserved in this way could be kept for several months or years.

The disadvantages are, first, the cost of the salt since a salt-to-fish ratio by weight of 1:2 is required and, second , the cost of constructing

cemented pits since the fish is to be stored in the solution and processed
further only before selling.

Sun drying of fish

The traditional method of sun drying by exposure to direct sunlight is
unhygienic and results in a loss of vitamins due to the long drying times. An
improved drying method would be required to:
  - shorten the drying times, thus reducing vitamin losses;
  - make the process more hygienic; and
  - dry fish to low moisture contents, thus increasing its shelf life.

Raised drying racks

Description and   One basic improvement in the traditional method of
design aspects   sundrying fish is by using raised racks or platforms.
                      These can take the form of permanent fixtures (fig.7.14) or
                      simply metal (wooden) tables. For large fishes the surface
                      of these racks can be made of wire and can be slanted to
                      allow drainage of water from the fish. For small fishes
                      flat topped racks with solid tops are preferable.

Materials and   Wood, bamboo sticks, metal rods, wire netting, bricks and
parts   clay, cement.

Manufacture   Can be owner built or by village artisan (mason or
                      carpenter).

Special advantages Hygienic.

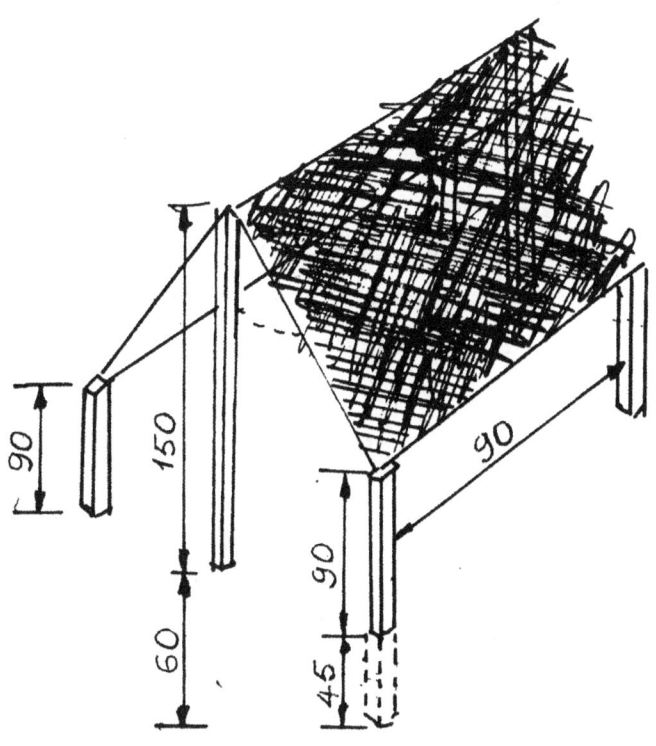

All measurements are in cm

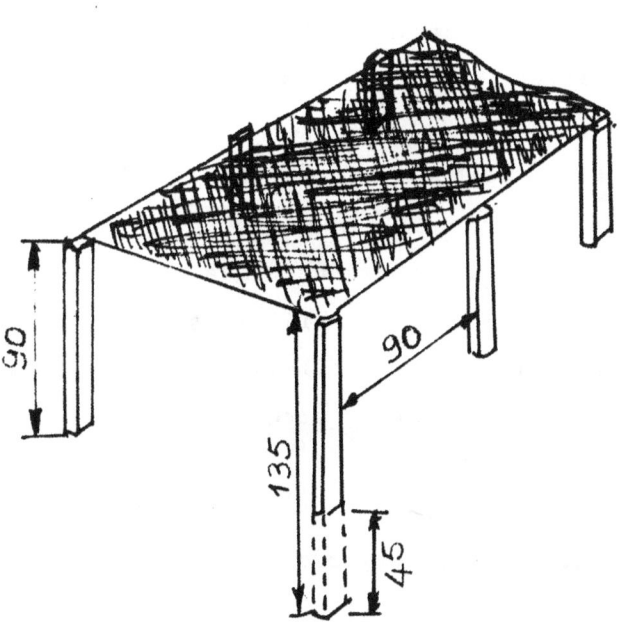

Fig.7.14 Fixed drying racks with flat and slanting tops

Solar dryers

The solar dryer (box type)

Description and
design aspects

Solar crop dryers could be used to dry fish. The crop
dryer consists of a flat wooden box (portable version) or
mud structure (fixed version) eight feet long, 4 feet wide
and 1 foot deep and covered with a "double-glazed" lid of
glass or pure polythene sheeting on a wooden or bamboo
frame (Fig.7.15). The inside of the box is painted black
and vent holes are made on the bottom and sides of the
box. Such a surface absorbs heat from the sunlight thus
attaining temperatures higher than the ambient. The fish
is dried by a flow of air which is brought about by
convection. Cold air enters through the bottom vent holes,
rises, gets hotter and flows out through the top vent holes.

Depending on the design of this type of dryer,
temperatures of up to 70°C can be attained within the box.

Materials and
parts

Wood or bamboo sticks, glass or polythene, cement or clay,
hinges.

Manufacture

Basic carpentry tools; basic masonry.

Special advantages

Hygienic. Sundrying times are considerably reduced. Also
high temperatures kill insects and their lavae which
normally cause spoilage. Vitamin destruction is reduced
due to absence of direct exposure to the sun's rays.

The solar tent

Description and
design aspects

This type of dryer can be built locally from local
materials. Clear and black polythene are used to form the
tent walls as shown in fig.7.16.

Materials and
parts

Bamboo sticks, wooden poles, ropes or nails for fastening
the frame. Clear and black polythene. A bamboo/wooden
fish rack.

Manufacture

Can be owner constructed or by village artisan using basic
tools.

Special advantages

Same as for solar box dryer above.

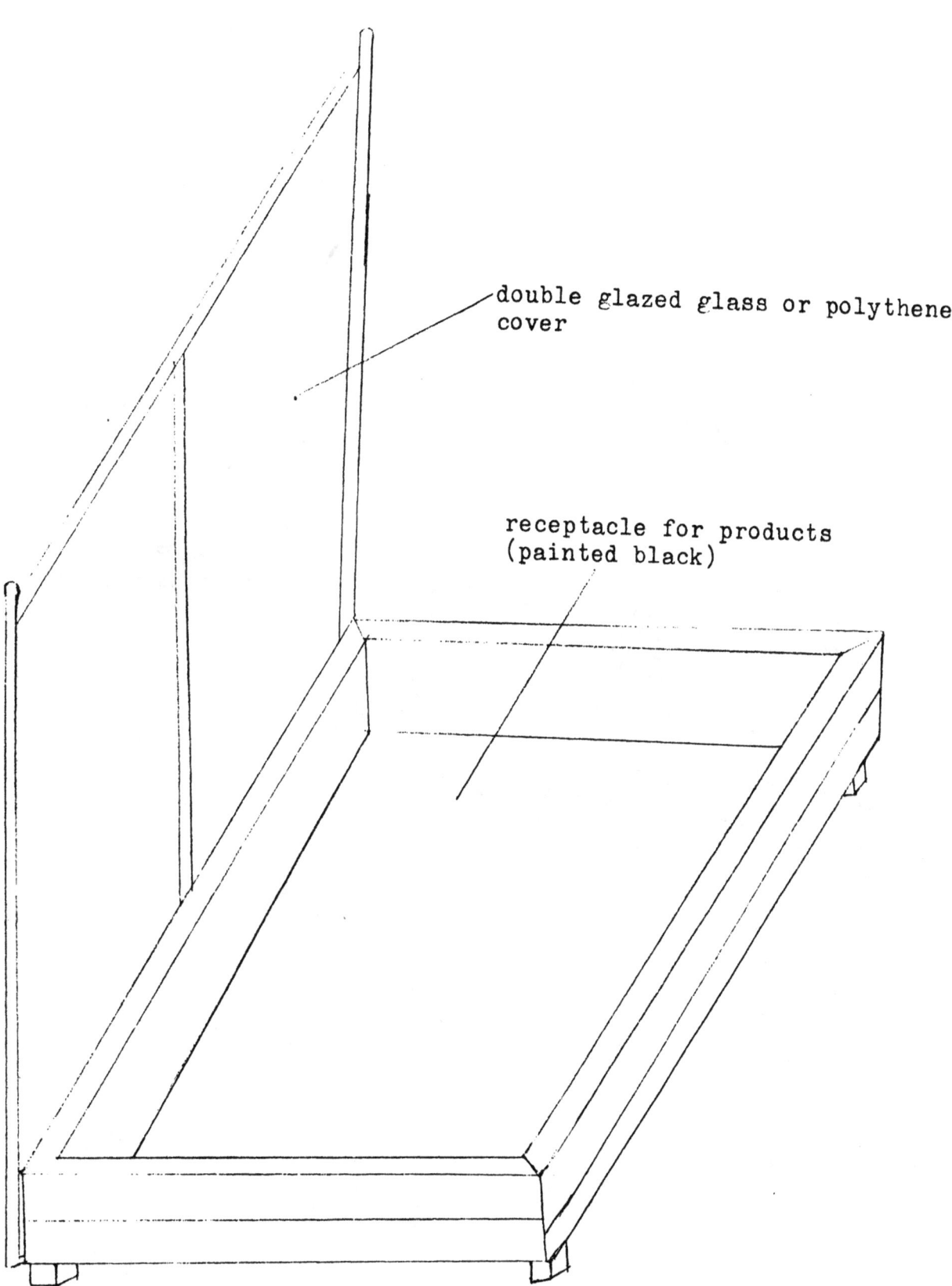

double glazed glass or polythene cover

receptacle for products (painted black)

Fig.7.15 A solar dryer
(vent holes and wire net tray not shown)

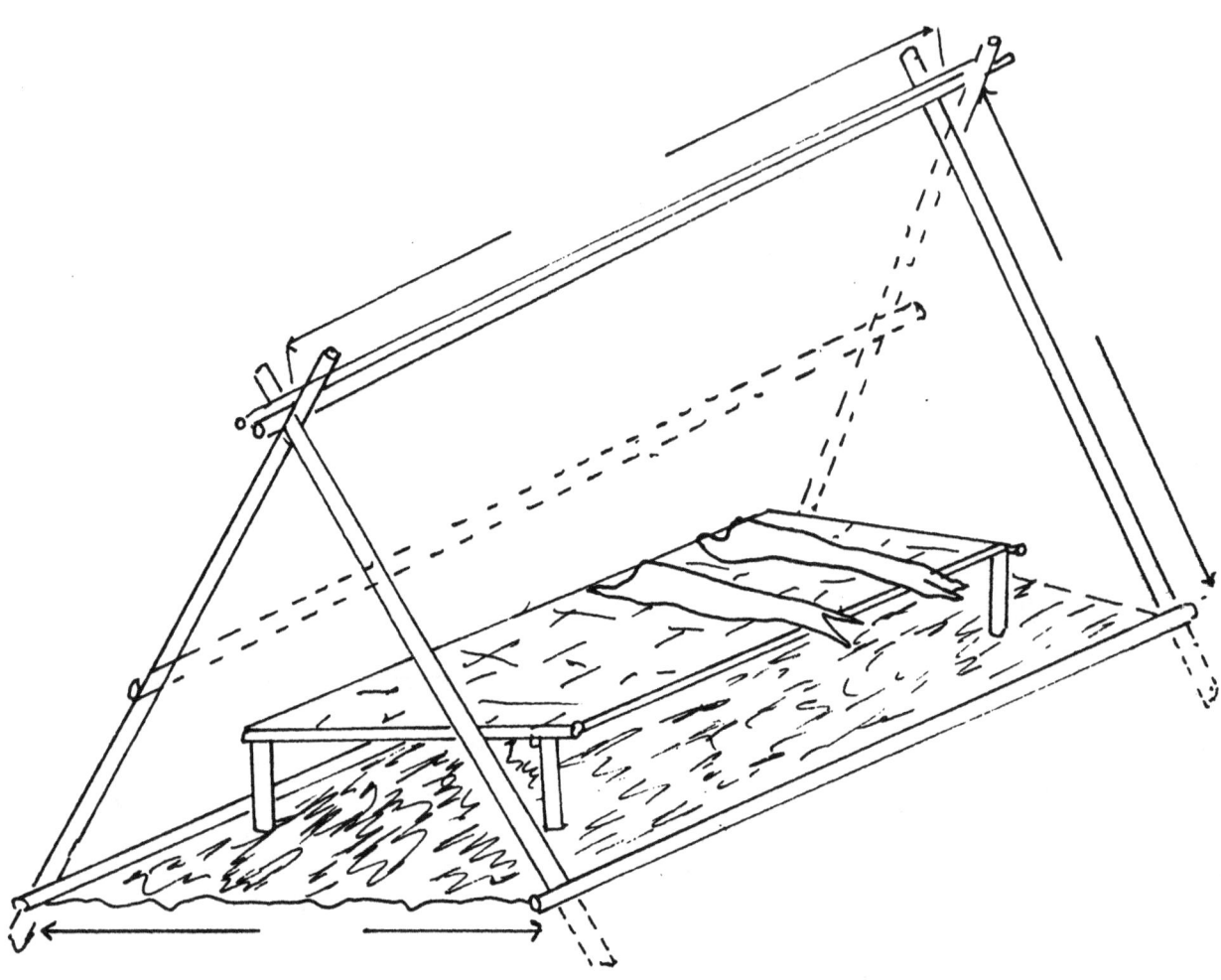

Fig.7.16 Small polythene tent dryer

Fish smoking

The traditional methods of fish smoking described in Chapter 10, although simple in construction and cheap, do not permit the efficient use of fuel and require turning over of the fish during smoking to ensure that both sides of the fish are smoked. Improved smoking methods which are available range from simple modifications of the traditional ovens to more sophisticated types, such as the Altona oven.

In order to improve on the traditional methods, an improved fish smoking method has to:
  (i) enable the more efficient use of fuel;
 (ii) eliminate the task of having to turn over the fish;
(iii) allow more fish to be handled at a time;
 (iv) reduce smoking times for fish;
  (v) regulate the heat/smoke ratio such that the fish is smoked and not
       scorched due to too much heat (this destroys much of the amino acids in
       the fish); and
 (vi) allow even distribution of smoke within the smoking compartment.

Oil drum oven

Description and
design aspects
This consists of a 44-gallon drum with a door at the bottom for the introduction of firewood. The fish can either be laid on a wire-mesh grill on top of the drum or hung by hooks on a webbed frame (see fig.7.17).

The only construction required is the cutting of a rectangular door at the bottom of the drum and the fitting of a hinged door. Holes are also cut at the top of the drum to accommodate wooden or metal rods which form the grill or frame.

Materials and
parts
44-gallon drum, bush sticks or wire netting, hinges.

Manufacture
Local artisan using basic boring tools.

Special advantages
A convenient distance is kept between the fish and the fire which minimises scorching of the fish. The oven is simple and inexpensive. The door allows more economic use of fuel as compared with the traditional method.

Fig.7.17 Oil drum oven

Oven from oil drum sections

Description and design aspects

Fig.7.18 shows a further modification of the oil drum oven. This consists of using a number of 44-gallon drum sections. The fish is hung by hooks in each of these sections and the sections are piled on top of each other over a fire. A large column can be obtained by using a large number of drum sections.

Materials and parts

44-gallon drums, bush sticks or wire, metal ribbons for handles.

Construction

To construct this oven, a number of 44-gallon drums are cut one-third of the depth from each end along the flanges so that these pieces can be placed on top of each other with ease. Drums which are badly damaged should be avoided as this might make the whole column unstable. A small opening 18 cm by 23 cm is made in the bottom drum piece for admitting the fuel.

Handles consisting of loops of strong wire are then passed through holes drilled in the sides of the section near the top. Alternatively, the handles could be made from metal strips rivetted or welded on to the sides. A damp cloth can be placed on the top of the pile to allow retention of the smoke during smoking.

Special advantages The fact that the fish are hung means that more fish can be smoked as compared to the traditional methods where the fish are laid on the grill.

Also hanging of the fish ensures that both sides of the fish are smoked evenly, which eliminates the need for turning over the fish.

No grill marks are left on the smoked fish.

After the initial work of loading the oven has been completed, supervision can be done by only one person who only needs to tend a single fire and to change the position of the sections to ensure that the fish in each section receive an equal share of heat and smoke.

Being light and portable, this oven can be used by fish processors who move from place to place with the fishermen who catch migratory fish.

Disadvantages Initial work on the preparation of the fish is increased due to the need to hang the fish on hooks.

The lower layer of fish can be scorched if placed too close to the fire. For this reason heat and smoke can be supplied to the oven through a trench from a pit in the ground holding the burning fuel (fig.7.19).

There can be loss of smoke at the places where the sections meet, especially if they do not fit well.

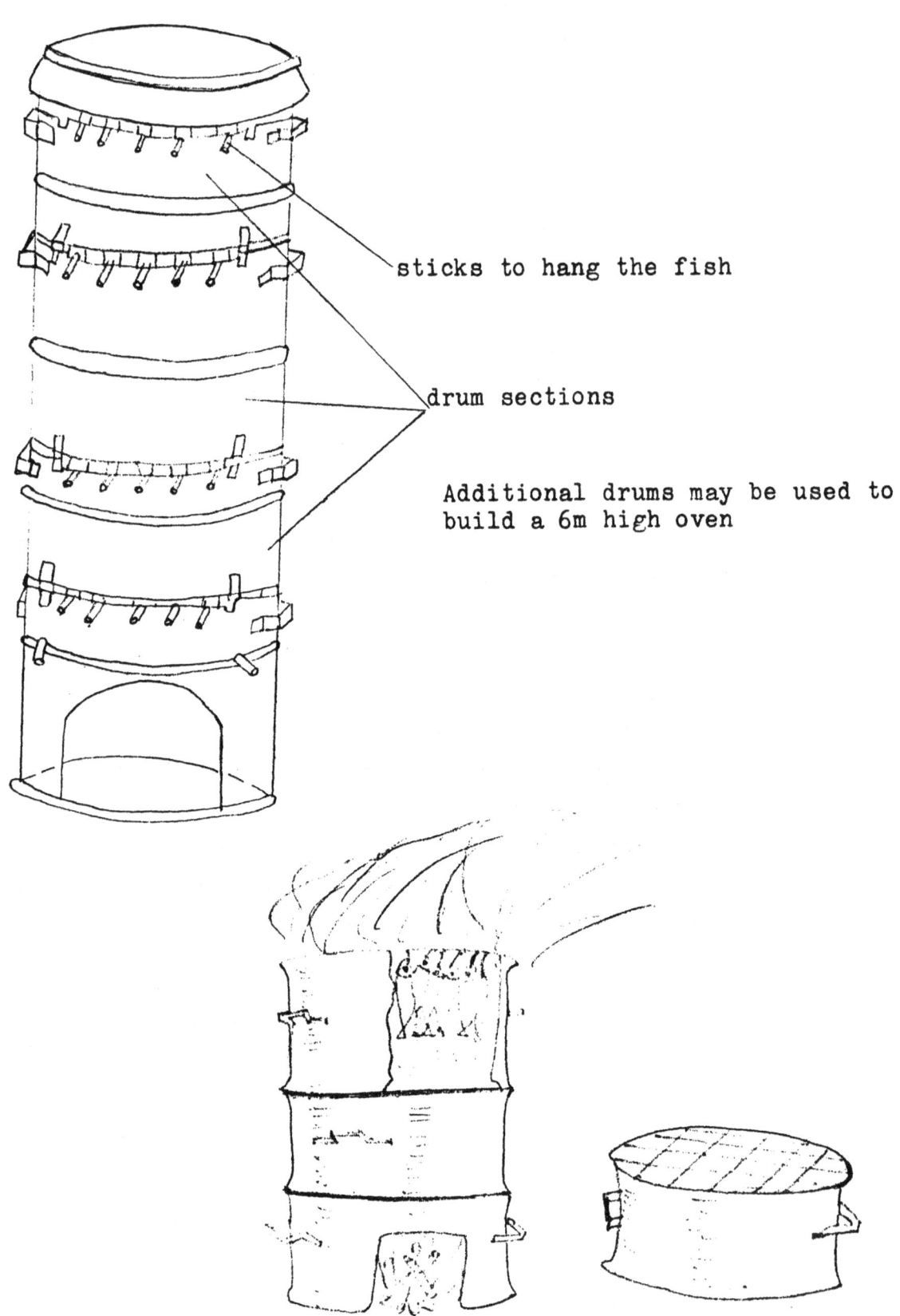

sticks to hang the fish

drum sections

Additional drums may be used to
build a 6m high oven

Fig.7.18 Drum sections oven

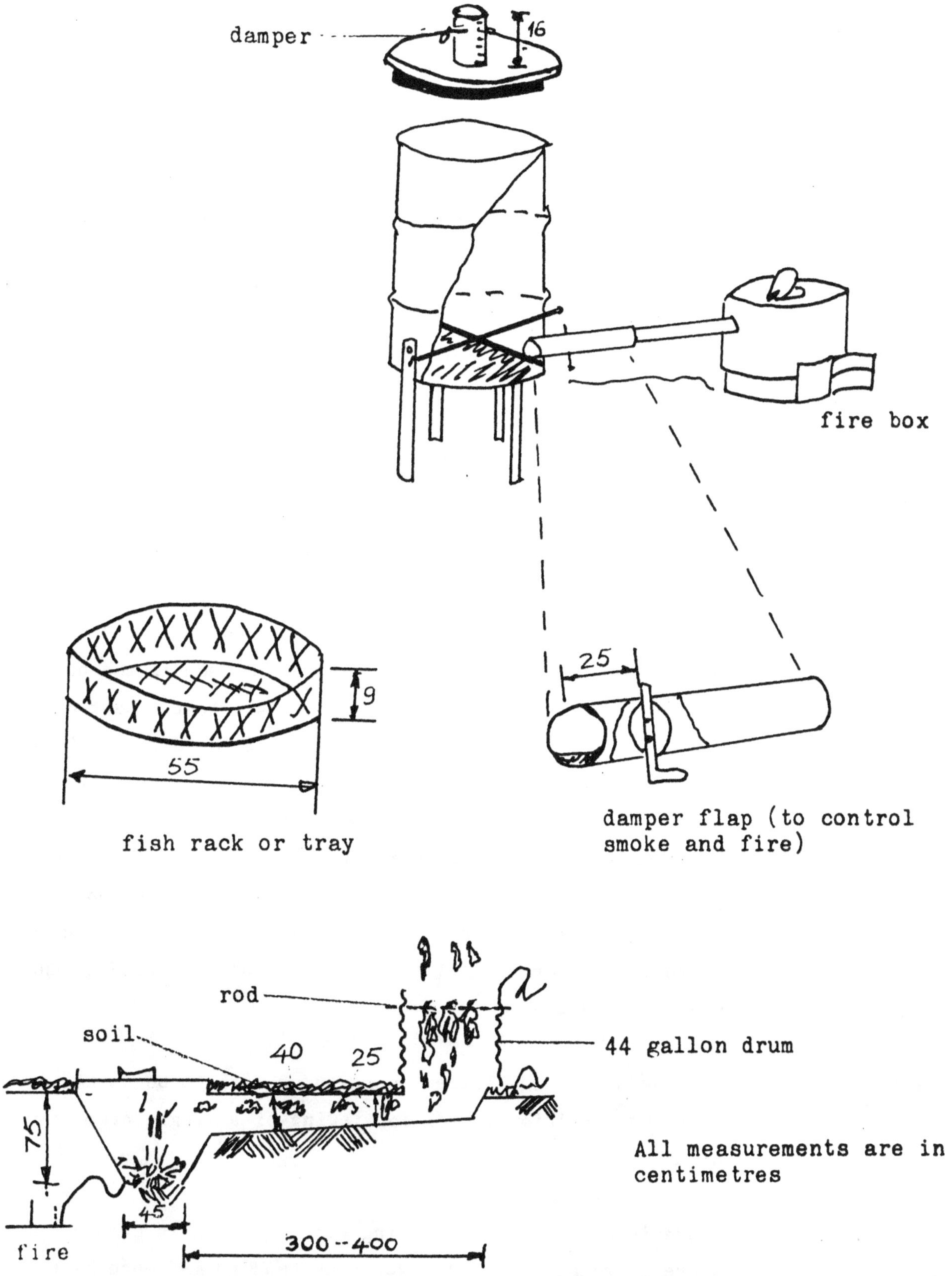

damper

16

fire box

9

55

fish rack or tray

25

damper flap (to control
smoke and fire)

rod

soil

40   25

44 gallon drum

All measurements are in
centimetres

75

45

fire

300--400

Fig.7.19 Arrangements for   smoking chamber

Improvised oil drum oven with door and trays

Description and design aspects	This type of oven is shown in fig.7.20. It takes the form of a 44-gallon drum with holes punched along the sides. The drum is divided into two chambers by means of a grill which enables the smoke to disperse during smoking. Two doors, one in each chamber, allow for loading both fuel and fish into the oven. The fish is loaded on trays made of wire mesh. These trays are fitted on the upper (smoking) chamber.
Materials and parts	44-gallon drums, hinges, metal ribbons, wire mesh.
Construction	An oil drum is used for the construction. The drum is opened at both extremities and two openings are made in it, as shown. The top opening should be two-thirds of the length of the drum. The lower opening should be about half the length of a drum section. Holes are made in the body of the drum at intervals of about 10 cm. Next, sheet metal is cut to fit into the inner diameter of the drum and holes are also punched in this sheet. It is then fitted into the drum one-third of the way up from the bottom. This grill separates the combustion chamber from the smoking chamber and serves as a disperser of smoke. Wire mesh strips are cut into shape and fitted in the smoking compartment to act as shelves for the fish. Finally, a door is fitted to the smoking chamber.
Special advantage	This oven allows a larger quantity of fish to be smoked than the traditional oven consisting of a single drum or drum section.
Disadvantages	There is a problem of ensuring that the fish is evenly smoked, as those in the lower tray tend to get more heat and smoke. It requires wire mesh which increases the cost. (Sticks arranged to form a trellis could replace the wire mesh). Fish in the lower tray might scorch if the fire is too big.

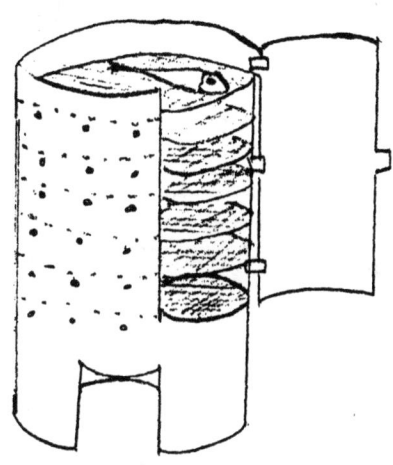

Fig. 7.20 <u>Improvised oil drum oven with doors and trays</u>

Fig. 7.21 <u>Wooden barrel ovens</u>

Wooden barrel ovens

Description and design aspects

Basically these do not differ from the oil drum ovens except that it becomes imperative to have the combustion chamber outside the wooden barrel to prevent it from burning. In the versions shown in fig.8.6(a) the combustion chamber is put underground. The fish can either be laid on a grill or hung by hooks on a frame. To minimise the effect of direct heat on the fish, the combustion chamber can be put some distance away and the smoke can be fed to the smoking compartment (the barrel) via a trench or pipe (see fig.8.6(b)).

Materials and parts

Wooden barrel, bricks, metal flute, wood or metal sheet.

Construction

Construction of the combustion pit can be done by digging a hole in the ground. This hole is cemented or lain with bricks or mud. In the case of the oven in fig.8.6(b), the trench can take the form of a metal pipe which is connected to a second cemented pit under the barrel, as shown. A square sheet of metal is cut and fitted with a handle to cover the combustion pit.

Disadvantages

Its main disadvantage over the oil drum ovens is the necessity of having an underground combustion chamber which makes it unsuitable for transportation.
Its cost includes that of the underground pits.
There is need for frequent replacement of the barrels due to weathering.

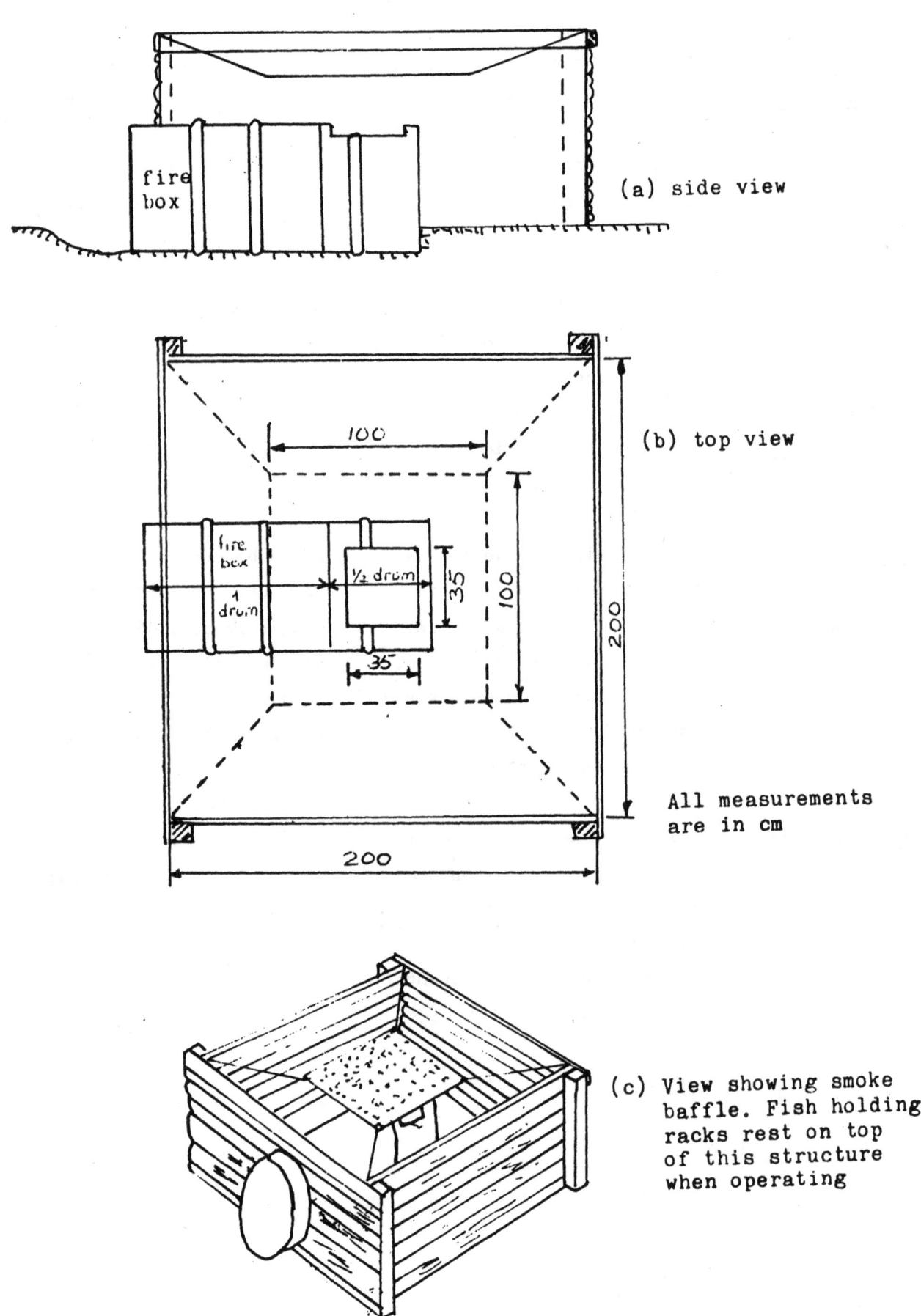

(a) side view

(b) top view

All measurements
are in cm

(c) View showing smoke
baffle. Fish holding
racks rest on top
of this structure
when operating

Fig. 7.22 Modified version of traditional oven- Ivory Coast kiln

Improved rectangular (square) ovens (fig.7.22).

Description and
design aspects

In this modification of rectangular ovens (see Chapter 5),
oil drums are used for the fuel chamber. The oven itself
can be constructed of any material (for example, wood,
corrugated iron, flattened oil drums, crates or mud
walls). The two extremities of the oil drum for the fire
are removed. One end of the drum serves as the fuel inlet
and also produces the draught. At the end of this drum is
placed another oil drum with a square opening, as shown in
fig.8.7. A perforated corrugated iron sheet is suspended
over this hole to allow the even dispersion of smoke in the
smoking chamber. The fish is placed on wire grills fixed
onto wooden frames.

Materials and
parts

44-gallon drums, corrugated iron sheets, concrete or mud
bricks, wood or flattened oil drum pieces.

Construction

An   oil drum is opened at both extremities and laid with
its side on the ground. Half of a second oil drum is then
cut and a square hole with sides of 35 cm is made at the
top of it as shown. The body of the oven is then
constructed around these drums, as shown, so that about 10
cm of its length is protruding outside of the oven. If the
oven is metallic, then it would require a wooden frame to
which the sides are fastened. For brick, cement or mud
bodies this frame is not required. This chamber is built
so that the square hole in the oil drum falls in its
centre. This hole permits the smoke to spread into the
central part of the oven.

A square piece of sheet metal is perforated with holes
of 2 cm at about every 6 cm and this sheet is suspended at
25 cm above the oil drums with wire, as shown. This sheet
acts as a disperser to spread the smoke evenly in the oven.

Wooden frames which hold the wire mesh grills are
constructed to fit over the ovens. A number of trays can
be constructed and fitted one above the other.

Special advantages Minimises fuel use.

Uniform smoking of the fish is achieved.

Cost is basically the same as that for the traditional square oven.

The fact that the oven body itself is kept away from the heat makes it possible to use cement, which prolongs the life of the oven.

Disadvantages   More skill is required in its layout and construction.

It is a fixed oven.

Sheet metal oven

Description and design aspects	Fig.7.23 shows an improved sheet metal oven with facilities for hanging the fish vertically. The combustion chamber is connected to the smoking chamber via a metal pipe duct underground to prevent scorching of the bottom layers of fish. The combustion chamber is cemented or lined with bricks in the same way as the chamber under the oven.
Materials	Sheet metal/wood/cardboard, bricks for fire box, metal flue, hinges.
Construction	The smoking compartment is made of sheet metal which is cut into shape and welded. Alternatively, wood could be used. Two holes are dug in the ground and cemented as shown. A sheet metal plate is cut to cover the fire pit. This could be fitted with a welded handle. An angle iron is fitted in the smoking chamber for holding the grates to which the fish are hung or stacked. The door is fitted via hinges.
Special advantages	Ease of use. Assembly of the oven is not required each time.
Disadvantages	Its manufacture requires a higher level of expertise, as well as a workshop (welding shop in the case of metal ovens and carpentry shop in the case of wooden ones). Also masons are required to prepare the underground pits. It requires a chimney or vent holes to allow free circulation of heat and smoke.

Simple altona ovens[8]

Description and design aspects	A simple altona oven is shown in fig.7.24. Here the lower chamber is built of brick and contains a door, as shown. The fish are put in wire grill trays with wooden frames which are, in turn, fixed to angle iron shelves in the upper chamber. The roof is made of corrugated iron which is raised to allow regulation of the draught. These ovens can smoke up to 180 kg of fish in 4 to 5 hours.

Materials and parts	Bricks or concrete blocks, wood, corrugated iron sheets, hinges.
Construction	The lower chamber is laid with bricks or cement blocks, or bricks according to the dimensions shown in figs.8.24(b), (c) and (d). In one version, fig.8.24(d), the framework of the upper chamber is made of angle iron, 33 mm in width. Layers of angle iron to hold 10 trays are fitted along the walls. The chamber is then lined with 1 mm sheet iron. The corrugated iron roof is raised 6 cm above the sides to allow for airflow as shown. In some versions a chimney is used for this purpose. Some models incorporate a valve at the top of the oven to allow for the regulation of the smoke.
Special advantages	It can hold a large volume of fish. Fuel use is minimised (about 50-60% of use for same size of traditional oven). Fish does not require turning over. Smoking times are considerably reduced. Greater smoke intensity to flavour. Greater durability.
Disadvantages	High cost of installation. It requires higher level of skill and technology for its construction. Variable temperatures require frequent rotation of trays. High initial capital outlay.

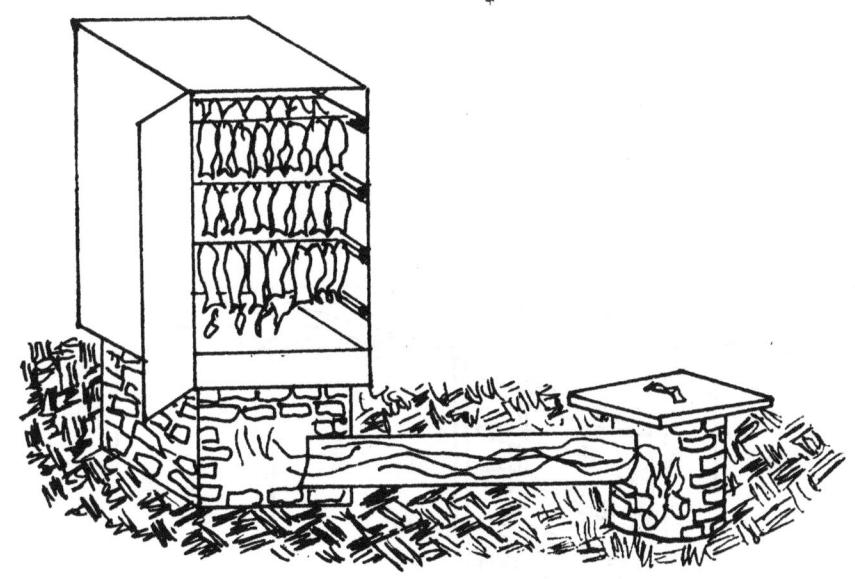

Fig.7.23 Sheet metal/wooden/cardboard oven

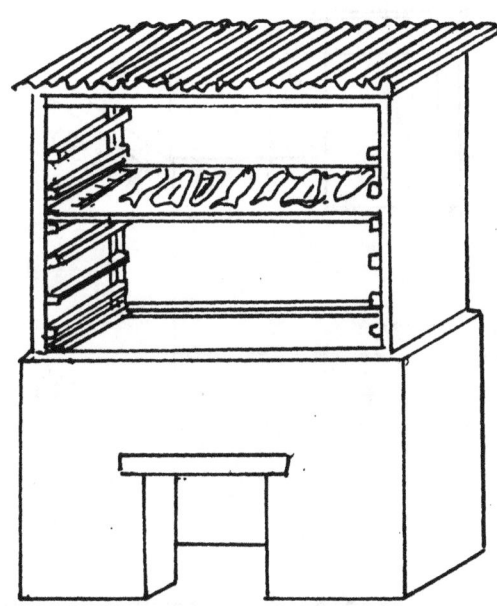

Fig.7.24(a) Simple Altona oven (doors not shown)

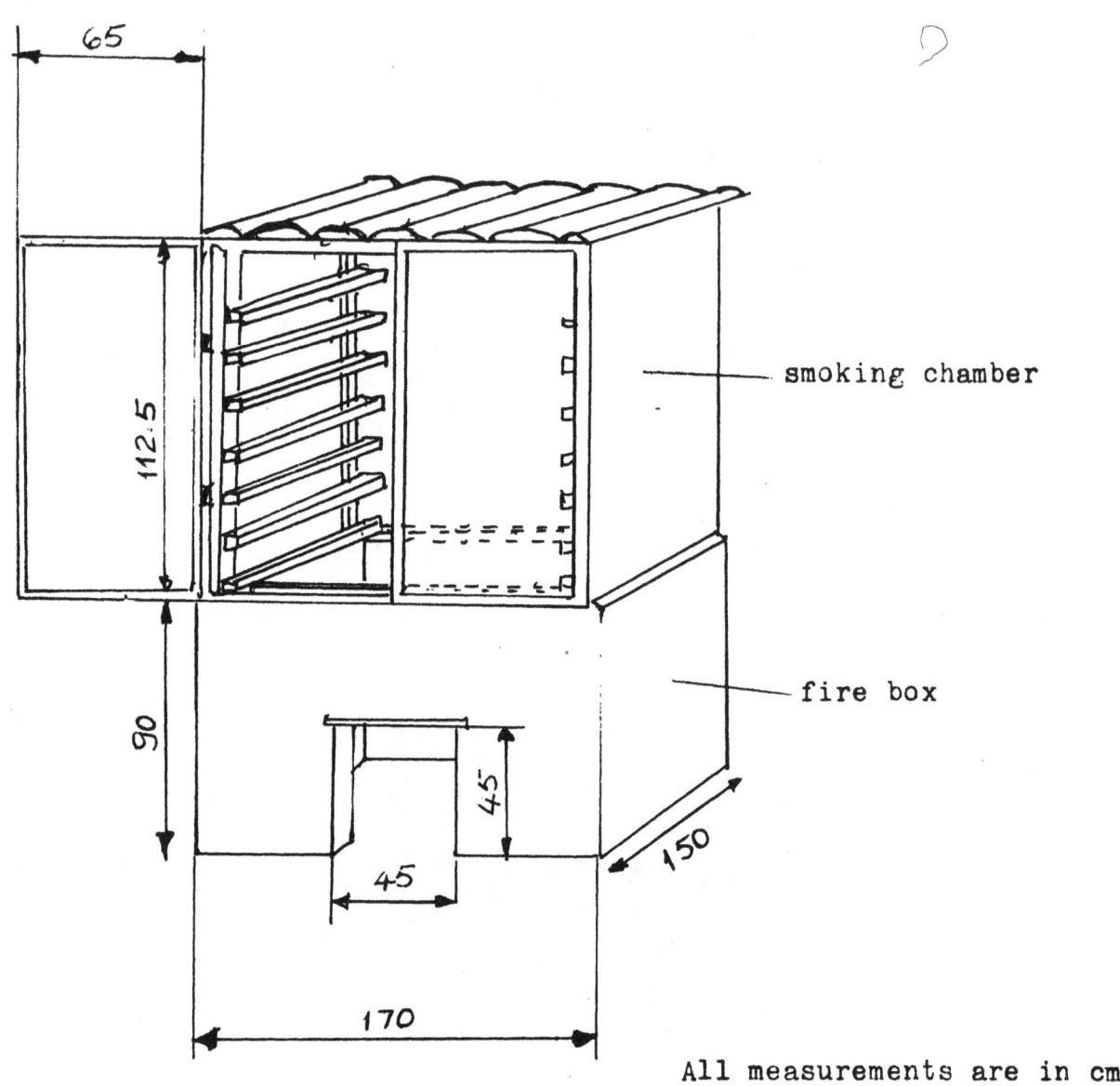

All measurements are in cm

Fig.7.24(b) Simple version of Altona-type oven with fire box
built from clay: overall view

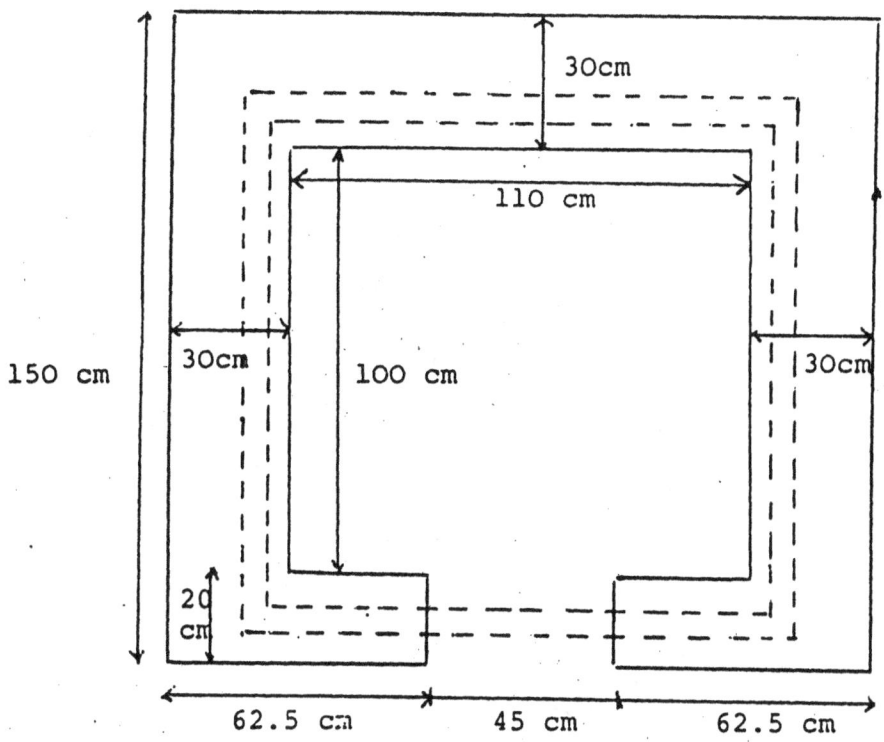

Fig. 7.24 (c)

Simple version of Altona-type oven with fire box
built from clay : Ground plan of fire box

Notes : 1. If the fire-box is constructed from sun-dried clay, blocks,
           the inside dimensions should be 120 x 110 cm, and the walls
           90 cm high and 20 cm thick.

         2. The materials needed to construct a simple Altona-type oven
           include (for fire-box built from dried clay blocks):

Item	Length	Pieces	Item	Length	Pieces
Wooden battens	130 cm	4	Clay blocks		
5x5 cm	122.5 cm	4	(dried)		
	112.5 cm	2	20x10x10 cm		300
	100 cm	2			
4x4 cm	122.5 cm	14	Hinges		
4x2.5 cm	112.5 cm	4	10 cm		4
Strip iron			Nails		
750x50x60 mm		2	7.5 cm		1.5 kg
Corrugated iron sheets			2.5 cm		0.5 kg
60 x 150 cm		10			

All measurements are in cm

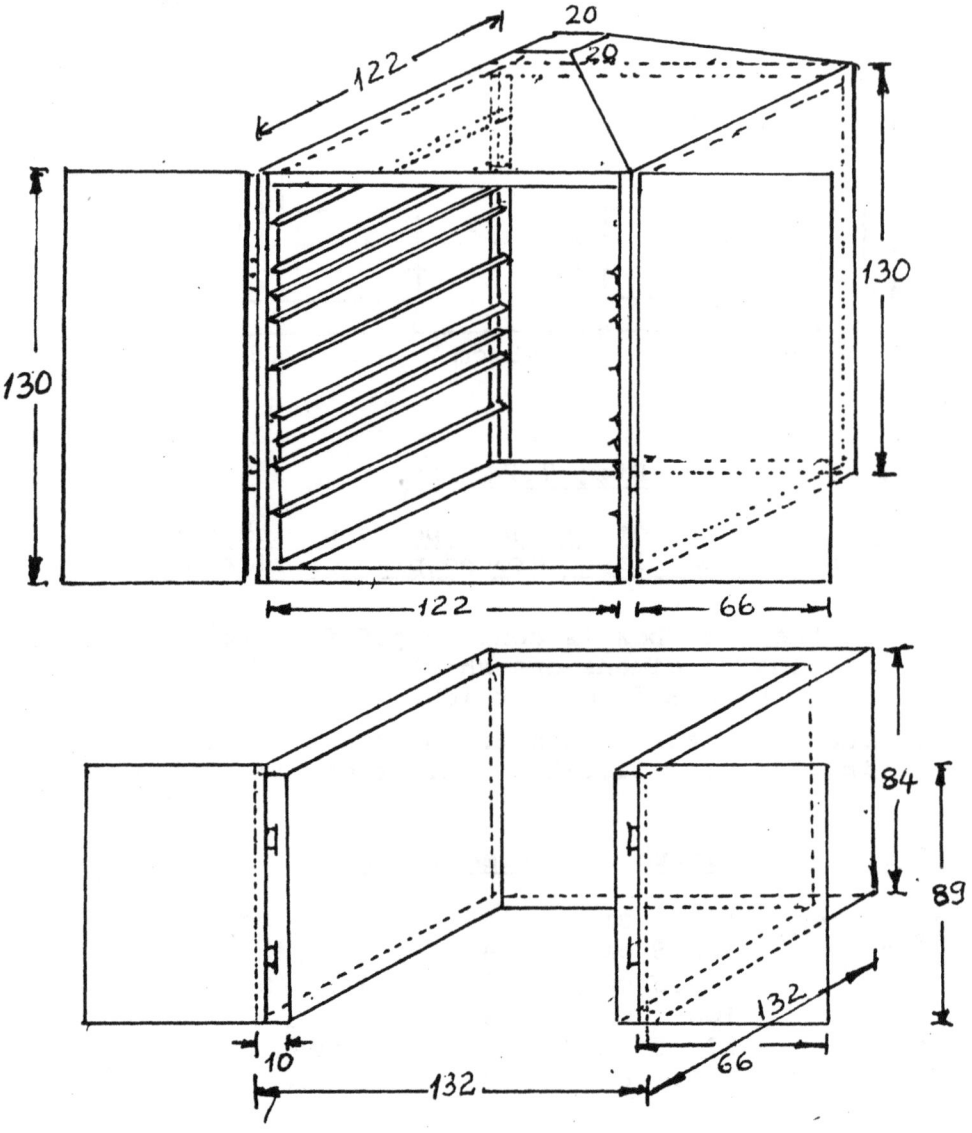

<u>Fig.7.24(d) An Altona oven</u>

(showing dimensions for construction)

Modified altona oven - adjetey oven

Description and design aspects	One modification of the altona oven is the adjetey oven. In this type the oven is constructed from heavy metal and the combustion chamber is located on the side of the smoking chamber with a flue connection to the latter. A baffle plate at the bottom of the smoking chamber acts as a disperser to spread out the smoke so that the fish is evenly dried (see improved traditional square oven described earlier).
Materials and construction	Same as for altona oven except for heavy metal body requiring welding.
Special advantages	Same as for the altona oven except that the smoke is more evenly spread.
Disadvantages	Higher cost imposed by the use of heavy metal and the flue connection.

COMPARATIVE PERFORMANCE OF IMPROVED AND TRADITIONAL TECHNOLOGIES

Due to the non-standardisation of the final product of fish-smoking, of the variations of the types, sizes and physical dimensions of the traditional ovens and the variety of fishes processed it is not easy to give a straightforward comparison of alternative ovens. However some sample values for concrete situations are given in table 7.2.

On the basis of smoking 1000 dozen herrings (sardinella aurita) of average weight 0.08 kg for 200 days, processing using the 'fante' oven will cost Le 15,000[9] in Sierra Leone, while using the altona oven, the cost is estimated at Le 6,500. Initial capital outlay of the banda is however lower (Le 50-400) at 1983 prices, while that of the altona oven is Le 900-1200[10].

Linsenmayer (1976) estimated the net profit from smoking (100lbs) 45.5 kg of smoked fish using the Altona oven as Le 0.34 as compared to Le 0.05 when the traditional oven is used. This large difference is due to the large savings in fuel. (According to Linsenmayer fuel costs constitute 44% of processing cost when the traditional banda is used).

Table 7.2 Comparison of some 'figures of merit' of traditional and improved smoking ovens

Type of oven	Smoking temperatures maintained	Smoking times	% weight reduction	Life of processed fish	Remarks
Ghanaian mud oven Sierra Leone 'Banda'	widely variable	1-48 hours 2-9 hours	42% (fish weighing less than 0.5 kg	up to 24 weeks 1-8 days	Lower figures refer to previously sun-dried fish
'Fante' oven		3-16 hours	24% fish weighing more than 0.5 kg	2-13 days	Type of fish herrings (sardinella avrila)
Oil drum oven	90-100°C (maintained)	3-4 hours	35-40%	2 months	Figures refer to fish sundried for 2 days before and after smoking
Altona oven	80-110°C (maintained)	12-24 hrs	23-30%	N/A moisture content 8-12%	Type of fish is bonga (ethmalosa spp).
Improved square oven	N/A	3 days	N/A	N/A	15 kg of wood is used for 100 kg of fish (traditional process requires 1100 kg of wood).

NOTES TO CHAPTER 7

1   Only these are referred to as 'salted' fish or 'stink fish' in Ghana.

2   The large variations are due to the particular taste and salt availability. There are no standards as regards traditional processing.

3   In most West African countries within each season (dry and rainy) atmospheric conditions remain virtually constant.

4   For dryer and hotter areas such as Senegal sundrying times for similar species of fish scarcely exceeded 2 days.

5   This is hot smoking of fish. Smoking temperatures range between 65°C to 120°C. Cold smoking is not suitable for this area.

6   Replacement of the trays made of bush sticks by wire netting material and the adoption of the Fante ovens have meant additional costs in terms of wire mesh and corrugated iron sheets.

7   Sixty-one per cent of oven users and 69 per cent of sand users utilised ovens of capacities not exceeding 60 kg of raw fish.

8   For detailed description of construction materials see FAO, 1971.

9   Le1 = $2.5 (US)

10 Figures obtained for altona ovens which are being used in the Tombo village in a German Government sponsored project.

Chapter 8
USES OF BY-PRODUCTS OF FOOD PROCESSING ACTIVITIES

USES OF BY-PRODUCTS IN SURVEYED AREAS

During the rural survey in Ghana and Sierra Leone information was sought on the use of the by-products of the processing activities examined in this manual. Table 8.1 summarises the types of by-products and the uses as stated by the respondents. As can be seen from this table very little use is made of these products in spite of the fact that they have properties which can enable them to find uses as fuels, fertilisers, animal feeds, starch, potash, in construction and handicrafts.

USES OF BY-PRODUCTS AS FUEL

Depending on its initial condition of moisture biomass can be converted to fuels through thermochemical and biological processes. Many of the wastes obtained from village processing activities in West Africa have low moisture content and lend themselves to the former type of processing.

Thermochemical processes

These include direct burning of wastes (combustion), pyrolysis (heating of wastes to high temperatures in the absence of air to produce a mixture of charcoal, liquid and gaseous fuels), gasification and liquefaction.

Traditionally some wastes in West Africa have been used directly as fuel. Coconut husks and shells, palm kernel shells, straws and other dry wastes are used to supplement firewood in traditional cooking. Indeed, these wastes have calorific values which are comparable to those of firewood (see table 8.2). However, the lack of adequate burning methods and stoves to burn these materials efficiently means a waste of these valuable fuels.

(a) Direct combustion of agricultural wastes

A few stoves for burning these fuels are being designed. Two such stoves utilising rice husk as fuel are described below. Such stoves could be used to burn ground groundnut shells or sawdust.

Table 8.1 Use of by-products of food processing

By-product	Use as fuel		Use as animal feed		Use as fertiliser		Other uses (specify)		
	Ghana	Sierra Leone	Ghana	Sierra Leone	Ghana	Sierra Leone		Ghana	Sierra Leone
1 Cassava peels	0	0	85	0	0	0			
2 Fluid from grated cassava during dewatering	0	0	0	0			To make starch	51	92
3 Fish scale and entrails	0	0	0	25	0	0			
4 Palm bunches and fibres	0	0	0	0	0	0	Preparation of potash for soap preparation	19	34
5 Palm kernel shells	57 (by blacksmiths)	88	0	0	0	0			
6 Palm kernel cake (chaff)	0	-	0	12	0	0			
7 Maize husk	0	-	0	-	0	-	For packaging kenkey	100	-
8 Liquid after boiling	0	-	0	-	0	-	Traditional cure for cough	50	-
9 Rice stalks	-	0	-	0	-	4	Preparation of potash for soap preparation	-	2
10 Rice husks and bran	-	0	-	2	-	13			
11 Coconut husks	-	85	-	0					
12 Coconut shells	-	100	-	0					
13 Coconut cake (chaff)	-	0	-	77					

Source: Rural survey in Ghana and Sierra Leone

- indicate that these activities were not studied in given country

Table 8.2 Burning properties of some convention fuels and
by-products of processing

By-product	Average calorific value (kcal/kg)	Moisture content (%)	Ash content (%)
Coconut shell	3774	13.9	negligible
Palm kernel shell	3903	14.8	negligible
Rice husk	3127	13.5	15.0
Groundnut hull	3682	17.8	10.0
Cow dung	3404	16.8	10.0
Wood	4910	13.8	negligible
Charcoal	6376	7.4	negligible

Source: Bassey (1981)

A simple rice hull stove

Description and
design aspects
: The stove is made of a 4-gallon kerosene tin or any
similar tin. A vent hole is cut at the bottom of the tin
as shown in fig.8.1. Two pices of wood are held in place
as shown and the stove is loaded with rice husks. The rice
husks are compressed with a piece of wood. When the
chamber is full up to 2.5 to 5 cm from the top, the pieces
of wood are carefully removed so that the holes remain.
The stove is now ready for use. To light it a piece of
wood is dipped in kerosene and pushed into the bottom
hole. This wood which should be at most half of the width
of the opening to allow for air flow, remains in place and
is pushed in from time to time as the end burns up. The
rice husks will burn along the inside of the hole. The
rice husk should be dampened if it is too dry and cannot
compact easily.

Material
: Old metal, 4-gallon kerosene tin or substitute.

Construction
: Can be owner made. Only cutting of vent hole and opening
of top of tin required.

Special advantages
: Allows for use of rice husks which are usually thrown away.

Disadvantages
: Problems in heat regulation.
Cannot be recharged until after one lot of fuel has
completely burned out.

Output
: Burning of a 4-gallon tin rice husk stove should last for
about 2 hours for one filling. This would of course depend
on the state of the rice husk and the position of the stove.

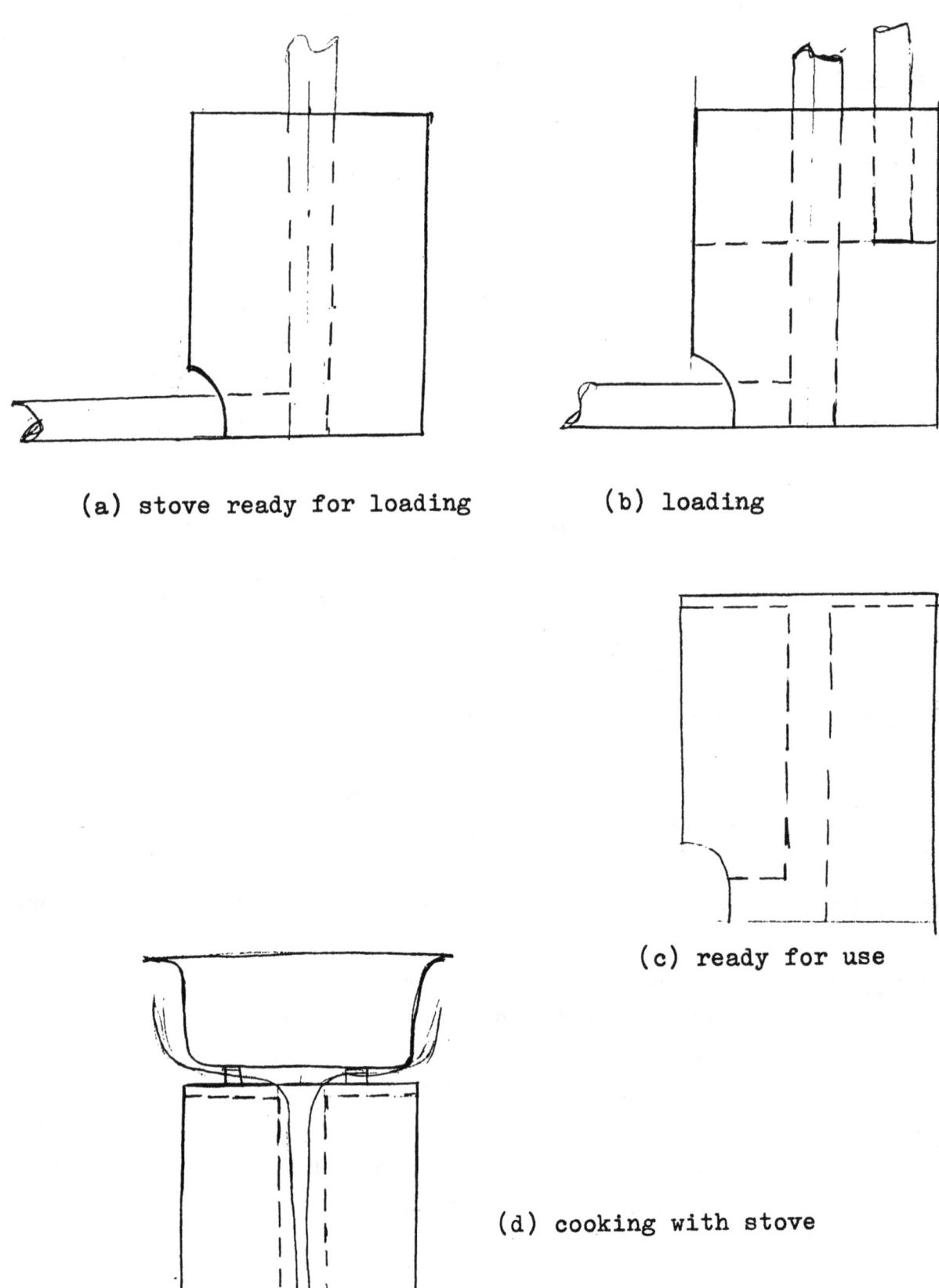

(a) stove ready for loading   (b) loading

(c) ready for use

(d) cooking with stove

Fig. 8.1. A simple rice husk stove

A conical rice husk stove

Description and design aspects	A diagram of this type of stove is shown in fig.8.2. It is a cone-shaped made out of old drums or sheet metal which is cut to shape and folded. Three vent holes are cut instead of one as in the other version. To use this stove one piece of wood is put in vertically and three pieces horizontally as shown. The rice husk is next put in and compacted. If necessary it is wetted. When the level is just below the vent holes, the four pieces of wood are carefully removed. The stove is lit by introducing a lighted stick dipped in kerosene in one or more of the vent holes. This stick can be removed when the rice husk is burning well. By closing one or more of the vent holes with a metal strip some control of the heat can be achieved.
Materials and parts	44-gallon drum, sheet metal (clay could be used), bolts for handles.
Manufacture	Basic metal working tools. All seams can be folded (no soldering required).
Special advantage	Some heat regulation is achieved by closing vent holes.
Disadvantage	Cannot be reloaded during cooking.
Output	2-3 hours of uninterrupted cooking.

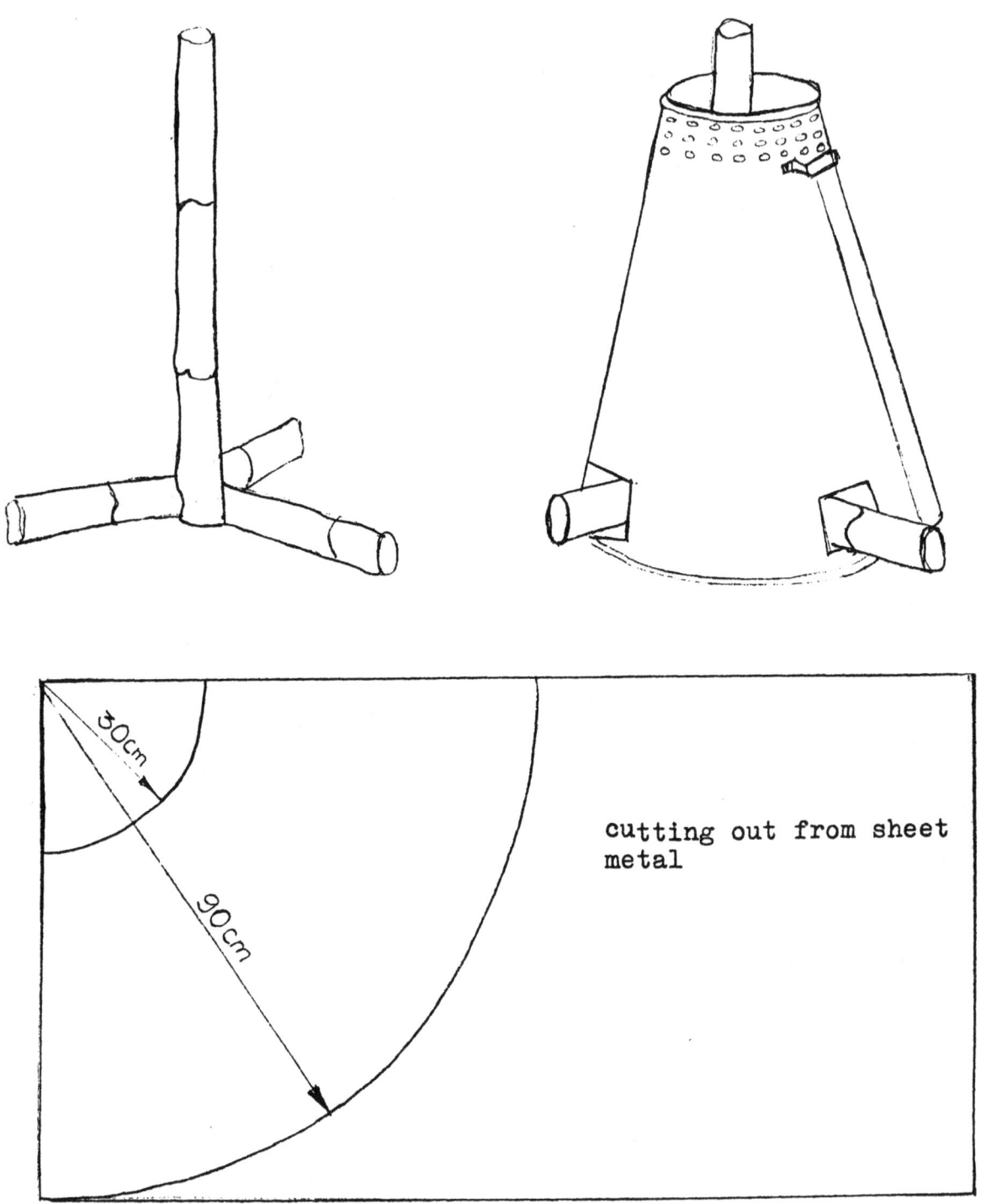

Fig.8.2. <u>A conical rice husk stove</u>

A new technology, <u>densification</u>[1], converts biomass to high density
pellets, cubes or logs. These products are called 'instant coal' and can be
easily transported or stored in this form. In Gambia groundnut shells are
ground and then compressed to form briquets which can be burned in normal
charcoal stoves. Briquets also enable this waste to be easily used.

The ashes obtained from direct burning of most of these wastes can be
used as fertilisers (see later paragraph on use of wastes as fertilisers).

(b) Pyrolysis of coconut and palm kernel shells and other wastes

As well as being directly burnt in open fires or traditional charcoal
stoves, coconut and palm kernel shells can be processed into charcoal which
can easily be transported and stored. Charcoal is prepared by burning the
shells in a limited supply of air. A simple pit for preparing this type of
charcoal is described below:

A hole 1 mm deep, 75 cm long and 75 cm wide is dug in the soil. The
shells (clean and free from husks) are placed inside this pit and lit. When
they are burning they are made into a pile and more shells are added until the
whole pit is filled. The pit is then covered with zinc or iron sheets and
made airtight with earth packed at the edges.

Different types of pits which can be used for charcoal preparation are
shown in fig.8.3. These pits can be lined with mud bricks. In locations
where the water table is high it might be necessary to use kilns which are
above ground (Fig.8.4). Small quantities of charcoal can be prepared in
44-gallon drum kilns. About 20,000 whole shells are required to make one ton
of charcoal. The calorific value of coconut shell charcoal is 7500 kcal/kg.

Shell charcoal is generally dense, very hard and highly retentive. Their
rate of absorption is generally higher than those of coal carbons due to their
pore structure. Apart from their use as fuel, in activated form[2], they can
be used as a catalyst in the dechlorination of water supply, for decoloration
and deodorisation in the refining of vegetable oils, for the removal of bitter
and mushy flavours from wines and spirits and as a general antipollutant.

In the methods of pyrolysis described above only the solid fuel
(charcoal) is recovered for use. Where vast quantities of wastes are
available, an arrangement which can also recover liquid and gaseous fuels can
be used. Fig.8.5 shows schematically one such a converter. In this
converter, wastes are fed into the 44-gallon drum kilns. Char and oil are
collected as shown while the hot gases are used to dry crops. Pyrolysis of
one ton of rice straw at 200-700°C gives 430 m^3 of gas, 42 litres of oil

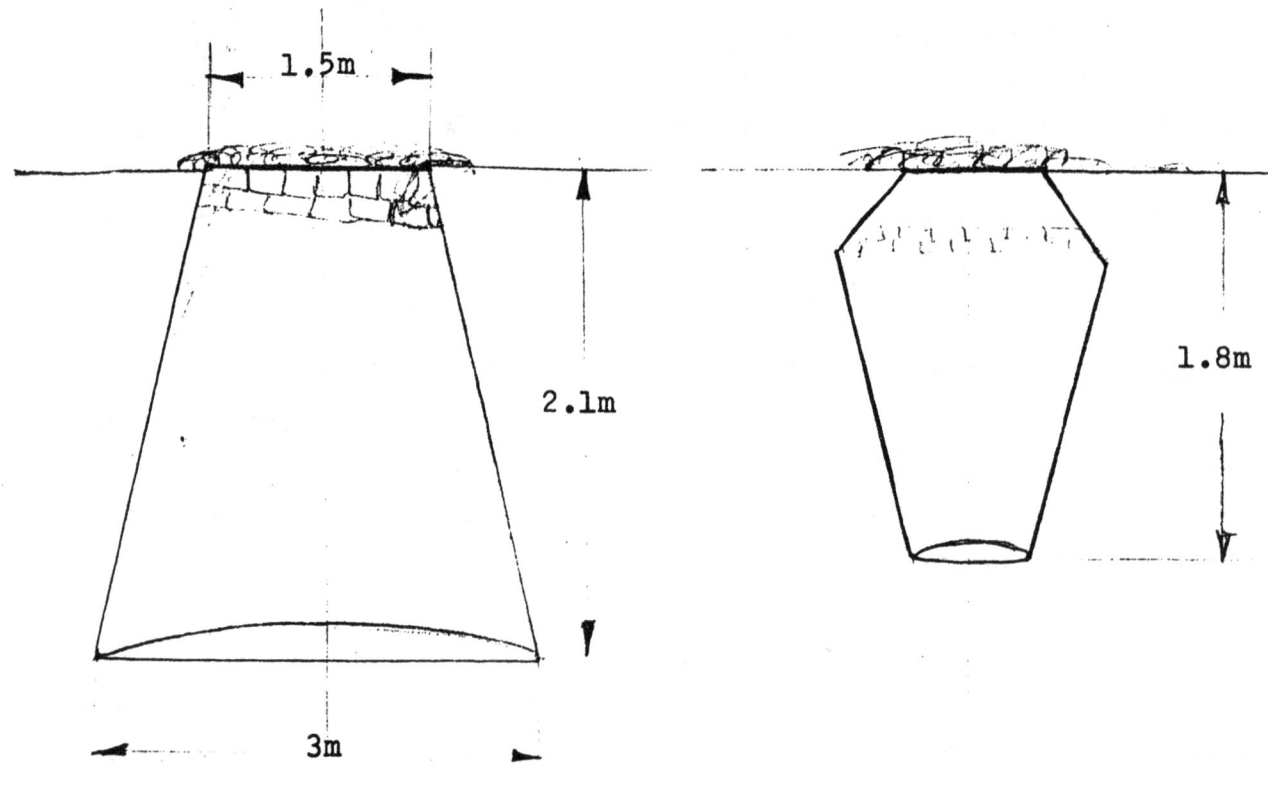

Fig . 8.3. <u>Pits for preparing shell charcoal</u>

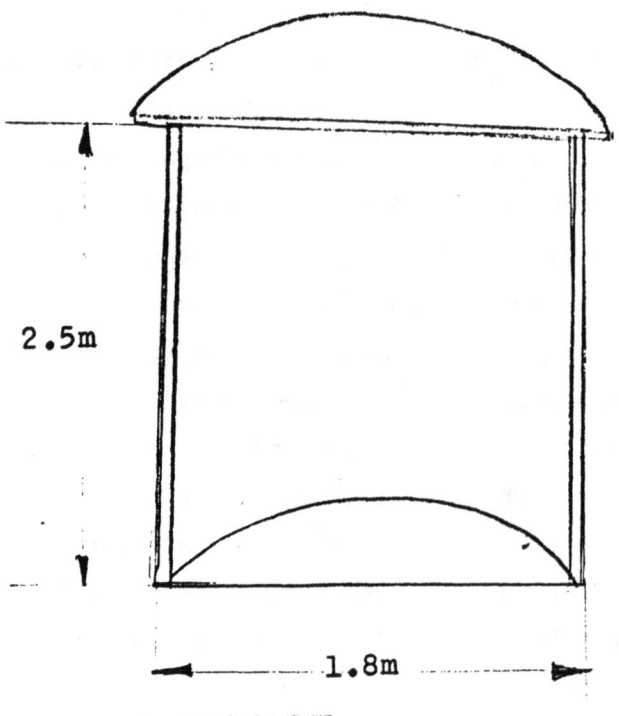

Fig . 8.4. <u>A cylindri cal charcoal kiln</u>

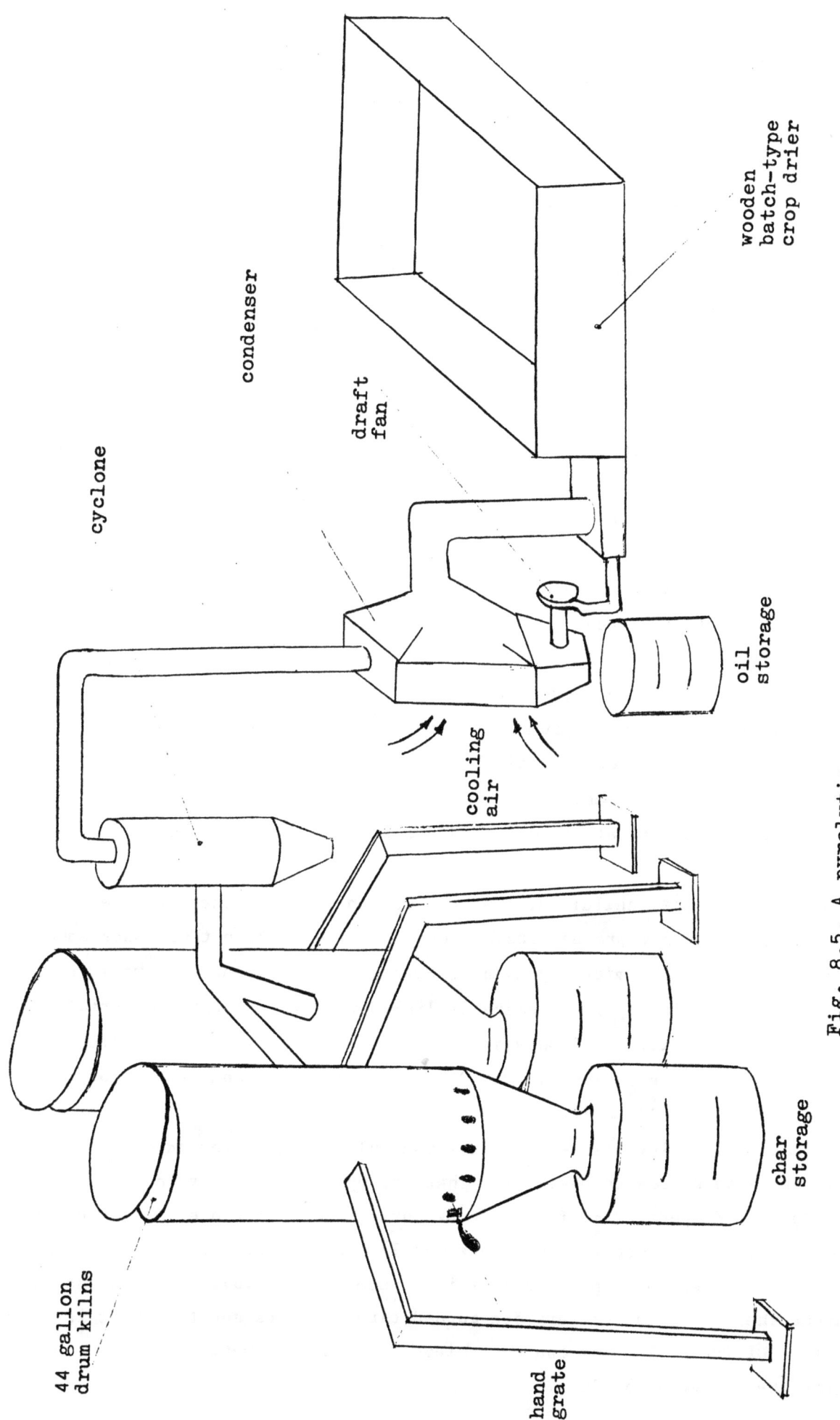

condenser

cyclone

draft
fan

wooden
batch-type
crop drier

oil
storage

cooling
air

char
storage

44 gallon
drum kilns

hand
grate

Fig. 8.5. A pyrolytic converter

and 363 kg of char. Experiments performed with rice husks in Indonesia showed
that 65 kg of husk can give 16 kg of char. If a converter of the type
described above is placed near a rice mill, it can utilise waste husks to
provide some of the power required to run the mill.

A small pyrolysis unit is currently being operated in Technology
Consultancy Centre in Ghana. Although it is fed by saw dust and wood chips
other agricultural wastes could be exploited by such a converter to provide
power for rural industries. In the TCC case the char is intended to be used
for cooking while the gas and oil will be used for firing a brick kiln.

USES OF SOME BY-PRODUCTS AS FEEDS

It is estimated that by-products or residues of food crops which can be
transformed into animal feed is equal or more than the human edible food
component. The proportion of such residues to the food obtained for human
consumption is as follows:

>   1.5:1 for roots and tubers
>
>   2:1 for cereal grains
>
>   6:1 for oilseeds
>
>   10:1 for sugar crops

In West Africa, although ruminants are allowed to feed on grazed or
browsed herbage, for dry periods of the year some means of providing
additional feed for these animals becomes necessary. Processing of various
organic wastes which are at present thrown away for animal feed would thus be
invaluable.

Cellulose and hemicellulose, the most common carbohydrates are present in
plant cells. Ruminants produce enzymes capable of digesting these substances
through fermentation by microorganisms. However in the plant cell walls these
substances are physically and chemically linked with indigestible materials
such as lignin and silica. Processing to rupture the cell walls improves the
feeding value of these residues. Both chemical[3] and physical methods of
rupturing the cell walls exist.

At the village level in West Africa the only feasible method of
processing these wastes is physical. That is, by chopping or grinding.

Simple hand-operated chaff and straw cutters have long been designed and
developed. One such cutter (Passmore's model) consists of cutting blades
attached at an angle on a pair of cast iron wheels (fig.8.6). When the handle
is turned the feed press rollers are turned through gears and the chaff is
drawn in. Different lengths can be achieved with a combination of gears and
changing the number of blades.

Fig. 8.6. <u>A chaff cutter for preparing animal feed</u>

Feed supplements for animals

Table 8.3 shows the % of energy and protein components in certain types of wastes from food processing.

<u>Table 8.3 Composition of some feed components</u>
<u>on dry matter basis</u>

	DM (%)	SE (%)	DCP (%)
Oil cakes	90	50-70	35-50
Grain by-products	80-90	40-60	10-30
Maize silage	27	16	1.3

DM   Dry matter component

SE   Starch equivalent defined as the amount of pure starch which has the same energy component as 100 kg of that feed

DCP Digestible crude protein - this is a measure of the nitrogen in the feed consumed, which is retained in the body after losses through faeces and urine. It is determined by digestibility trials.

(a) <u>Poultry feeds</u>

Oil cakes, rice bran, shells of shellfish and bones are valuable components in poultry feed. The poultry which are raised in the rural areas of West Africa are mainly free-range poultry who find food by scavenging. Many of these animals are small and many die very young due, among other things, to improper feeding. Proper feeding can be achieved by discriminate use of some of these wastes which are available in the village. The oil cakes contain a lot of protein and 10-15 per cent of poultry feed could consist of these cakes. A typical mixture for industrially produced poultry feed in Ghana is as follows:

Maize	57%
Oil cake	10%
(groundnut or	
palm kernel)	10%
Wheat bran	7%
Oyster shell	5%
Fish meal	10%
Premix	5%
Rice Bran[4]	6%

Poultry feed mixers are manufactured by Agrico Ltd. of Ghana. Design and development of feed mixers have also been undertaken by some R & D institutions (see Chapter 9).

(a) Supplementary feeding of ruminants

Suggested supplementary feeds for goats and sheep during the rainy season contain the following:

Table 8.4 Components of supplementary feeds

for goats and sheep

	Pregnant ewe or she-goat	Suckling ewe or she-goat	Goats and sheep undergoing fattening
Rice bran	100 g	400-500 g	
Oil cake (coconut or palm kernel cake)	300 g	600 g	350 g
Grass	2 kg	2 kg	2 kg
Cooked cassava	-	200-900 g	

In the dry season grass can be replaced by 1 kg of hay and 500 g of silage.

USE OF BY-PRODUCTS AS FERTILISERS

Many agricultural wastes can be used to return nutrients to the soil. This is because they contain nitrogen and minerals which are required by the soil. Tables 8.5 and 8.6 show the percentages of nitrogen and potash (both valuable substances for soil nutrition) in some wastes produced as a result of food processing.

While direct application of these wastes is possible it is advisable that proper composting be done to provide a balanced nutrient. It is not recommended that certain wastes such as palm kernel and coconut shells and coconut husks be burnt specifically to produce ash to be used as fertilisers since the ash content of such materials is very small. However, ash obtained as a by-product of using these as fuels would be useful in preparation of humus through composting.

Table 8.5 Nitrogen content of some wastes

	Nitrogen content (%)
Coconut cake	3
Groundnut cake	7
Fish scraps	6.5-10

Table 8.6 Potash content of some wastes (%)[5]

	Potash content (%)
Ash from coconut shells	50
Ash from coconut husks	25-35
Coconut cake	2.4
Rice husk ash	2.3

Composting

Composting is an aerobic biological process through which organic wastes are converted into humus by the activity of a complex of interacting soil organisms. The factors that effect composting are pH value, carbon: nitrogen ratio and the availability of phosphorus, potasium and other mineral elements and temperature. Water is also important in composting and a water content of 50-70% is usually adequate.

Many village wastes can be used in composting. An old formula for composting is: a 6-inch layer of plant wastes (for example rice straws, rice husks, peanut hulls and palm fruit fibres, cassava peels), a second layer of another plant material, a layer of animal manure (fish cleanings or dung), a thin layer of soil, a sprinkling of ashes (from burning wood or other waste products) and water. Then the whole process is repeated until the pile is about 4 to 6 feet high. The material should be turned once in a while to allow air into the pile to enable the materials to rot more quickly. The resulting natural fertiliser should be ready in 2-3 weeks if tender green plants are used as plant material. If straw and dry materials are used up to three months may be required. In general, the fertiliser is ready for use when the temperature of the pile drops to atmospheric.[6]

Compost heaps can be made in the open but to protect them from effects of rain they can be enclosed in a structure. This could take the form of a bush-wood enclosure of measurements 8 feet long, 4 feet wide and 4 feet high.

OTHER POSSIBLE USES OF BY-PRODUCTS

In addition to the uses described above wastes could be utilised as follows:

Coconut husks

- as mulch for the conservation of moisture in the soil. A ring of husks is placed in a ring from about 0.3 m to 2.1 m from the base of palm trees. This also prevents weeds from growing around the trees when fertiliser is used.
- coir fibre obtained from the fibrous mescocarp can be used for spinning coir yarn for mats and ropes, material for brushmaking and can serve as a stuffing for mattress and upholstery.

Coconut shells

- use by craftsmen in making ornaments
- to build roads, for lining wells during drilling
- the flour prepared by grinding clean coconut shells to a fine powder can be used as filler in construction
- the flour can also be used as a mild abrasive (to clean piston engines) and is incorporated in hand cleaners and as a dilutent for potent insecticides.

Rice husks

- rice husk ash, because of its high silica content (93%) can be used in conjunction with powdered fats to produce an admixture suitable for cleansing soap.
- making cement from rice husk ash. Preliminary figures showed that this could be some 30-50% cheaper than conventional cement. It can be produced at village level.[7]

NOTES TO CHAPTER 8

1 This process consists of drying, crushing and mechanical compression.

2 Shell charcoals could find export market to countries such as U.K., U.S.A., Federal Republic of Germany, the Netherlands and Japan which have facilities for production of activated carbons widely used in pollution control.

3 Rice straw for instance can be treated with urea. Alkalis and acids can be used to hydrolyse cell wall constitutents causing the cellulose to swell thus increasing digestability.

4 The rice bran must be separated from the husks as the use of rice husk as poultry feed is not recommended not only because of its lack of digestive nutrients but also because of its abrasive action on the intestinal tracts.

5 Because of their high potash content some of these wastes can be used for making soft soaps as a substitute to caustic soda. Research on qualities of such soaps have yet to be done.

6 During decomposition heat is produced and in large composts this heat can even be exploited.

7 See Appropriate Technology Vol.6 No.4 for details.

PART III: CONCLUDING

Chapter 9

PROBLEMS OF DESIGN, DEVELOPMENT AND MANUFACTURE

OF IMPROVED EQUIPMENT: EXPERIENCE FROM GHANA AND SIERRA LEONE[1]

INTRODUCTION

In the preceding chapter improved equipment which could be used in rural women's activities was described and assessed. This chapter attempts to evaluate the capabilities of existing institutions and enterprises within the countries to design, develop and manufacture improved tools and equipment for these activities. It aims to determine the constraints which have hitherto hindered the wide-scale supply of improved equipment in these countries and suggests some potential solutions to alleviate the problems involved. In order to do this, the facilities available to institutions which are involved in improved technology design and development in the two countries and the scope within these countries for the manufacture of improved equipment and tools are examined. Fig.9.1 shows a self-explanatory flow chart which analytically describes steps for the generation and supply of improved equipment. This analysis will be concerned with institutions which undertake design and/or development (elements 1-14 on the flow chart) and of manufacture (elements 15 and 19 of the flow chart).

DESIGN AND DEVELOPMENT OF IMPROVED EQUIPMENT

General

In the two countries studied, development of tools and equipment has been carried out for decades.[2] Such work has been carried out on a trial-and-error basis without any sound scientific and engineering thinking. Thus by trial-and-error methods local artisans have arrived at tools and equipment which perform given operations, however inefficiently. Commendable though their efforts may be, for the maximisation of benefits from time and material resources and in order to ensure that the technical performance of tools and equipment are optimal, a coherent and scientific approach to their design and development is vital.

This approach requires trained expertise and proper laboratory facilities to perform research and tests. The tools and equipment which result are conceived, designed and developed on the basis of some scientific and engineering principles and/or as a result of basic scientific research.

Fig.9.1 Flow chart for design, development and manufacture
of improved equipment

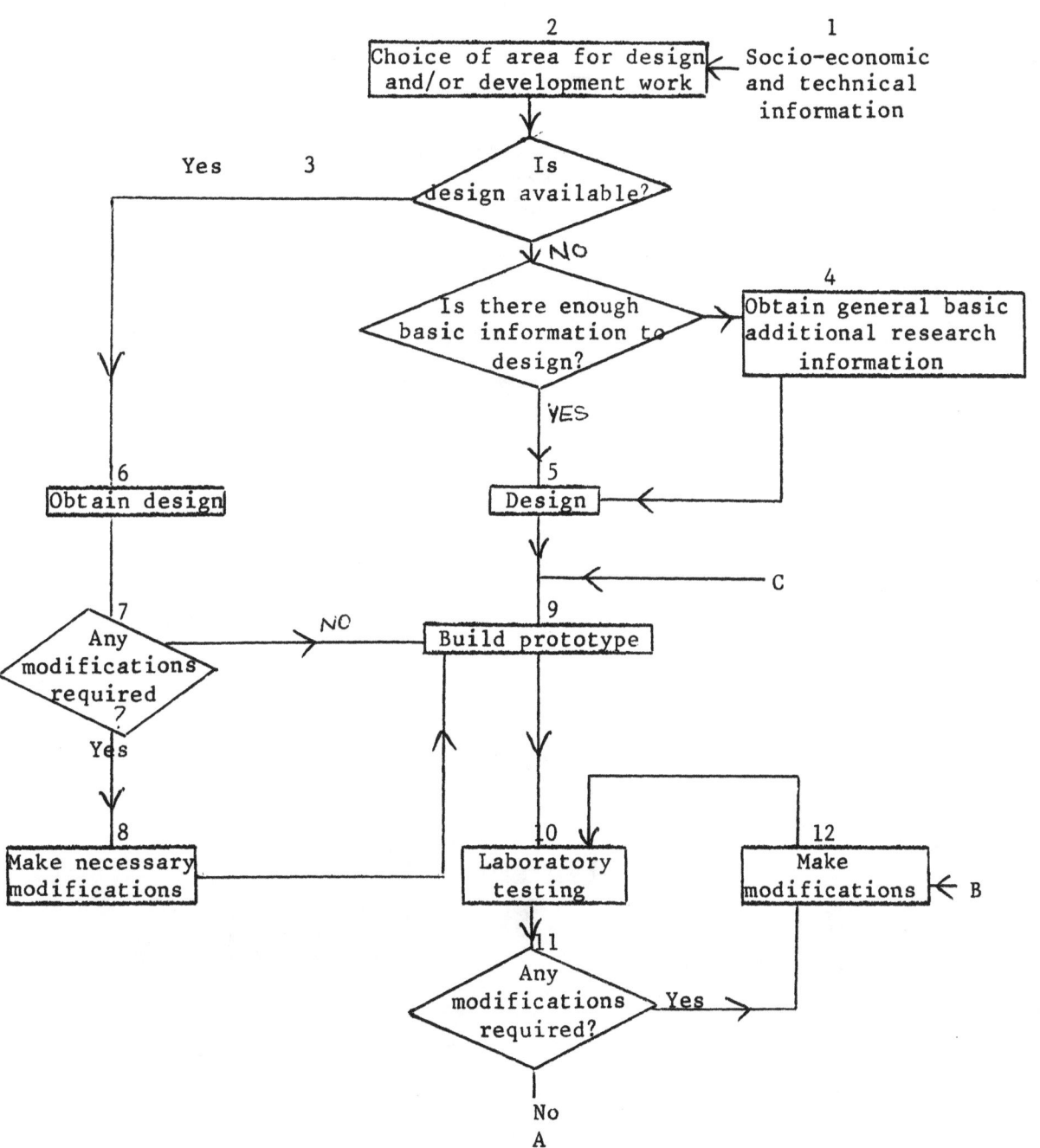

Fig.9.1 Flow chart for design development and manufacture of improved equipment

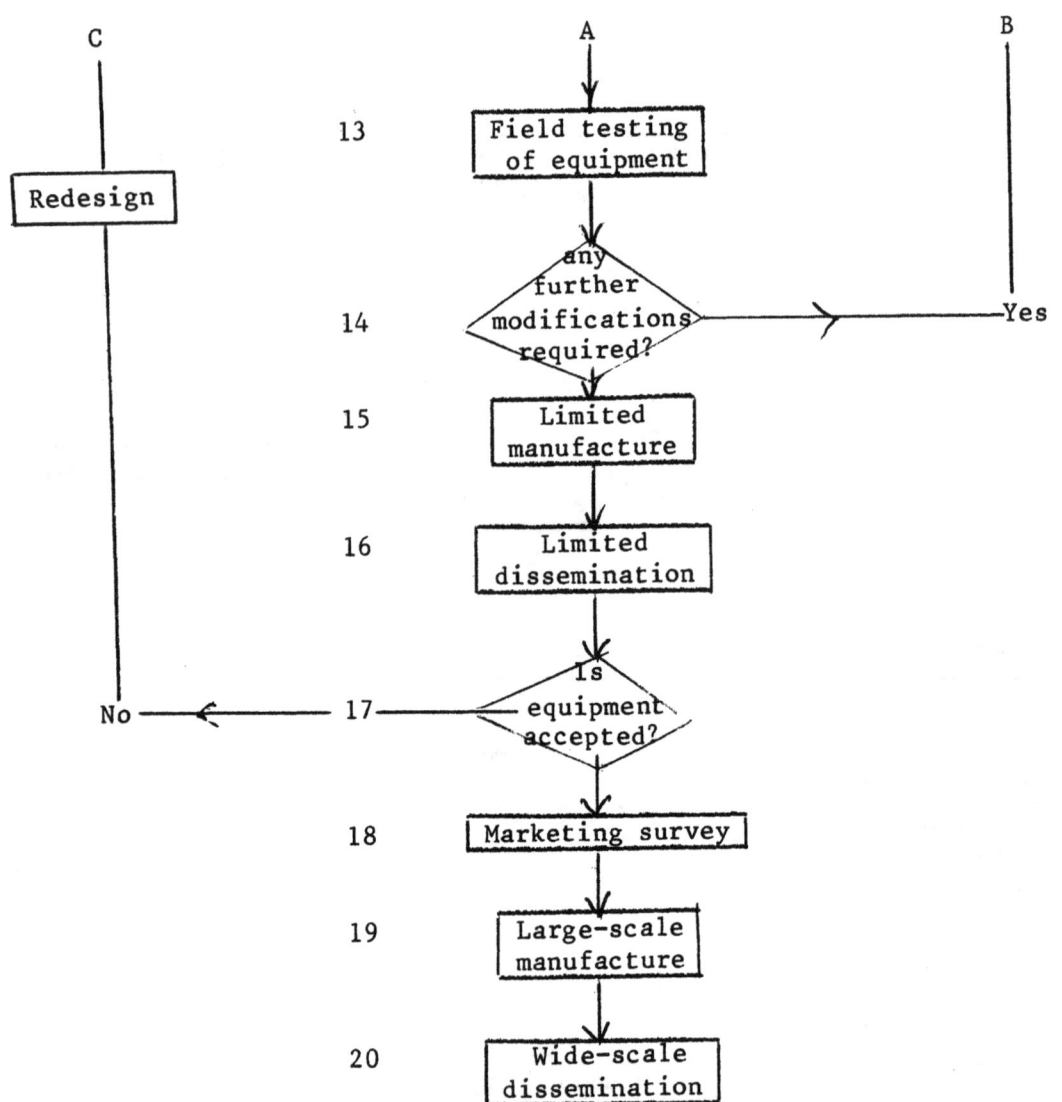

Basic research can be undertaken in all branches of science as, for instance, in the chemistry of materials (as in the case in determining properties of locally-produced potash for soap preparation, for example), the physics of processes (for example the determination of the calorific values of different fuels to be used for stove design) and meteorological phenomena (such as the collection and analysis of solar radiation data for the design of solar collectors). Results of such research are used to determine the type of technology to be applied, the size, shape and physical form of equipment and tools as well as the material and technology to be utilised in their manufacture.

From the above, it is obvious that design and development of improved technology can only be carried out within established institutions of science and technology which possess the necessary manpower and infrastructural facilities for doing so. It is these institutions which are of interest in this study.

Although it is recognised that every country does not have to reinvent the wheel, such facilities for design and development should be available in each country for the purpose of providing solutions to local problems and for adapting "imported" solutions.

In this section an attempt is made to assess the capability for design and development of improved village technology in two countries of West Africa. The criteria for assessment are:

(a) Financial resources.

(b) Manpower resources.

(c) Research and testing facilities.

(d) Exchange of information through conferences, seminars and publications among similar institutions both within and outside the country.

(e) Links with manufacturing institutions.

(f) Facilities for socio-economic research.

Types of design and/or development institutions

Data was collected on 10 institutions through interviews, mailed questionnaires and analysis of documentary material. These institutions are listed in table 9.1. On the whole, they represented the major institutions involved in the design and development of improved equipment prototypes[3] in the two countries.

As can be seen from table 9.1, six of the institutions in the sample are university departments/faculties or separate branches within universities, two

Table 9.1: Design and development institutions studied

No.	Name of institution	Country	Type of institution	Activities involved in	Comments
1	Agricultural Engineers Ltd., (Agrico Ltd.)	Ghana	Private	Design, development and large-scale manufacture	Interview and filled in questionnaire
2	Technology Consultancy Centre University of Science and Technology, Kumasi (TCC)	Ghana	University (separate AT unit)	Design, development, small-scale manufacture	Documentary material
3	Department of Nutrition and Food Science, University of Ghana, Legon (DNFS)	Ghana	University Department	Research, development	Filled in questionnaire
4	Agricultural Engineering Division, University of Ghana, Legon (AED)	Ghana	University Department	Design, development, small-scale manufacture	Filled in questionnaire
5	Home Science Department, University of Ghana, Legon (HSD)	Ghana	University Department	Design and development	Filled in questionnaire
6	Food Research Institute, Council for Scientific and Industrial Research (FRI)	Ghana	Governmental	Research, design and development	Documentary material
7	Advisory Services for Technology, Research and Development, Faculty of Engineering (ASTRAD)	Sierra Leone	University Departments	Research, design, development and small-scale manufacture	Interview and filled in questionnaire
8	Department of Agricultural Engineering, Njala University College (DAE)	Sierra Leone	University Department	Research, design and development	Interview
9	Tikonko Agricultural Extension Centre (TAEC)	Sierra Leone	Charity (United Christian council)	Design, development and small-scale manufacture	Interview and filled in questionnaire
10	National Workshop (NW)	Sierra Leone	Governmental	Design and development	Interview and filled in questionnaire

are governmental, one is a private charitable organisation supported by the Methodist church. The separate unit within the Kumasi university is set up to work specifically on appropriate technology.

Sources of funding for design and development

Funding for design and development work within university institutions was obtained in most cases only from annual departmental votes/subventions. In these cases, due to other departmental commitments[4], the proportion of funds allocated to improved technology work was reported to be minimal and far from adequate. Some institutions received grants from national, foreign and international organisations and private individuals. The TCC in Ghana which is the university institution with the highest capital for improved technology work received in 1978/79 grants from the British Ministry of Overseas Development (ODM), the Canadian International Agency (CIDA), the United Nations Educational Scientific and Cultural Organisation (UNESCO), the United States Agency for International Development (USAID) and a private individual totalling C307,447[5]. This, combined with the University Subvention (C148,524), and income from consultancy and production (C441,141) brought their total income in 1978/79 to C897,112.[6] Another university institution in Ghana which reported receipt of an overseas grant was the Home Science Department, University of Legon. This grant was from USAID.

In Sierra Leone, ASTRAD received grants from the United Nations Industrial Development Organisation (UNIDO) and the Canadian Industrial Development and Research Council (IDRC) to the tune of US$60,000. The Department of Agricultural Engineering at Njala is to benefit from some of the funds donated to the Adaptive Crop Research Project (ACRE) sponsored by USAID.

The governmental organisations were funded mainly by the governments through the national councils of science and technology (as is the case in Ghana) and a government ministry as in Sierra Leone. These institutions were not only involved in design and development of improved equipment[7] but combine these activities with basic scientific and industrial research, consultancy work, as well as advice on the transfer and adaptation of technology.[8] It was therefore not easy to say explicitly that funds are allocated specifically to improved technology design and development. In 1980 the National Workshop had approximately Le 180,000[9] after deducting its wage bill from the total income it obtained from repair, maintenance and the sale of finished products.

Agrico Ltd., in Ghana worked on an annual budget of C4,000,000 which is used for design, development and manufacture of improved equipment for food production and processing. The TAEC in Sierra Leone received donations from church organisations and other charities.

Design and development manpower resources

In the university institutions which were teaching departments, the staff combine their normal teaching duties with research, design and development. In these cases, there is a concentration of expertise, especially since the services of staff members from other university departments could be solicited. However, all of these institutions attributed their slow rate of work to the fact that the staff were overloaded with normal teaching duties and laboratory supervision and were therefore finding it difficult to devote time to improved technology work. Some departments (Home Science Department, University of Legon and the Department of Nutrition and Food Science, Legon (Ghana) and the Department of Agricultural Engineering, Njala (Sierra Leone)) reported that there was no full-time staff in the 1980/81 academic year working on equipment design and development. Only ASTRAD had appointed one engineer and three technicians who worked full time on solar and solar/sawdust crop dryers.

The TCC employed 88 people in 1978/79 including three engineers at PhD level, six research fellows with university degrees in engineering, science or agriculture and 26 technical workers (technicians, machinists, welders and apprentices). The TCC also benefited from the services of the staff of university departments of science, engineering and social sciences.

In the Labour Saving and Rural Technology Programme of the Food Research Institute (Ghana) at least three research officers worked full time on equipment design and development for food processing. The National Workshop (Sierra Leone) had a total staff of 480, of which only five were trained engineers, 110 are skilled workers and 100 technical or trade apprentices.[10]

Agrico Ltd., (Ghana) had a staff of 150 consisting of engineers, technicians and non-technical workers who worked in design, development and the manufacture of equipment. The TAEC (Sierra Leone), had a total staff of 32 of which 10 (2 engineers and 8 technical workers) worked in its Small Farm Equipment Unit which was engaged in design, development and the small-scale manufacture of equipment.

Research and laboratory testing facilities

For the design of equipment prototypes it is usually necessary to perform basic research which is also required to test the quality of raw materials which are to be processed by the equipment as well as the final products obtained from processing by using equipment prototypes. The type of research (and hence the research laboratory facility required), depends on the concrete tool or equipment which is being designed and/or developed.

The development of equipment from a first prototype to the final design requires a considerable amount of laboratory testing. For this reason laboratory facilities are of importance if an acceptable degree of performance is to be guaranteed, over a range of operating conditions.

The university institutions used laboratory facilities both within the departments/faculties or centres and from other university departments. Thus, provided that the teaching and research laboratories within the universities were well-equipped, these institutions had no problems for research facilities. However, this was not always the case, as the equipment required for particular tests might not be available at the appropriate laboratory. The institutions which were engineering faculties in these countries could boast of mechanical engineering, civil engineering and electrical engineering laboratories and reported using other laboratory facilities within their universities such as those available in the chemistry, physics and botany departments for basic research. The agricultural engineering departments were physically separated from mechanical, electrical and civil engineering departments since these were in a university (Ghana) and college (Sierra Leone) which do not possess these departments.

The mechanical, electrical and civil engineering laboratory facilities of these agricultural engineering departments were not as developed as those of established departments of mechanical, electrical and civil engineering. However, they had access to chemistry, physics and botany departmental laboratories within their campuses. The TCC worked hand in hand with the engineering and science departments and used their laboratory facilities for research work, thus making it possible for it to run only testing laboratories for testing equipment prototypes. The institutions interviewed complained of inadequacy of laboratory facilities for basic research.

The Department of Nutrition and Food Science at Legon had microbiology, chemical analysis and food-processing laboratories, while the Home Science Department had no laboratory facilities but had a small improvement centre where improved kitchen equipment undergoes trials.

The governmental research institutes had specialised laboratories. The FRI (Ghana) concentrated on food research and had its own food laboratory facilities. The Institute's Labour Saving and Rural Technology Programme benefited from results obtained from basic research carried out within the Institute. The Programme also utilised the Institute's mechanical workshop where the equipment was developed.

The governmental non-research institution, National Workshop (Sierra Leone) had no research laboratories but could boast of sophisticated workshop facilities which could be used for testing. Agrico Ltd., (Ghana) and the TAEC (Sierra Leone) also did not have laboratory facilities, but possessed mechanical workshops.

The absence of laboratory facilities in the above three cases was understandable as most of the designs of their machines were foreign and they concentrated mainly on development and manufacture. They depended on the clients to test the devices developed by them.

Access to information on improved technologies

The source reported for access to information were study tours, visits from experts, meetings, publications and personal correspondence. The meetings (internal, national, regional and international) took the form of seminars, conferences and workshops.

Only the TCC reported organised study tours of its staff members as well as visits from overseas experts to the Centre. Thus its staff members had been able to acquire direct useful information from overseas which had enhanced their work on design and development of improved equipment.

The research institutions (university and governmental) held internal seminars through which they shared their experiences with colleagues within their institutions and receive useful suggestions and criticisms. Within the two countries, exchange of information between institutions had been done through national seminars to which all institutions have participated at one time or another. Such seminars have been arranged in the case of Sierra Leone by the National Association on Appropriate Technology[11] to which all institutions studied belong. In Ghana a workshop on appropriate technology was held in 1981.[12] In addition, the Economic Commission for Africa has held national seminars and/or workshops in the two countries. These national meetings brought together designers and developers of improved technology devices within the countries.

At the regional level, the West African Science Association holds biennial conferences. In 1976 it organised an appropriate technology regional conference in East Africa. The Commonwealth Secretariat has also organised rural technology "meets" in Gambia, Nigeria and Zambia. All these meetings

had representation from the two countries. In Sierra Leone, an international
conference on appropriate technology was held in 1978.[13] This was the first
of its kind in tropical Africa, and it brough together researchers, designers
and developers of improved technology devices from 13 countries in Africa,
Asia, Europe and North America. All the appropriate technology institutions
in Sierra Leone participated in this conference.

The research institutions (university and governmental) were equipped
with libraries to keep up-to-date information on improved technologies. All
the institutions in Sierra Leone and Ghana complained of financial constraints
to purchase reading material and difficulty in obtaining foreign exchange for
ordering overseas publications. The major source of publications on improved
technologies reported was the ITDG.[14] All the institutions studied had
received ITDG publications. VITA[15] and IDRC[16] were the next popular
sources of information. For most of the institutions these were the only
three sources of publications on improved technologies. At least one
institution in the study received publications from the following
organisations: FAO, WHO, UNICEF, ILO, the Tropical Products Institute (TPI)
and the International Institute for Tropical Agriculture (IITA). There does
not seem to be much exchange of publications between these institutions and
their counterparts in developing countries. Indeed none of the institutions
interviewed reported receiving publications from any institution of improved
technology in developing countries.

Choice of areas for design and development work and socio-economic studies of
target groups

Table 9.2 shows the areas of work of the institutions. All of the
institutions studied had designed and/or developed tools and equipment for
food production and processing. By virtue of their terms of reference some of
these institutions only worked on equipment in this area. The choice of this
area had been governed by a common awareness of the need to improve
productivity and quality of crops as well as to lessen the time and labour
involved in traditional food-processing activities.

Conservation of energy and exploitation of renewable energy sources is
the second area which had attracted much attention. Work had been undertaken
on design and development of improved cooking stoves and ovens, on solar
collectors for cookers, dryers, water heaters and distillation plants, on the
use of biogas as a source of fuel and on using agricultural and industrial
wastes as domestic fuel. Preliminary work on design and development of
micro-electric generating plants had also been undertaken.

Table 9.2: Areas of work of equipment design and development institutions

No.	INSTITUTION	EQUIPMENT DESIGNED AND/OR DEVELOPED				
		For food production and processing	For energy exploitation (excluding use in food processing)	For non-farm rural employment	For rural construction	Other
1	Agrico Ltd., (G)	Gari plants. Palm oil plants. Corn milling units. Feed mixing plants. Sugar-cane crushers. Rice mills. Irrigation pumps. Vegetable oil mill.				
2	Technology Consultancy Centre TCC (G)	Palm oil press. Screw press for pressing water from brewer's spent grain. Rice threshers.	Fuel dryer. Pyrolytic converters.	Broadloom. Glass bead plant. Soap-making plant. Brass foundry. Iron foundry.		Bullock carts. Water pump. Water tanks. Gate hinges. Perfume distiller.
3	Department of Nutrition and Food Sciences, Legon (G).	Improved Ghanaian oven				
4	Agricultural Engineering Division, Legon (G).	Cassava grater. Feed mixer. Hand maize sheller. Grain dryer. Oil palm press/nut cracker.				
5	Home Science Department, Legon (G).	Smokeless stoves. Improved oven.				Improved water pots and coolers. Kitchen racks.
6	Food Research Institute (G).	Cassava grater, smoker/dryer. Screw press. Maize sheller. Equipment for separating grains from pebbles.				

Table 9.2: Areas of work of equipment design and development institutions (continued)

No.	INSTITUTION	EQUIPMENT DESIGNED AND/OR DEVELOPED				
		For food production and processing	For energy exploitation (excluding use in food processing)	For non-farm rural employment	For rural construction	Other
7	Advisory Services for Technology Research and Development (SL)	Palm oil press. Palm kernel cracker. Solar crop dryer. Fuel crop dryer. Solar cooking.	Solar distiller. Solar water heater. Small charcoal/wood fired boiler. Mini-hydropower generator. Biogas generator.		Laterite concrete.	
8	Department of Agricultural Engineering Njala (SL)	Rice parboiling unit. Rice thresher. Fuel rice dryer. Press for opening cocoa pods.				
9	Tikonko Agricultural Extension Centre (SL)	Groundnut sheller. Cassava graters. Rice threshers. Rice winnowers. Hand tools.		Concrete block making machine. Blacksmith's blowers.		Barrow-type trolley. Water pumps. Wheel chairs. Bird scarer.
10	National Workshop (SL)	Hand tools. Wood and charcoal burning stoves.			Block-making machines.	Household utensils, mineral working jigs. Charcoal-making kiln.

The development of non-farm rural industries has been another area of concern. The TCC had concentrated a great deal of attention on designing improved plants and units for rural production of soap, glue and glass beads while the TAEC had worked on the design of blacksmith's blowers.

The next area of concentration had been in rural construction. ASTRAD of Sierra Leone had undertaken research into the properties of lateritic concrete.

Identification of areas for design and development in no case involved socio-economic studies. There was reported to be "general awareness" of the needs of the rural people and design and development had been undertaken on this basis. In some cases (TCC, Ghana, TAEC, Sierra Leone) these areas had been identified by the rural people or individuals and special requests had been made to them to find technical solutions to specific problems. No institution reported in-house social scientists although at least one institution (TCC) has sought the services of the Economics Department at the Kumasi University.

Problems in design and development expressed by the institutions

One problem which was reported by most of the institutions was that of ensuring that the final price of the equipment was not prohibitive. This problem had arisen because of the cost of components which had to be imported. Cutting down on the cost of the equipment sometimes led to using materials which did not give an acceptable performance.

Another difficulty faced by the teaching departments of universities was that of the unavailability of staff time to devote to design and development work. In Ghana and Sierra Leone the staff were, in most cases, already overloaded with teaching duties and could not therefore spend as much time in design and development work as as they would have liked to.

Links between design and development institutions and manufacturing enterprises

In spite of the fact that some equipment had been designed by indigenous institutions, bulk of this equipment had failed to pass the field testing stage (see fig.9.1). A lot of work had stopped at the stage of laboratory testing. The only devices which had been manufactured on a limited scale had been those designed and developed by institutions which had the manufacturing capacity to embark on small-scale production. In none of the countries was there evidence of wide-scale manufacture of equipment designed and developed within the countries. Table 9.3 shows the number of pieces of equipment

Table 9.3: Annual production of equipment developed by institutions studied

Name of Institution	Equipment	Annual Production (No)	Manufacturers
1 Agrico Ltd., (Ghana) (Annual production figures are average for 15 years)	Gari plants Palm oil plants Corn milling units Feed mixing plants Sugar cane crushers Rice mills Irrigation pumps Vegetable oil mills Implements for tractors	19 5 57 19 34 6 34 1 560	Self
2 Technology Consultancy Centre TCC (Ghana)	Palm oil presses Caustic soda plants Soap boiling plants Wheels for bullock ploughs	5 4 16 110	Self
3 Agricultural Engineering Division, Legon (Ghana)	Feed mixer	2	Self
4 ASTRAD (Sierra Leone)	Palm oil presses	15	Self
5 TAEC (Sierra Leone)	Rice thresher Winnowers Cassava graters Blacksmith's blowers Agricultural hand tools Trowels Well pulleys	1 3 4 2 335 90 150	Self
6 National Workshop (Sierra Leone)	Agricultural tools Cooking stoves and ovens	N/A	Self

designed and developed within the countries which had been manufactured and disseminated on a limited scale. As can be seen from the table, these devices were all manufactured by the design and development institutions. Institutions which did not have adequate workshop facilities did not feature in this table because most of the equipment they developed existed only as prototypes. The small numbers of pieces of equipment manufactured in university workshops was explained by the fact that even though workshop facilities existed in the universities the latter could not effectively embark on manufacture due to constraints imposed by the other commitments of university departments. Indeed, all the university institutions interviewed expressed no desire to take up large-scale manufacture of equipment. What then accounts for this apparent bottleneck between development and manufacture of equipment?

When questioned about how they ensured the manufacture of their prototypes, some institutions (for example, the Food and Nutrition Science Department, the Home Science Department, Legon and the TAEC) responded that their designs were made simple to enable the local artisans to copy them with ease. Although this approach is commendable, the limit imposed by the village artisans' equipment and training adversely affect their capacity to produce some of the simplest equipment in large numbers.[17]

In the situations which existed in the countries, design and development required a great deal of personal effort and dedication on the part of the designer. The only reward he expected to get was some recognition of his work. The non-availability of patenting facilities within both countries was a major setback in encouraging a designer to release his designs to manufacturers, since he had no guarantee that he would be given credit for them. In both countries intellectual properties can only be patented in the United Kingdom. This placed an undesirable burden (financial or otherwise) on the indigenous inventor who could not afford the means to pay in foreign currency for patent grants or to contest in foreign patenting courts. It also meant that inventions are subjected to the jurisdiction of foreign bodies whose interests did not always coincide with those of the countries concerned.

On the other hand, there was much scepticism on the part of manufacturers to engage in the production of equipment which had not been "well proven". They would normally require some guarantee as to the acceptability of these devices which, unfortunately, have never left the laboratory for field tests.

MANUFACTURE OF EQUIPMENT AND TOOLS FOR FOOD PRODUCTION AND PROCESSING

General

Every tool or equipment requires for its production:
- tools and machinery to perform a given set of technological operations;
- skilled personnel to operate the machinery and/or use the tools,
- a given set of materials and components.

The quality of the equipment would depend on the suitability of the above three elements and would be reflected in its performance and life.

An equipment manufacturing industry is restricted as to the type of equipment it can produce by its access to raw materials, its existing tools and machinery and the level of skill of its personnel. For the purpose of assessing the capability of local manufacturing enterprises in the three countries studied one can distinguish three broad groups of industries (see table 9.4).

The main basis for the distinction into groups is the capacity to perform technological operations at a given level depending on the machinery available within the industry. This is related to the types of raw materials which can be handled and the types of skills which are required. The machinery available also dictates the types of equipment which can be produced economically within each of the groups.

It is interesting to note that this classification is not unrelated to those which differentiate between "formal" and "informal" or those which categorise these industries into "small", "medium" or "large", depending on the number of employees, as can be seen from table 9.3.

For food production and processing activities in the three countries all three types of industries produced tools of varying degrees of complexity. Due to the capacity in each of these groups the types of equipment which were produced varied between groups. Thus the industries in Group I (usually the traditional blacksmiths) produced most of the rudimentary tools such as cutlass and hoe, while the industries in Group III produced sophisticated equipment such as hydraulic press.

In addition to manufacture, these industries could also repair equipment. Depending on the kind of repair required, the services of all the three groups could be used. Besides, it was not always necessary to obtain repair services from the group type which manufactured the device. Thus a village blacksmith can perform simple repairs which required only forging operations to equipment manufactured by a Group III or Group II type industry and all three groups could also repair imported equipment.

Table 9.4: Types of manufacturing enterprises

Group	Machinery and tools	Power Source	Types of raw materials	Number of employees	Source of skill acquisition of employees	Sector
I	Basic forging tools: forging hammer, chisel, anvil, file, blowers, soldering iron, hacksaw, pincers	Hand-operated tools	Scrap metal, old oil drums and tins	1-10	Informal mainly on-the-job	Rural informal
II	Basic forging tools as for I. Also hand drills, screw vice, wracking iron, welding set, grinding machine, plate shears	Hand and power-operated	Scrap metal and unused materials and	5-30	Formal and informal	Rural and urban formal and informal
III	All machinery and equipment in II as well as lathes, milling machines, equipment for sheet-metal work (bending, folding, coiling) (may or may not contain equipment for electro-plating, galvanising, metal spraying, foundry facilities)	Power-operated machines (except for tooling)	Usually unused components and material	30+	Formal training	Urban formal

The types of manufacturing firms

The major concern was food production and processing, and the choice of
industries to be studied was governed by this.

For Group I industries the village artisans in the sample villages were
interviewed, while in Groups II and III only firms who had produced equipment
for the food-processing activities covered in this manual were included in the
study. In the case of Group III these represented the largest industries
within the country which manufactured (or which had the capacity to
manufacture) equipment for food production and processing on a large scale.
The case studies are presented in this sub-section.

Group I type firms

This type of industry could only perform forging operations (apart from
those who possessed soldering irons). They therefore faced limitations as to
the type of materials they could utilise and the equipment they could
produce. They depended on scrap pieces which were close enough to the shapes,
forms or sizes required for the manufacture of their tools and equipment.
This minimised the tasks of cutting and shaping which were very arduous given
the rudimentary tools they possess.

Thirteen of the nineteen villages surveyed had resident firms of the
Group I type (blacksmiths' workshops).[18]

In villages with blacksmiths' workshops the ratio of blacksmiths'
workshops to the total population ranged from 1:83 to 1:2,500.[19] The latter
figure represents communities close to the towns or non-farming communities.

Seven blacksmiths were interviewed in the two countries. Their ages
ranged between 18 and 65 years. The blacksmith who was 18 years of age was a
cripple and because he could not engage in farming had learnt the trade from a
tender age. The other blacksmiths were, however, over 30 years old.[20] Of
these, five had been working in the trade for over 20 years while one had been
in it for less than ten years. Three blacksmiths had been trained within
their villages, three in nearby villages and only one in the town. Six out of
the seven were trained by kinsmen on an informal basis who were blacksmiths.
The main products which were manufactured in the blacksmiths' workshops were
hoes, cutlasses, spears and other hand tools, metal stoves, buckets and
cooking pots. The basic raw materials were old, 44-gallon drums, used tin
cans, scrap iron, parts from motor vehicles and wooden pieces for making
handles. Apart from the wooden pieces (sticks) the other materials were
obtained from the towns. The basic tools possessed by these blacksmiths were
hammers, chisels, vices, files, manual shears, drilling tools and blacksmiths'

blowers. They used charcoal and palm kernel shells as fuel for heating metal pieces.

All the blacksmiths repaired their own products, as well as items such as imported hand tools, buckets and bicycles, when such repairs involved only forging operations, for which they possessed vast skills. The blacksmiths' shops employed between one to nine people, mainly as apprentices, and work in the open or under suspended roofs or in make-shift workshops.

When questioned about the problems they encountered in the manufacture and repair of equipment, six complained of the non-availability and high prices of raw materials, five reported that the job was too strenuous, three were unhappy about the lack of machines and spare parts for tools. One had problems with apprentices who would not stay long enough and one required adequate premises for his workshop. Only one blacksmith reported no problems in his work.

Group II type firms

These are firms which operated in both rural and urban areas. They possessed more varied types of machinery than the firms of Group I and were therefore more diversified in their activities. Table 9.5 gives the typical products they manufactured in both countries.

Country	Typical products
Ghana	Animal-drawn implements, ploughs, wheelbarrows, manual cement block making machines, corn mills[21], cassava graters[21], flour mixers[21], coal pots, palm kernel crackers, pepper and tomato grinders, nuts and bolts.
Sierra Leone	Coal pots, metal window frames, rice threshers, rice winnowers, cassava graters.

These industries only manufactured on a small scale. Usually one item of equipment is the main product and the other types are made to order. In the latter case the equipment was usually made to customers' specifications, which implied a unit production system.

The firms in this group usually copied designs of imported machinery, which was normally done by dismantling the sample and reproducing each part with modifications which were necessitated by available materials and machinery. Some parts such as bearings, which could not be manufactured locally since the technology for their production was very sophisticated, were obtained from motor vehicle and other scrap. Parts which could be made from sheet metal and iron rods created less problems as these could be purchased in the countries.

Due to the classification, this type of firm varied considerably in its scale of operation. To give a picture of the extreme cases of firms in this group two firms (one informal and the other formal) were interviewed.

The first[22] had a duplicating key machine, a grinding machine, a drilling machine, vice, anvil, forging hammer and a welding plant. Although it produced mainly tools, it also engaged in the repair of locks and safes and chain saws. Five people worked in the firm and the proprietor had had his education in Israel. The main problem of this firm was the lack of more sophicticated machines which prevented it from embarking on the production of more sophisticated equipment. No financial record was kept by this firm.

The second firm[23] in this group which was interviewed possessed a mechanical hacksaw, a drill press, two saws, an electric arc welder, as well as blacksmithing and carpentry tools. It produced rice threshers, winnowers, cassava graters, blacksmiths' blowers, hand tools and well pulleys. It had a staff of ten, of whom two were engineers, two had had formal technical training, five had had on-the-job training and one was an apprentice.

It utilised raw materials in the form of sheet steel, galvanised pipe, screws, nails, bolts, timber, angle iron and flat bars, all of which are new. Other parts such as bicycle chains and bearings were obtained from railway, tractor and motor vehicle scrap. Sources of energy were electrical (20 hp machinery) and charcoal for blacksmithing.

This firm had made modifications in the original designs which were usually foreign. For example, in the ox-cart, steel shafts were used instead of wood (as in the original ITDG design). Also, instead of timber, bush stick hitch-poles were used and the metal wheels were replaced by wooden ones. These modifications were found necessary in order to adapt the design to suit available workshop facilities and to meet customers' needs and local conditions. Although the firm was reported not to be used at full capacity there was no enthusiasm to expand its operations until the power supply situation was improved. The products from this firm were sold to farmers, schools, institutions teaching agriculture and aid programmes all over the country.

The main problems faced by the firm were those of lack of raw materials, competition from foreign products and the difficulty in making a two-way contact between the workshop and its customers, dissemination of information on its products, which would eventually lead to expansion of its activities and the short supply of electricity. Income from the sale of equipment of this firm amounted in 1980 to approximately Le 5,000.

Group III type firms

The Group III type of firms were few in number in the two countries.[24]

In Ghana Agrico Ltd. was perhaps the best-known firm which manufactured equipment for food production and processing. Agrico had the following workshops and sections: forging shop, machine shop, foundry carpentry shop, sheet metal section, implements manufacturing section, trailer manufacturing section, processing machinery section and testing section, which are served by a total of 150 workers. It imported iron and steel components as well as finished machine components from Europe, the United States and India and depended (apart from tooling) on electrical energy for production. It had facilities for quality control and final testing. The different types of equipment which it manufactured (see table 9.3) were produced from its own designs and were made to order or for stock. Buyers for its products were farmers and government agencies all over the country, as well as in neighbouring Guinea, Nigeria, Liberia, Togo and Upper Volta.

The firm did not think it was fully utilised, the reason being the lack of inputs in the form of raw materials and spare parts. This represented the major problem it faced. However it had plans to increase its output of present products, as well as to produce new products, if this problem could be overcome. At the time of the interview, it was finding it impossible to meet the demands for its products.

Agrico operated on a working capital of C4,000,000. In 1981 its estimated income from the sale of equipment was C5,500,000.

In Sierra Leone the only equipment manufacturing firm which belonged to this group was the National Workshop. It had a total number of 449 employees, of which its 110 skilled technicians represented some 10 per cent of the national capacity in this area.

There are 14 shops in operation: the machine shop, tool room, millwright shop, electrical maintenance shop, heavy-duty maintenance shop, light-duty maintenance shop, coppersmiths' shop, welding shop, plating shop, saw mill, carpentry and joinery shop, the foundry, blacksmiths' shop and heat treatment shop. The Workshop depended on railway scrap for components and parts[25] and bought sheet metal as well as bars from the local market.[26]

It depended on its own designs as well as customers' samples to produce equipment. In the case of the latter, modifications had been made to suit the workshop facilities, to meet the customers' needs and local conditions, and to improve the original designs. The main source of energy was electricity, although charcoal was used as in the blacksmith's shop and imported coke was used in the foundry.

Some goods were manufactured to customers' orders and others were manufactured for sale to the general public all over the country. Although it

was able to meet demand for its products, its capacity was not considered to
be fully utilised. The main reasons given for this were the limited market,
inadequate skilled labour and the lack of some raw materials, critical
supplementary production facilities and capital to import bulk materials,
spares and basic tools. Plans were underway to manufacture new products once
the conditions were improved.

Apart from the problems listed above the firm complained of the
non-availability of credit facilities and consumers' ignorance of some of its
products. It stressed the need for trained technicians for the Workshop. The
necessity of having final testing of its products had been recognised and
plans were now underway to embark upon quality control which had hitherto been
lacking.[27]

The income from the sale of products and maintenance and repair of
equipment for 1979-80 was reported to be Le 518,000.

Manufacture and repair of farming equipment in use in the areas studied

Table 9.7 shows the percentage of households in the rural areas surveyed
which reported the use of traditional and improved equipment for farming
operations. In Sierra Leone most of the equipment was traditional.[28]

For land preparation the traditional equipment were mainly hoes and
cutlasses, while the improved equipment reported were tractors (in the case of
Ghana) and improved tools (cutlasses, rakes, shovels, pick-axes, spades and
machets) in both countries. For planting and weeding both traditional and
improved equipment were basic hand tools.

Table 9.7 Use of traditional and improved farming equipment in the villages/sub-units

Country	Activity	Percentage of households using:		Total number of reported cases
		Traditional	Improved	
Ghana	Land preparation	63	37	151
	Planting	81	19	155
	Weeding	95	5	154
Sierra Leone	Land preparation	94	6	112
	Planting	93	7	112
	Weeding	92	8	97[29]

Village artisans accounted for the manufacture of most of the traditional equipment in use in farming. For improved equipment table 9.8 showed the places of manufacture reported by the households. Tables 9.9 and 9.10 showed the places of minor and major repairs of farming equipment in use. As can be seen from the tables, most of the minor repairs to equipment in use could be done within the villages. The only exception is that for land preparation equipment in Ghana, where 58 per cent of the respondents reported that minor repairs had to be done in the towns. This can be explained by the fact that this equipment were mainly tractors which require, even for minor repairs, skills and facilities not available within the villages. Since Group I type manufacturing firms were the only type in the villages one can conclude that, apart from tractors, this group of firms can cope with minor repairs, even of imported farming equipment.

For major repairs (table 9.10) for each operation and country, the dependance on the towns generally increased as one moves along the table from implements manufactured by the village artisans to imported equipment. This trend shows that for major repairs the improved farming equipment, imported or manufactured mainly by Group II and III firms (see table 9.8), the villages depended more on the facilities available in the towns for their major repairs. This applied even to hand tools (those used for planting).

This latter fact has implications for promoting the use of improved technologies in the rural areas. It suggests that unless the facilities and skills of the rural craftsmen are improved, they would lose their jobs, with the widespread use of improved equipment. The provision of these skills and facilities in the rural areas would also relieve the firms of Groups II and III from repair work, thus allowing them to concentrate on the manufacture of equipment.

Problems of equipment manufacturing firms

Raw material procurement

For the Group I firms the main raw material used was scrap metal. This could be purchased from the urban areas, usually through dealers. In Ghana there were two main markets for scrap metal[30] where artisans could bargain for goods. In Kenya and Sierra Leone various scrap dealers in the towns engage in the trade. However, this meant that the rural blacksmiths had to travel to the towns to buy scrap metal and arrange for its transportation to the villages. The recent growth in the number of Group II firms which also used some scrap had meant that the village artisans had to compete with them for the purchase of scrap.

Table 9.8 Sources of improved farming equipment in use in the
villages/sub-units as reported by households

| Country | Activity | Types of equipment | Percentage of households utilising equipment manufactured by: | | | Total no of reported cases |
			(Group I) Village artisan	(Groups II and III) Local factory	Imported	
Ghana	Land pre-paration	Hand tools and tractors	0	4	96	56
	Planting	Hand tools	7	13	80	30
	Weeding	Hand tools	0	43	57	7
Sierra Leone	Land pre-paration	Hand tools	0	33	67	6
	Planting	Hand tools	0	33	67	6
	Weeding	Hand tools	16	17	67	6

Table 9.9 Places of minor repairs of equipment for land preparation
and planting reported by householders

Manufacturers	% of households reporting place of minor repairs as:			Total number of respon-dents	Activity	Country
	Within village/ sub-unit	Nearby village/ sub-unit	Town			
Village artisan (Group I firms)	81	19	0	36	Land pre-paration	Ghana
	89	11	0	55	Planting	
	98	2	0	87	Land pre-paration	Sierra Leone
	94	5	1	84	Planting	
Local factory (Group II and III firms)	80	8	2	50	Land pre-paration	Ghana
	72	23	5	62	Planting	
	75	25	0	75	Land pre-paration	Sierra Leone
	93	7	0	93	Planting	
Imported	29	13	58	13	Land pre-paration	Ghana
	81	11	0	11	Planting	
	0	100	0	4	Land pre-paration	Sierra Leone
	100	0	0	0	Planting	

Table 9.10 Places of major repairs of equipment for land preparation
and planting reported by householders

Manufacturers	% of households reporting place of major repairs as:			Total number of	Activity	Country
	Within village/ sub-unit	Nearby village/ sub-unit	Town	respon- dents		
Village artisan (Group I firms)	49	24	27	34	Land pre- paration	Ghana
	67	16	17	52	Planting	
	81	17	2	87	Land pre- paration	Sierra Leone
	77	21	2	83	Planting	
Local factory (Group II and III)	40	24	36	47	Land pre- paration	Ghana
	49	26	25	59	Planting	
	60	0	40	10	Land pre- paration	Sierra Leone
	67	17	16	12	Planting	
Imported	5	11	84	63	Land pre- paration	Ghana
	74	7	19	31	Planting	
	0	50	50	4	Land pre- paration	Sierra Leone
	100	0	0	4	Planting	

Ghana had a steel plant which produced iron rods, iron plates and angle iron form scrap and imported iron while in Sierra Leone there were no ferrous metals industries.

Paradoxically, statistics from Sierra Leone show that scrap metal is in fact exported from the country. In Sierra Leone 42,340 tons of railway scrap metal alone, in the form of locomotives, track material and other miscellaneous items were exported between 1971 and 1977 at an average price of $22.00 a ton (National Workshop, 1980). Since these were exported as whole items, it cannot be argued that all the parts could not have found use locally in equipment manufacturing. When this is compared to the average price of Le 600 per ton which the country pays for imported iron and steel materials in the form of mere sheets and rods (Central Statistics Office, Sierra Leone, 1979) it would appear that, in the long run, the exportation of scrap metal can only give a false sense of gain in foreign exchange earnings.

In Sierra Leone, the industries manufacturing equipment for food production and processing in Group II and the National Workshop did not have licenses to import materials and had to purchase from the local shops. It was estimated that the average price per ton of iron and steel sheets and rods was Le 1,500 per ton.[31] Thus, the National Workshop exported scrap metal at US$22, a ton but bought iron and steel materials at Le 1,500 per ton. The cost of raw materials to equipment manufacturing firms could be reduced by

- setting up recycling plants for scrap metal;

- providing equipment manufacturing firms with import licenses;

- establishing controlled and/or subsidised prices for equipment components.

Machinery and spare parts procurement

For Group I and some Group II firms who generally depend on scrap material to construct their own machines, the problems of the acquisition of scrap and other raw materials have been discussed earlier. The purchase of second-hand machinery by Group II type firms has been affected since the Group III firms from which machines are generally purchased are finding it difficult to get replacements for their machines due to lack of foreign exchange.

The foreign exchange problems in Ghana and Sierra Leone have affected the purchases of new machines and spare parts for existing machines by Group II and Group III type firms. The lack of specialised machinery has meant that certain parts could not be produced locally, thus limiting manufacturing activities. For example, implements such as farming tools, which are at present imported in large numbers could be manufactured if the appropriate machinery could be made available.

A feasibility study[32] done by the National Workshop in Sierra Leone (National Workshop, 1980) showed that the unit price of agricultural implements (taking into account factory building works, machinery cost and installation, tools and implements, electricity, fuel, water and salaries) would be half that which the country pays for imported varieties.[33] Studies of this type would demonstrate that foreign exchange can, in fact, be saved by allowing the importation of machinery and spare parts by equipment manufacturing firms.

Credit facilities

For Group I and some Group II type firms the main source of capital is personal savings and loans from relatives and friends. It is not clear whether these smaller firms would require loans to extend their operations if there is increased incentive brought about by the availability of raw materials and machinery but, for the existing scale of activities as noted by Chuta, 1976, for Sierra Leone and Norcliffe et al, 1980, for Kenya, capital is not the overriding constraint facing small industries. In the case of equipment manufacturing industries this can be explained by the fact that manufacturing by smaller firms is mainly done to order, for which prepayments are made. If, however, these artisans are to increase their production, loans would become necessary. The small credit schemes of all three countries appear to have had a limited impact on Group I type firms. In Ghana and Sierra Leone there are no separate lending schemes for small artisans and whatever small schemes are available go mainly to farmers and traders[34] (Bank of Sierra Leone, 1978).

For the larger firms, the services of commercial banks are available if the necessary collaterals can be provided. However, in the past, it has granted most of its loans to commercial enterprises.[35]

Skilled personnel

For the informal sector firms' training is done on the job. Apprentices learn the job this way because the technological operations involved are simple and can be learned in one or two years.

However, the more sophisticated the machinery and technological operations which are involved, the greater the demand for formal training. In all three countries there are technical institutes and trade schools which cater for technicians. In Ghana there are the state-run polytechnics, and other establishments such as the Ghanaian-German Technical Institute and the Opportunity Industrialisation Centre. The National Vocational Training Institute is a joint ILO/Ghanaian Government project which, by 1978, had trained 500 people in the Kumasi area alone in welding, straightening, engine mechanics, electrical works and spraying.

In Sierra Leone the Freetown Technical Institute and the University of
Sierra Leone offer middle-level technician training, while craftsmen's courses
are offered at the Kenema Technical Institute and the trade centres at Kissy
and Magburaka.

One problem of these training institutes is that the numbers of trainees
are very small to cope with the requirements within the countries. For
instance, the total enrolment at the Sierra Leone institutions listed above in
1978 was 872, out of which 172 were in the final grade. It was estimated that
the annual output of trained technicians and craftsmen was 900-1000(JASPA,
ILO, 1978). Taking the figure of graduate engineers from the University of
Sierra Leone in 1977 (39), it can be seen that the ratio of trained engineer
to trained technician is 1:3.[35] Assuming that industries can absorb the
graduate engineers this ratio suggests a shortage of trained technicians to
work with the engineers.

Technical training has been believed to be for "misfits" who could not
enter universities. The students themselves go to these instututions already
considering themselves failures, a fact which does not help them to acquire
the devotion required for the successful completion of their courses. This
also means that only second-rate students enter the technical institutes, thus
resulting in high drop-out rates and graduates of mediocre quality.

These institutions have been criticised for not providing the right type
of graduates required for the existing industries which complain that the
courses are mainly theoretical and do not concentrate on practical issues.
Practical training is costly in that machinery has to be provided. Technical
schools have not always had the necessary financial support in order to
provide adequate practical training. In Sierra Leone, for example, only 1.9
per cent of the total recurrent expenditure of the Ministry of Education goes
to technical education (JASPA, ILO, 1978). In Ghana technician training has
received a great deal of national and international support in recent years.

The importance of formal training seems to be underplayed in the
literature (see, for example, King, 1977). While informal apprenticeship has
a role to play in training people in the use of basic tools and machinery,
formal training allows for the use of more sophisticated machines and for
greater adaptability of the trainees. Thus, a formally-educated technician
can utilise new machinery with greater ease than an informally trained,
on-the-job apprentice who has to be trained to use each machine.

The bulk of apprentices is to be found in Group I type firms and informal
firms of the Group II type. In Ghana, for instance, it is estimated that only

800 out of the 31,000 apprentices are to be found in the formal sector Group
II and Group III firms (Hakam, 1978). Whereas the informal sector firms can
train on the job as the technological operations become more complicated, the
time and effort in training becomes a full-time job in itself, a job which can
best be done at centres of training, that is, institutes.

Infrastructural facilities

There is no doubt that the infrastructural facilities available within
the countries affect the scale of operation of manufacturing firms. For Group
I and Group II type firms in the rural areas, the operations they can perform
are limited by the available source of power. For instance, machines to
perform operations not now done by these firms might require electricity,
diesel and gas supply or a steady flow of cooling water, and unless this is
readily available the range of technological operations they can perform
cannot be increased substantially. It is argued (King, 1977) that even if the
power is brought to these firms they cannot afford the cost of the machinery
needed to be able to use it. Although this is true one should consider that
if the quality of their products is to be improved, and if they are to
increase the range of their goods, their performance of certain operations
would become imperative. Loans schemes planned for artisans at this level
should take cognizance of this fact.

The Technology Consultancy Centre at Kumasi, Ghana also has a pilot rural
blacksmith's workshop in which it makes rural blacksmiths familiar with new
techniques and equipment. The coverage of the Ghanaian scheme has been
limited.

Limited market

This is one of the constraints experienced by manufacturing firms in
both countries. While it is true that this is a problem in all developing
countries, the condition is made worse by the fact that there appears to be an
excess of firms producing one sort of equipment, while there are virtually
none producing other types which could also have large demand.

Production for export to neighbouring countries would help to alleviate
the problem of the limited market. Thus, within economic communities such as
the Mano River Union and the Economic Commission of West African States
(ECOWAS), agreements regarding the sort of equipment to be manufactured by
firms in member States to supply other States could lead to a wider market for
equipment manufacturers.

NOTES TO CHAPTER 9

1 This was as a result of a survey undertaken in the two countries in 1981.

2 Blacksmiths have been known, for instance, to develop cutting machines from motor vehicle scrap.

3 See Technology in the Commonwealth - A Directory of Organisations. Commonwealth Secretariat, 1980. Only institutions designing and/or developing improved equipment for village use.

4 This applies to institutions which are teaching departments within universities. The TCC in Ghana is a separate appropriate technology unit, the university votes are devoted solely to appropriate technology.

5 C2.75 = US$1.00.

6 In the past the TCC had received grants for AT work from the Rockefeller Brothers Fund; Oxfam, Quebec; Oxfam, UK; and the Canadian Industrial Development Council (IDRC).

7 Indeed, evidence suggests that equipment design and development in all cases only account for a small proportion of their activities.

8 The National Workshop in Sierra Leone engages in repair of equipment as well.

9 Le 1 = US$0.9 (1980).

10 These figures are total staff who spent very little time in development work.

11 The National Association for Appropriate Technology was formed to bring together institutions within the country which are working on (or interested in) improved technology.

12 This workshop was organised jointly by the Centre for Development Studies, University of the Cape Coast and the David Livingstone Institute, Glasgow.

13 This conference was organised by ASTRAD and the Sierra Leone Institution of Engineers and sponsored by ITDG and UNESCO.

14 Intermediate Technology Development Group, Great Britain.

15 Volunteers in Technical Assistance.

16 International Development Research Council.

17 See the next section on manufacture of equipment and tools e.g. the equipment developed by the TAEC requires welding which many village artisans cannot do with their available facilities.

18 The communities which do not have blacksmiths are fishing communities. These villages however possess carpenters for construction and repair of boats. Whatever blacksmithing services are required are obtained from nearby villages/sub-units or towns.

19 The ratio of blacksmith workshops to the total rural population in Sierra Leone according to Liedholm and Chuta is 1:400. In Kenya a rural survey revealed that 2.2% of sampled households was involved in tool and equipment manufacture and repair (G. Norcliffe et al.). These ratios might be smaller where blacksmiths' services are used by neighbouring villages.

20 Average age of 50 years.

21 Of the three countries only Ghana possesses a steelworks which produces steel rods from recycled scrap, but recently this industry has only been operating at 30 per cent capacity. All metal components such as galvanised sheet steel and mild steel plates, which are imported items, can be purchased locally in the three countries.

22 This is in one of the villages studied in Ghana.

23 Tikonko Agricultural Extension Centre's Small Farm Equipment Unit.

24 Although a number of workshops exist with the facilities of Group III firms specified in table 9.3, these workshops are not basically manufacturing workshops. For example the workshops of the Ministries of Agriculture are mainly for the maintenance and repair of tractors and other agricultural equipment. The workshops in teaching institutions are mainly for teaching and training purposes and are discussed in a later section.

25 This workshop was formerly the railway workshop. The railway has been phased out and, since 1978, the workshop now operates as a government workshop. Plans are underway to improve its facilities so that it can produce light engineering products to service the local industries.

26 The workshop itself does not import materials.

27 Goderich is not included in this analysis.

28 Some respondents weed only by hand.

29 In Accra the "scrap" market is known as Kokompe and in Kumasi as The Magazine (Agboage, 1982).

30 For example, one galvanised steel sheet 8' x 4' x 1 mm cost Le 40.00 in 1980 (estimates are made on the basis of an iron density of 7.8 g/cc).

31 This was based on estimated annual requirements of hand tools from import figures.

32 Since some of these costs are local the savings in foreign exchange is effectively more than the figure suggests.

33 This applies to the rural banks in Ghana and the National Development Bank Rural Loans Scheme in Sierra Leone.

34 In 1978 only 20 per cent of its grants went to industry as a whole (Kilby, 1981).

35 The same ratio would apply to engineers/skilled craftsmen. For developing countries a ratio of at the most 1:6 could be considered ideal.

Chapter 10
CONCLUDING REMARKS

IMPROVED TECHNOLOGY ADOPTION

This manual describes a wide range of improved equipment which can be adopted by women in the rural areas of West Africa. The selection of equipment in concrete cases would depend on the scale of production required, the specific features of interest and the available capital. Given the low scale of production of the women[1] and their limited capital, it is advocated that some of the equipment described could only be owned on a communal basis or by individual entrepreneurs.[2] Recommendations on the types of ownership of equipment described in this manual are given in Table 10.1.

The power-driven machines described in this manual are at present mainly driven by means of diesel or petrol engines. The exploitation of locally available sources of energy such as solar, wind and water to operate these machines could be invaluable in areas where diesel and petrol are scarce or expensive.

It is to be noted that the outputs obtained from some of the hand-operated equipment are comparable to those of the traditional methods. In these cases selection of such equipment should only be made when certain specific features of the traditional methods (other than output) are to be improved. Thus in cases where the traditional method is particularly strenuous improved equipment could be introduced to relieve the strain even though the output would remain virtually unaffected.

Other hand-operated equipment which increases the outputs could be recommended for poorer women who could not afford to buy or pay for the hire of power-driven equipment or whose scales of production are low.

Some large processing plants are only discussed briefly in this manual as it is felt that they are beyond the means of most female rural processors. However, assuming that the improved equipment would lead to increased incomes and large-scale production incorporating plantations for raw materials, a transition to such plants would be inevitable.

CONSTRAINTS IN DESIGN, DEVELOPMENT AND MANUFACTURE OF IMPROVED EQUIPMENT

The constraints of design and development institutions and manufacturing enterprises which have affected the availability of improved equipment in West Africa can be highlighted.

Design and development facilities

Most of the financial support obtained for improved technology development is from foreign and international organisations. This reflects the lack of awareness on the part of the governments of the need for design and development of improved equipment. Whatever funds have been available from government sources have been minimal when compared to the enormity of the problems associated with research and the design and development of improved equipment. A lot more funding would have to be provided for research, design and development work in these countries if meaningful results are to be obtained.

The bulk of the countries' manpower and laboratory facilities is found in the research institutions. In the universities, where the expertise and facilities exist, unfortunately a shortage of staff has meant overloading the existing staff who therefore do not have enough time to spend on design and development work. From the TCC example one can conclude that in teaching institutions, unless a separate unit is created to concentrate on the design and development of improved technologies, design and development work might suffer as a result of teaching commitments.

Efforts should be made to improve the facilities in associated laboratories (such as engineering, chemistry and physics) so that design and development institutions have access to at least one well-equipped laboratory in these disciplines where basic research could be carried out.

There is an urgent need for greater interchange of information and publications. The seminars/conferences/workshops which are being held are sometimes too general in nature to enable scientists from different disciplines to benefit from the experiences of their counterparts. More specialised conferences, for instance, on design and development of wood stoves, which would bring together researchers from different countries working on wood stoves, would provide a good forum for a useful inter-change of ideas. Such specialised meetings are to be preferred to general meetings which attempt to consider a whole range of issues.

From the types of equipment designed and developed (table 9.2), it can be seen that there is a great deal of duplication of efforts, even within each individual country. This unfortunate situation, considering the limited resources available, can be the result of the haphazard approach to design and development within the countries and emphasises the need for institutions to get together and distinguish areas of speciality in order to best utilise the scarce resources available.

The problem of the non-existence of patenting rights within the two countries has been mentioned. When an inventor produces an original design he deserves some recognition for his work. The introduction of patenting rights within these countries would encourage scientists to increase their design and development activities and to make their designs available to manufacturers.

Yet another problem in the transition from the design and development stage to the manufacturing stage is encountered as a result of inadequate resources for field testing of equipment. All too often manufacturers are sceptical about embarking on production of devices which have not been well-proven in the field. As a result many equipment prototypes of potential benefit to the rural people have never left the laboratories.

The "missing link" between designers and manufacturers could be provided by institutions which are interested in the widespread adoption of improved technologies. Thus national and international organisations should sponsor projects aimed at field testing devices already developed so that their chances of adoption can be determined. After successful field tests, manufacturing firms would be assured of the profitability of embarking upon large-scale manufacture.

Manufacturing facilities

Procurement of raw materials and parts is a major problem in production. It places a severe strain on the firms and affects their annual output (most of the firms studied had experienced a downward trend in equipment production due to this problem).

For blacksmiths, for whom the raw material is scrap metal, institutional arrangements are to be made to ensure an efficient supply of such scrap in the rural areas. For the firms in Group II and Group III governments and other concerns are to be urged to establish steel recycling plants for the conversion of scrap metal into sheets or rods which could be used for equipment manufacture. Alternatively, import licences for the purchase of raw materials should be made available to these industries.

In some countries, where there are foreign exchange problems, equipment manufacturing firms have suffered from lack of foreign exchange facilities to enable them to import machinery required for specific technological operations or for replacement. Feasibility studies would however reveal that foreign exchange could be saved by providing these firms with these facilities so that items of tools and equipment which are now being imported can be manufactured locally.[3] Equipment manufacture within the countries also has employment implications as it would mean that more employment would be provided for qualified engineers, trained technicians and unskilled workers.

The promotion of the manufacture of equipment within the countries could serve not only the role of import substitution but also one of export promotion. Agrico Ltd., in Ghana exported equipment to neighbouring Guinea, Nigeria, Togo, Liberia and Upper Volta on a small scale. If its production could be increased or raised to full capacity it would be able to cover local demand as well as increase its exports. Production for export to neighbouring countries would help to alleviate the problems of limited market. Thus, within economic communities such as the Mano River Union and the Economic Commission of West African States (ECOWAS), agreements as to the sort of equipment to be manufactured by firms in member States to supply other States could lead to a wider market for equipment manufacturers.
In Sierra Leone, the National Workshop could be improved by supplementing existing facilities to enable it to supply the other countries of the Mano River Union with light engineering products.

Extension of credit facilities to equipment manufacturers needs to be given some consideration by govenment and banking institutions. In recent years agricultural credit schemes have evolved due to an awareness to promote agriculture in these countries. In the same way, recognition of the need for the provision of equipment and spare parts within the countries to enhance the success of agricultural schemes should lead to special credit schemes for the expansion of existing firms, as well as for the setting up of new ones. Where credit schemes for manufacturing firms exist, much is to be gained by ensuring that equipment manufacturers get a fair share in the facilities offered, taking into account the fact that these firms require, as a rule, a larger capital, when compared to other types of manufacturing firms. In granting credits, precautions should also be taken to ensure that there is no overproduction of a single type of equipment as this would lead to a saturation of the market.

The problems of providing personnel with adequate training to work in industries do not exist as a result of a lack of training institutions. It would seem that the existing institutions are handicapped by lack of proper training workshops, as well as trained teachers in practical work. One way to alleviate this problem is to organise sandwich courses in which trainees are given an opportunity to spend a few months a year in industry to acquire the "adequate" training required by these industries. This would require cooperation from the manufacturing firms but would ensure that at the end of the training period these industries would have technicians with appropriate practical knowledge.

In order to ensure employment for the artisans of Group I type firms, their basic capacities in terms of skills and equipment would have to be increased. Appropriate equipment for welding, manual cutting and bending machines would have more appeal to these artisans than the power-driven tools and precision lathes.

Village artisans might not possess the necessary skills and equipment required for maintenance and repair of improved equipment. They would then, of necessity, require some added skills and equipment if they are not to lose their sources of income. Programmes aimed at introduction of improved equipment should take cognisance of this fact. Group III type firms would have a role to play in the manufacture of appropriate equipment for use by members of Group I type firms as they upgrade their capacities to meet the new consumer demands for maintenance and repairs.

Specialisation by groups of manufacturing firms is desirable. While some firms of the Group II type have been known to build equipment which could perform operations such as metal cutting, it should be noted that these random successes cannot be used to indicate that these firms are capable of producing sophisticated equipment. Within the technological capability which each firm possesses, product types should be determined which would ensure that the equipment produced would be reliable and guaranteed to give good and lasting performance. On the other hand, the Groups II and III type firms should embark on more sophisticated equipment types which they have the facilities to produce. Some of these firms manufacture only items such as agricultural hand tools, thus competing with the artisans of Group I type firms.

NOTES TO CHAPTER 10

1   Even at ten fold increase in production in most cases would not justify possession of this equipment due to its high capacities.

2   Capital costs may be high but in the long run there is a saving due to the use of free fuels.

3   In Sierra Leone, for instance, tools, household equipment and appliances, agricultural hand tools and farming implements account for about 25 per cent of total domestic imports.

LIST OF EQUIPMENT SUPPLIERS

A. WEST AFRICAN SUPPLIERS

Agricultural Engineers Ltd. (Agrico Ltd.)
Ring Road West Industrial Area,
P.O. Box 3707,
ACCRA,

    (Ghana).

Agro Machines Ltd.,
Liberia Industrial Free Zone,
P.O. Mail Bag 9047,
MONROVIA,

    (Liberia).

Fabrication Engineering and Production Company,
Projects Development Institute,
3, Independence Layout,
P.O. Box 609,
ENUGU,

    (Nigeria).

SISCOMA,
B.P. 3214,
DAKAR,

    (Sénégal).

Technology Consultancy Centre,
University of Science and Technology,
University Post Office,
KUMASI,

    (Ghana).

Tikonko Agricultural Extension Centre,
P.O. Box 142,
BO,

    (Sierra Leone).

B. OTHER AFRICAN SUPPLIERS

Agrimal (Malawi) Ltd.,
P.O. Box 143,
BLANTYRE,

(Malawi).

Brown and Clapperton Ltd.,
P.O. Box 52,
BLANTYRE,

    (Malawi).

Manik Engineers,
P.O. Box 1274,
ARUSHA,

    (Tanzania).

Nduma Ltd.,
P.O. Box 62,
GILGIL,

    (Kenya).

Ubingo Farm Implements,
P.O. Box 2669,
DAR-ES-SALAAM,

    (Tanzania).

United Engineering Works,
P.O. Box 3082,
ARUSHA,

    (Tanzania).

C. ASIAN SUPPLIERS

Allied Trading Company,
Railway Road,
Ambala City 134 002,
MARYANA,

    (India).

CECOCO Ltd.,
Chou Bocki Goshi Kaisha,
Central Commercial Company,
P.O. Box 8,
Ibaraki City,
OSAKA PREF 567,

    (Japan).

Cossul & Co. PVT Ltd.,
Industrial Area,
Fazalgury,
KANPUR,

    (India).

Dandekar Brothers,
Engineers & Founders,
Sangli,
MAHARASHTRA,

  (India).

International MFG Co. (Regd).,
Hospital Road,
Jagraon,
Ludhiana,
PUNJAB,

  (India).

Kumaon Agri-Horticulture Stores,
P.O. Kashipur,
Distr Nainital,
U.P.

  (India).

Melanesian Council of Churches,
P.O. Box 80,
Lae
PAPUA,

  (New Guinea).

Mohan Singh Harbhajan Singh,
G.T. Road,
Goraya 144 409,
Distr Jullundur,

  (India).

Mohinder & Co. Allied Industries,
Kurali,
Distr Ropar,
PUNJAB,

  (India).

Rajan Trading Co.,
P.O. Box 250,
Madras 600 001,

  (India).

Rajasthan State Agro Industries Corporation Ltd.,
Virat Bhawan,
C. Scheme,
Jaipur 302006,
RAJASTHAN,

  (India).

EUROPEAN SUPPLIERS

The Alvan Blanch Development Co. Ltd.,
Chelworth,
Malmesbury,
Wiltshire SN 169 SG,

      (U.K.)

E. H. Benthall & Co. Ltd.,
Maldon,
CM9 7NW,
Essex,

      (U.K.)

ETS A Gaubert,
16700 Ruffee,
23, rue Gambetta,

      (France).

John Gordon & Co. Ltd.,
196, High Street,
EPPLING,
Essex,

      (U.K.)

ABC Hansen Comp A/S,
Hauchsvej 14,
DK-1825 Copenhagen V,

      (Denmark).

Harrap Wilkinson Ltd.,
North Phoebe Street,
SALFORD,
M5 4EA,

      (U.K.)

R. Hunt and Co. Ltd.,
Atlas Works,
Earls Colne,
COLCHESTER,
Essex   CO6 2EP,

      (U.K.)

IRUSWERKE DUSSLINGEN,
7401 Dusslingen,
Postfach 128,

      (West Germany).

RENSON ET CIE,
B.P. 14,
59550 Landrevies,

(France).

S.A.M.A.P.,
B.P. 18,
Horbourg-Wihr,
6800 Colmar,

(France).

REFERENCES (by sources)

A. ILO

ILO: Small-scale Processing of Fish, Technology Series, Geneva, 1982.

--- Guide to Tools and Equipment for Labour-based Road Construction, Geneva, 1981.

Aboagye, A.A.: Technology and Employment in the Capital Goods Industry in Ghana, (Geneva, World Employment Programme research working paper, restricted).

Adder Associates: Processing Cassava into Gari (Kent, mimeographed).

Akande, A.: Participation of Women in Rural Development (Geneva, unpublished).

Baron, C.: Technology, Employment and Basic Needs in Food Processing in Developing Countries, (Oxford, Pergamon Press, 1980).

Bhalla, A.S.: Towards Global Action for Appropriate Technology, Oxford, Pergamon Press, 1980.

Date-Bah, E.: Rural Women, Their Activities and Technology in Ghana: An Overview, (Geneva, ILO mimeographed World Employment research working paper, restricted, 1981).

Hakam, A.N.: Technology Diffusion from the Formal to the Informal Sector, (Geneva, ILO mimeographed World Employment Programme research working paper, restricted).

JASPA: Sierra Leone: Ensuring Equitable Growth, (Addis Ababa, ILO, Jobs and Skills Programme for Africa, 1978, Confidential Report to Sierra Leone Government, restricted).

Longhurst, R.: Rural Development Planning and Sexual Division of Labour: A Case Study of a Moslem Mausa village in Northern Nigeria, (Geneva, ILO, 1980, mimeographed World Employment research working paper, restricted.

Stevens, Y.: Technologies for Rural Women's Activities: Problems and Prospects in Sierra Leone, (ILO, 1981, mimeographed World Employment Programme research working paper, restricted).

Tadesse, Z.: Background Paper ILO Tripartite Regional Seminar on Rural Development and Women, (Dakar, Senegal, 1981).

Traore, A.: L'accès des Femmes Ivoriennes aux Resources - Les Femmes et la Terre en Pays Adiokrou, Background Paper, ILO Tripartite Regional Seminar on Rural Development and Women, (Dakar, Senegal, 1981).

Woillet, M.J.C.: Appropriate Technology, Scope for Co-operation among the Countries of the West African Economic Community, (ILO, Geneva, 1979).

B. FAO

Aten, A., Faunce, A.D. et al.: Equipment for Rice Processing, FAO Agricultural
        Development Paper No. 27, Rome, 1953.

Gariboldi, F.: Rice Parboiling, FAO Agricultural Development Paper No. 97,
        Rome, 1974.

Grimwood, B.E.: Coconut Palm Products, FAO Agricultural Development Paper No.
        99, Rome, 1975.

Thieme, J.G.: Coconut Oil Processing, FAO Agricultural Development Paper
        Rome, 1968.

Rawson, G.C.: A Short Guide to Fish Processing, FAO, Rome, 1966.

Better Farming Series 1977 Edition: Sheep and Goat Breeding No. 12, Keeping
        Chickens, No. 13, FAO, Rome, 1977.

C. UNICEF

UNICEF Teknologi Tepat Guna, untuk di Pedesaan, UNICEF, Jarkata, 1981.

Langley, P. Ngom, M. and David, P.: Technologies Villageoises en Afrique de
        l'Ouest et du Centre, UNICEF (Abidjan) et ENDA (Dakar) (undated).

National Research Council: Food, Fuel and Fertiliser from Organic Wastes,
        National Academy Press, Washington, 1981.

UNICEF: Appropriate Village Technology for Basic Services, A catalogue of
        devices displayed at UNICEF/Kenya Government, Village Technology
        Unit, Nairobi, Kenya, (undated).

D. Other UN

Carr, M.: Appropriate Technology for African Women, UNECA, 1978.

United Nations: Animal-driven Power Gear, UN, Geneva, 1975.

E. ITDG (Intermediate Technology Development Group, 9 King Street,
LONDON, WC2E 8HN)

Abbot, E.: Rasulia Animal Drawn Roller Thresher, Agricultural Equipment and
        Tools for Farmers designed for local construction series, (London,
        undated).

Boyd, J.: Tools for Agriculture: A Buyer's Guide to Low-cost Agricultural
        Implements, ITDG, London, 1976.

Holterman, S.: Intermediate Technology in Ghana: The Experience of Kumasi
        University Technology Consultancy Centre, ITDG, Rugby, 1981.

Melanesian Council of Churches: Foot Powered Thresher, Agricultural Equipment
        and Tools for Farmers designed for Local Construction Series, (London
        undated).

ARTICLES FROM JOURNAL APPROPRIATE TECHNOLOGY

Ahmad, M., and Jenkins, A.: Traditional Paddy Husking - an Appropriate Technology under Pressure, Appropriate Technology, No. 2, Vol. 7, 1980.

Asian Institute of Technology: A Simple Solar Dryer, Appropriate Technology, Vol. 5, No. 2, 1978

Boatwright, J.H.: A Wedge Press for Oil Extraction, Appropriate Technology, No. 6, Vol. 2, 1979.

Chanco, M.P.: The Rice Husk Stove Appropriate Technology , Vol. 5, No. 3, 1979.

Cook, D.J.: Using Rice Husk for Making Cement-like Materials Appropriate Technology, Vol. 6, No. 4, 1980.

Donkor, P.: A Hand Screw Press for Extracting Palm Oil Appropriate Technology, Vol. 5, No. 4, 1979.

Exell, M.P.: A Low Cost Solar Rice Dryer, Appropriate Technology, Vol. 5, Vol. 1, 1978.

Geddes, A.M.W.: Palm Oil Mill Project in Sierra Leone Appropriate Technology, Vol. 3, No. 2, 1976.

Hilton, D.J.: A Maize Sheller for Every Household, Appropriate Technology, Vol. 3, No. 2, 1976.

Holloway, R.: Making Coconut Shell Buttons: A Labour-intensive Technology, Appropriate Technology, Vol. 8, No. 3, 1981.

Mehta, P.: Technology Alternatives for the Use of Rice Husks, Appropriate Technology, Vol. 9, No. 4, 1983.

Pinson, G.: An Inexpensive Maize Sheller, Appropriate Technology, Vol. 9, No. 4, 1983.

Rana, A.A.: A Simple Manual Maize Shelling Device, Appropriate Technology, Vol. 2, No. 1, 1975.

Shaw, R.: Solar Drying Potatoes, Appropriate Technology, Vol. 7, No. 4, 1981.

Stuart Clark, C.: A Solar Food Dryer for Bangladesh, Appropriate Technology, Vol. 8, No. 4, 1982.

Unruh, W.: A Cone-type Hand-Operated Rice Huller, Appropriate Technology, Vol. 6, No. 3, 1979.

Williams, B.D. Jnr.: A Foot-Powered Thresher for Rice and Small Grains, Appropriate Technology, Vol. 2, No. 2.

F. VITA (**Volunteers In Technical Assistance**, 3706 Rhode Island Avenue, Mt.
       Ranier, Maryland, U.S.A. 20822).

Attfield, H.N.H.: How to Make Fertiliser, Technical Bulletin, No. 8, Maryland, (undated).

Sanbolle Bertrand: Small Corn Sheller, Technical Bulletin Nol 21, Maryland, (undated).

--- Rice Thresher, Technical Bulletin, VITA, Maryland (undated).

VITA: Village Technology Handbook, VITA, 1978.

G. COMMONWEALTH SECRETARIAT

Ellman, A., Mackay, B., Moody, M.: Guide to Technology Transfer in East, Central and Southern Africa, Commonwealth Secretariat, London.

Mackay, B.: Rural Technology in the Commonwealth: A Directory of Organisations, Commonwealth Secretariat, 1980.

H. OTHER SOURCES

Agrico Ltd.: Agrico Handbook on Mechanisation in Africa, Agrico Ltd., Accra, 1977.

--- Agrico 15th Anniversary, Accra, 1981.

Ampratwum, D.B.: Promotion of Technology for Rural Life in Ghana, Paper presented at UNECA Workshop for Trainers and Planners on Village Technology for the Rural Family, Bo, 1979.

Bank of Sierra Leone: Report on the National Workshop on Agricultural Credit in Sierra Leone, Bank of Sierra Leone, Freetown, 1978.

Bassey, M.W.: Heat values of locally available solid fuels in Sierra Leone (mimeo), Freetown, 1981.

Brace Research Institute and Canadian Hunger Foundation: A Handbook on Appropriate Technology, Ottawa, 1979.

Braconner: Nouveau Larousse Agricole, Librairie Larousse, Paris, 1952.

Central Statistics Office, Sierra Leone Government: Annual Statistical Digest, Freetown, 1977.

Darrow, K., Keller, K., Puck, P.: Appropriate Technology Sourcebook, Vols. I and II, Volunteers in Asia Publication, 1981.

De Lepelière, G., Krishna Prasad, K., Verhaarf, P., Visser, P.: A woodstove compendium (TH-Eindoven/TNO-Apeldoom, 1981).

Food Research Institute, Ghana: Newsletters: Vol. i, Nos. 1, 2, 3 and 4, Accra, 1977.

--- Newsletters: Vol. 9, Nos. 1, 2, 3 and 4, Accra, 1978.

--- Newsletters: Vol. 10, Nos. 1, 2, 3 and 4, Accra, 1979.

Gandhian Institute of Studies in India: Directory of Appropriate Technology (mimeo), Varanasi, 1973.

Government of Ghana: Preliminary Economic Survey, 1977-1979, Central Bureau of Statistics, Accra, 1980.

Hale, P.R. and Williams, B.D.: Liklik Buk, Melanesian Council of Churches, Papua, New Guinea, 1978.

Hoda, M.M.: Appropriate Technology: Directory of Machines, Tools, Plants Equipment, Processes and Industries, Appropriate Technology Development Association, Lucknow, 1977.

Hibi, S.: How to Measure Maintenance Performance, Asian Productivity Organisation, Tokyo, 1977.

Jéquier, N.: Appropriate Technology: Problems and Promises OECD, Paris, 1976.

Kaniki, M.: Economical Technology Against Technical Efficiency in the Oil Palm Industry in West Africa, Development and Change, Vol. II, 1980.

King, K.: The African Artisan, London, Heineman, 1977.

Korthals Altes (in W. Reidgh): Appropriate Technology for Developing Countries, Delft University Press, 1979.

Lawson, R.M. and Kwei, E.: African Entrepreneurship and Economic Growth, A Case Study of the Fishing Industry of Ghana, Ghana University Press, Accra, 1974.

Leidholm, C. and Chuta, E.: Economics of Rural and Urban Small-Scale Industries in Sierra Leone, Michigan State University, African Rural Economy Paper, 1976.

Linsenmayer, D.A.: Economic analysis of alternative strategies for the development of Sierra Leone marine fisheries, Working paper No. 18, African Rural Economy Programme, Michigan State University, East Lansing, 1976.

Macormack, C.P.: "Control of land, labour and capital in rural southern Sierra Leone" in Ray, E. (ed.) Women and work in Africa, (Colorado, Westview Press, 1982).

National Workshop Government of Sierra Leone: Report on Caretaker Committee for Railway Assets (Establishment of the National Workshop).

Okori, J.V.: A Guide to Lifestock Production in Nigeria, Macmillan, 1978.

Rao, P.V.S.: A Search for an Appropriate Technology for Village Oil Industry, Appropriate Technology Development Association, Lucknow, 1980.

Situri, T.: A Rice Hull Burning Cook Stove, ATOL, Belgium, 1979.

Smith, V.E., Lynch, S.: <u>Household Food Consumption in Sierra Leone</u>, Michigan State University, Rural Development Series Working Peprs, East Lansing, 1979.

Spencer, D.S.C., May-Parker, I. and Rose, F.S.: Employment, Efficiency and Income in the Rice Processing Industry of Sierra Leone, Michigan State University, African Rural Economy Working Paper, No. 15, East Lansing, 1976.

Tikonko Agricultural Extension Centre: <u>Annual Report, 1980/81</u>, mimeographed Bo, 1981.

University of Science and Technology, Kumasi, Ghana: Technology Consultancy Centre: Annual Review, Nos. 3-7, (Kumasi 1974-75; 1976-77; 1978-79).

APPENDICES

A1.1 <u>Annual Production of Cassava, Copra, Palm Kernel,</u>
<u>Palm Oil, Rice, Maize in West Africa</u>
(in 1000 MT)

	Cassava	Copra	Palm kernel	Palm oil	Rice	Maize
Benin	600	3	80,000	35,000	20	250
Cameroon	831	-	48,500	83,500	20	350
Gambia	105	-	270	2,500	29	4
Ghana	1,850	10	32,000	21,000	65	350
Guinea	500	-	12,000	40,000	400	320
Guinea Bissau	-	5	7,000	4,700	60	3
Ivory Coast	700	19	38,000	135,000	430	325
Liberia	272	2	14,300	252,000	264	3
Mali	40	-	-	-	270	85
Niger	180	-	-	-	34	7
Nigeria	10,844	9	375,000	680,000	580	1,450
Senegal	137	-	5,000	5,800	127	47
Sierra Leone	91	-	50,000	50,000	500	17
Togo	485	2	15,000	18,000	23	151
Upper Volta	1,100	-	-	-	32	101

Source: Agrico Ltd. 1977

Table A1.2 Annual Production Of Fish In Some West African Countries

	in 1000 MT
Gambia	2
Ghana	235
Senegal	35

Table A2.1 Main Receptacles In Use
In Traditional Food-Processing Activities Studied

Receptacle	Usual capacities (litres)	Uses
1. Forty-four gallon oil drums	200 l	Storage of water Boiling of palm fruits Sterilisation of palm oil Storage of palm oil Storage of palm-kernel oil Storage of coconut oil Parboiling of rice
2. Enamel pans	13.4 l (3 gallons)	Water collection Water storage Salting of fish Storage of fish Mixing pound palm fruits with water
3. Four gallon buckets	17.8 l	Water collection Water storage
4. Cast-iron pot	Usually 17.8 l and 35.6 l	Boiling of palm fruits Sterilisation of palm oil Roasting of palm kernels Boiling of water/ground palm kernel mixture Boiling of water/ground coconut mixture Cooking of maize dough for kenkey preparation Boiling of kenkey
5. Earthernware containers	Variable	Water storage Boiling of palm fruits Sterilisation of palm oil Roasting palm kernels Roasting of gari

Table A2.2 Scoopers And Stirrers Used
In Food Processing Activities Studied

Scooper/stirrer	Uses
Small calabash	Scooping of palm oil from boiling mixture and pit Scooping of palm kernel oil Collecting water from stream
Small metal pan 'three penny pan'	Scooping of palm oil from boiling mixture Scooping of palm kernel oil Scooping of coconut oil Stirring of gari during roasting
Calabash pieces	Stirring of gari during roasting
Wooden spoon	Stirring of palm kernels during roasting Stirring of gari during roasting Stirring of maize dough for kenkey
Metal spoon	Roasting of gari Scooping of palm oil from boiling mixture Scooping of palm kernel oil from boiling mixture Scooping of coconut oil

Table A2.3 Traditional Technology In Use In The Food
Processing Activities Studied

Traditional equipment it is used	Food processing activity for which	Operations for which it is employed
1. Pestle and mortar	Palm oil production	Pounding of palm fruits for separation of exocarp from the nuts
	Palm kernel oil production	Pounding of kernels
	Cassava processing	Pounding of soaked cassava for foofoo
	Rice processing	Dehusking rice
	Maize processing	Milling maize
2. Perforated metal sheet grater	Cassava/coconut processing	Grating of cassava and coconut
3. Palm oil pit (Ghana)	Palm oil preparation	Separation of palm fruit pulp and fibre
4. Palm oil pit (Sierra Leone)	Palm oil preparation	Separation of palm fruit pulp and fibre
5. Stone set for cracking palm kernels	Palm kernel oil preparation	Cracking of palm kernels
6. Pressing with stones	Cassava processing	Processing of grated cassava
7. Pressing with sticks held together by ropes	Cassava processing	Pressing of grated cassava
8. Raffia sieve	Cassava processing	Sieving grated cassava
9. Metal sieve	Cassava processing	Sieving grated cassava

Table A3 Maximum Reported Weekly Scale Of Food Processing In Sample Villages In Ghana And Sierra Leone[1]

Activity	Ghana			Sierra Leone		
	Mean	Mode	Range	Mean	Mode	Range
1. Fish processing (kg)	1000	400 (8%)	10-4000	700	80 (19%)	10-6000
2. Palm oil production (gallons)	12.3	20.0 (25%)	3-20	31.9	16.0 (17%)	1.220
3. Palm kernel oil production	6.0	4.0 (50%)	1-16	4.5	4.0 (28%)	2-12
4. Gari production (kg)	230.0	80.0 (35%)	10-480	136.0	100.0 (29%)	20-500
5. Foofoo production (baskets)	-	-	-	8.1	2.0 (19%)	2-21
6. Kenkey production (4 gallon bucketfuls)	30.2	80.0 (15.8%)	3-90	-	-	-
7. Rice threshed	-	-	-	13.1	2.0 (16%)	1-50
8. Rice parboiled and sun dried (bushels)	-	-	-	10.9	20.0 (22%)	1-80

1 Source: Household survey October-December 1981. Figures in parenthesis represent respondents reporting modal values

290 -

Table A4 Estimated Values Of Average Firewood Use
In Food-Processing Activities Studied (excluding fish smoking)

		Performance figure	Mean value of performance figures as reported	
			Ghana	Sierra Leone
Three-stone cooking (Estimated efficiency 10%)				
Palm oil preparation	Boiling palm fruits Sterilising of fruits	Fuel use (kg/gallon palm oil produced	8.98 (10.256)	7.04 (9.57)
Palm kernel oil	Roasting of palm kernels and boiling of oil/water mixture	Fuel use (kg/gallon of palm kernel oil produced	6.69 (5.399)	6.07 (3.753)
Coconut oil preparation	Boiling of oil/water mixture	Fuel use (kg/gallon of coconut oil produced)		8.2 (10.032)
Cassava processing	Roasting of gari	Fuel use (kg/kg of gari produced)	3.33 (6.71)	3.964 (4.63)
Rice processing	Parboiling	Fuel use (kg/bushel of rice parboiled)		3.9 (4.598)
Maize processing	Cooking of maize dough and final boiling of kenkey	Fuel use (kg/gallon fluid capacity of kenkey produced)	2.64 (2.275)	

- One firewood bunch (consisting of 10 sticks) is assumed to weigh on the average 4.4 kilograms (see notes to conversion in the Appendix)

- Figures in brackets indicate the standard deviations

Source: Rural Survey in Ghana and Sierra Leone

Table A5 Average Water Use In Traditional Food Processing Activities

Activity	Water Use	
	Ghana	Sierra Leone
Coconut oil preparation		9.6 gallons/gallon of oil (7.904)
Palm oil preparation	21 gallons/gallon of oil (28.560)	22 gallons/gallon of oil (27.312)
Palm kernel oil preparation	4.7 gallons/gallon of oil (3.148)	9.16 gallons/gallon of oil (10.036)
Maize processing into kenkey	3.53 gallons/4 gallon bucketful of kenkey (5.83)	
Gari preparation	0.2 gallons/kg of gari (0.265)	0.3 gallons/kg of gari (0.3)
Rice parboiling		3.74 gallons/bushel of rice (4.892)

Source: Rural Survey in Ghana and Sierra Leone

Figures in parentheses are standard deviations

A6 Suggested Areas For Design And Development
Of Improved Equipment In Food Processing

- Centrifugal presses for pressing cassava dough and vegetable oil pressing
- Efficient ovens and stoves for food processing
- Mechanical roasters for products
- Harnessing solar power by means of photovoltaic cells for powering food processing equipment
- Use of alternative fuels in cooking and food processing
- Solar parboiling of rice
- Small scale preservation of fruits and vegetables

www.ingramcontent.com/pod-product-compliance
Lightning Source LLC
Chambersburg PA
CBHW080842270326
41928CB00014B/2877